NANDSHANKAR

Vinayak Mehta (1885–1940) was the author of *Nandshankar Jeevan Chitra* (1916), the earliest modern father-son biography in Gujarati, and *Ko Jagari*. He was educated at Elphinstone College in Bombay (now Mumbai), at Kings College of Cambridge University, and briefly at Heidelberg University in Germany. As a member of the Indian Civil Service posted in Eastern United Provinces (present-day Uttar Pradesh), he wrote an important report on the peasant revolt of 1919–1920. Two articles on the 'Agricultural Sayings of the United Provinces' (1916 and 1917), a treatise on rural reconstruction *Gram Sanghatan* (1936), and a recently recovered paper on famines sum up his concern for the peasants of India. He died in Allahabad (now Prayagraj) in 1940.

Radhika Jayakar Herzberger is an Indologist, educationist, writer, and former Director, Rishi Valley Education Centre, Chittoor District, Andhra Pradesh. She is the author of *Bhartrhari and the Buddhists: An Essay in the Development of Fifth and Sixth Century Indian Thought* (1986, 2011).

NANDSHANKAR

A Portrait in Nineteenth-century Surat

VINAYAK NANDSHANKAR MEHTA

Translated from the original Gujarati by
RADHIKA JAYAKAR HERZBERGER

Orient BlackSwan

NANDSHANKAR: A PORTRAIT IN NINETEENTH-CENTURY SURAT

ORIENT BLACKSWAN PRIVATE LIMITED

Registered Office
3-6-752 Himayatnagar, Hyderabad 500 029, Telangana, India
e-mail: centraloffice@orientblackswan.com

Other Offices
Bengaluru, Chennai, Guwahati, Hyderabad, Kolkata,
Mumbai, New Delhi, Noida, Patna, Visakhapatnam

© Orient Blackswan Private Limited 2021
First published by Orient Blackswan Private Limited 2021

The portrait of Nandshankar Mehta and the artwork depicting a
'General View of Surat, India, in 1900' used herein are as available
in the public domain.

ISBN 978-93-5442-143-3

Typeset in
ITC New Baskerville Std 10.5/12.5
by Manmohan Kumar, Delhi

Printed in India at
Thomson Press, New Delhi 110 020

Published by
Orient Blackswan Private Limited
3-6-752 Himayatnagar, Hyderabad 500 029, Telangana, India
e-mail: info@orientblackswan.com

*I dedicate to my supremely adored mother
this biography of my revered father
and the times in which he lived.*
—Vinayak

On the eighth day of Navaratri,
the festival of the Great Mother

CONTENTS

ACKNOWLEDGEMENTS

Nandshankar Jeevan Chitra, one of the early modern biographies in Gujarati, was published in 1916. Its author, Vinayak Nandshankar Mehta, was born in Surat in 1885, educated at Elphinstone College in Bombay, at Kings College in Cambridge, and studied German language and literature at Heidelberg University in Germany. He joined the Indian Civil Service in 1907, with a posting in Eastern United Provinces (present day Uttar Pradesh).

I undertook the translation of *Nandshankar Jeevan Chitra,* a largely forgotten text, as a filial duty to Vinayak Mehta, who died in 1940 when I was less than two years of age. My grandmother Iravati kept his memory alive for the next thirty-eight years, all along exhorting her grandchildren not to forget the lyrical man of noble vision. It was she who gave me a rare copy of *Nandshankar Jeevan Chitra.* My first debt is to her.

I owe special thanks to Aban Mukherji, whose nuanced understanding of the Gujarati language and its literature kept me within the bounds of accuracy. She gave of herself with unstinting generosity as we went over the original text line by line. I am grateful to Moyna Mazumdar, my editor, for suggestions with respect to translation as well as presentation of the text; to Tulsi Vatsal, Maya Herzberger and Sunanda Herzberger for valuable suggestions and to Santhi Narasimhan for editorial support. My thanks to John Irons, for permission to use his translation of Goethe's poem '*Über allen Gipfeln*'.

TRANSLATOR'S INTRODUCTION

Nandshankar Jeevan Chitra—a picture of Nandshankar Tuljashankar Mehta's life—was written by his son Vinayak Mehta in 1916. It was a tribute to the first Gujarati novelist, in which he outlines the course of Nandshankar's personal life as steeped in purity and goodness, with responsibility to extended family members, and to the larger society. Vinayak fills in the sketch with colour drawn from Nandshankar's historical novel *Karan Ghelo*, the story of the Muslim conquest of Gujarat in the twelfth century. The novel's chief protagonist, Madhav, is Nandshankar's second self. Like Nandshankar, he is portrayed as belonging to Nandshankar's sub-caste, married to a much younger woman, as an eminently able administrator, and a committed rationalist. In *Karan Ghelo*, Madhav betrays his king to the Muslim emperor, Allauddin Khilji, becoming an agent of Gujarat's downfall. Nandshankar and his son both raise the question of Madhav's guilt, but the question is raised defensively, within the abstract philosophical issues of free will versus the will of the deity, in order to mitigate Madhav's culpability. The biographer, however, does not explore in any depth whether guilt accrues to Nandshankar for serving the East India Company, the Raj, or in any other context.

Given the patriarchal character of the time, it is perhaps unsurprising that the biography is written with extreme reverence for the father, and themes of betrayal and guilt are insufficiently explored. In fact, Vinayak Mehta adopts the accepted practice of never referring to one's father directly by name, as it would be considered disrespectful. Instead, he uses inflected versions of the reflexive pronoun—*poté, potānu*—a locution without a counterpart in English usage, and awkward even in Gujarati.

Vinayak Mehta's is not an intrusive presence in the biography. In significant sections the distance between the biographer and his subject dissolves, the narrator's voice fuses with the subject and a thoughtful and vivid voice speaks to the reader. There is only a rare hint of the more complex relationship between father and son, unlike the angle that is the mainstay of modern father–son biographies.

The adult Vinayak's acquaintance with his father Nandshankar was relatively brief. He was born in his father's late middle age, when Nandshankar was almost fifty years old and, at the age of twenty, left for England in 1903. Nandshankar died two years later. Vinayak returned to India in 1906 to join the Indian Civil Service. 'Given the significant lapse of time and the absence of diaries', he was unable to recover his father's 'involvement with municipal affairs, or unearth the articles' that he had written for newspapers (p. 110). How Vinayak could have recorded in conversational details Nandshankar's voice as teacher, writer and administrator remains a mystery, as he himself admits. One possible source could be the correspondence between father and son during the years Vinayak was abroad, or the source could perhaps be a product of Vinayak's prodigious memory filtered through his imagination. Unfortunately, Vinayak's papers, with the exception of a few diaries and photographs, are lost.

In 1913, Vinayak sent the completed manuscript of his father's biography to his elder brother Markandrao in Dumas, a seaside suburb of Surat, where the Nandshankar clan gathered in winter. Hansa Mehta, his niece, recalls family members avidly discussing the book, their feeling that the biography would remain a unique contribution to Gujarat's literature, and their doubts whether it would be within reach of the common reader.[*] For Vinayak was aware that readers may find the form he had adopted for his biography—vividly satirical conversations interspersed with abstract philosophical reflections, all framed within a myth from

---

[*] See Hansa Mehta 1916[1979]: 9.

the *Vishnu Purana*—difficult. He had requested his brother to edit, 'to add or to subtract from' the text. Unfortunately, Markandbhai, suffering from an acute asthmatic condition, died before finishing the task. 'I sent the manuscript to the printer without refashioning it any further,' Vinayak writes in his preface to the book. The result is a rich and occasionally obscure text, its obscurity compounded by the allusive nature of the multi-lingual content.

What follows is an overview of *Nandshankar Jeevan Chitra* (*NJC*) based on my translation of the original Gujarati text. I present each of the five chapters of the biography more or less in their original sequence: Nandshankar's forebears and boyhood; the impact of modern colonial education on the poets, critics and reformers of mid-nineteenth century Surat; Nandshankar as author of an historical novel; Nandshankar as administrator; Nandshankar in retirement. My intention is to trace Vinayak sketch a hundred years of Surat's social history, and the changes that occurred as one governing regime replaced the next. I have, in addition, referenced the Indian and European poets and thinkers that frame Nandshankar's portrait with the help of footnotes. In short, my concern throughout has been to read between the lines, and uncover Vinayak's intentions in relating the story of his father's life.

Nandshankar did not belong to a particularly distinguished lineage. His forebears, unlike some other members of the Nagar brahmin caste to which he belonged, were not *diwans* in the *Nawabi*, nor did they serve in the *kachairies* (courts) of the time. His grandfather Amritlal Mehta was 'either a clerk or aspiring to be one', a shrewd man about town, a fashionable ne'er-do-well and 'a jocular man, given to telling tall tales' (p. 4).

The feckless Amritlal died at the age of twenty-six, leaving behind a widowed Umiyakunvar and a son, Tuljashankar. She was made of sterner stuff than her husband, too independent to surrender to traditional norms imposed on widows, for 'how could she tolerate being holed up in some corner of a small room, in a place where she had neither family nor friend?' Vinayak describes the young woman strapping her son to her back, and swimming across the Tapi river to her parents' home in Olpad. 'Before leaving', the author dryly notes, 'she wrote a message in charcoal on the front door: "Do not look for me. I have gone to Olpad," proving, at the very least, that the women of the time were literate' (p. 5). In Olpad, the determined young widow succeeded in arranging Tuljashankar's marriage to the wealthy landlord Surajlal Desai's daughter, and so, forever changing the direction of her family's life.

That Vinayak venerated womankind is displayed throughout the biography. A rare passage respectful of women from the *Manusmriti*: 'The gods delight [in homes] where women are honoured,' animates the description of his parental household. He praises the independent women of Surat, who translate public events into *garba* songs, and who, seated on the threshold of their homes, with boundless curiosity plie passersby with an unending series of question upon question.

Umiyakunvar's move to Olpad and her success in negotiating a good match for her son, Tuljashankar, enabled him to set up house in Surat, and to send his only son, Nandshankar, to the newly opened English School. Nandshankar proved an able student, who attracted the favour of his teachers. His career unfolded under the aegis of the newly established education department. He began as a school master of the English School, then became headmaster, and subsequently head of the Teacher Training College. At the urging of Sir Theodore Hope, he next joined the lower rungs of government service as *mamlatdar*. His rise in the services was steady; in due course, he became Diwan of Kutch.

At the age of twenty-one, Nandshankar married the ten-year-old Nandgauri. Unlike the poet Narmadashankar, a contemporary of his father's, Nandshankar became a householder, reaching 'the other shore' without the usual struggle accompanying adolescence and, in his case, a relatively late marriage. There are hints of a brief struggle, given that Nandshankar's first suit was rejected, and the young girl to whom he was affianced married into a family of greater standing.

In Vinayak's telling, Nandshankar sailed through the rest of life on an even keel, with a family of wife and six children bonded in affection. He quotes a current homily describing what makes a satisfactory life:

> To be fit in body is the first happiness,
> To have sons at home is the next,
> To have gold is the third,
> And an excellent wife is the fourth. [p. 19]

Measured against these standards, Vinayak concludes, 'Father had acquired bodily health, progeny, money, and perhaps, best of all, an excellent wife' (p. 20).

In 1868, while still headmaster of the English School, and a passionate reader of Walter Scott and Bulwer Lytton's historical novels, Nandshankar wrote *Karan Ghelo*. The novel is set at a turning point in Gujarat's history, when the Muslim emperor of Delhi, Allauddin Khilji, defeated Gujarat's Rajput king, Karan Vaghela. The defeated king lived to see his queen preside over the Muslim emperor's seraglio, and his daughter marry Allauddin's son. The event is fraught with emotional and moral ambiguities, since Madhav, Karan's first minister, who betrayed Gujarat to the Muslim emperor, belonged to Nandshankar's Nagar caste.

The book was initially commissioned by a colonial government anxious to provide their newly arrived Haileybury civil servants with suitable reading material in the Indian vernacular languages. A fresh reprint of *Karan Ghelo* was later offered for use in government schools, 'provided all mention of spirits and ghosts is removed'. The rulers' civilising mission was to rid their Indian subjects of superstition, hence their insistence on ridding the text of irrational belief; the author's was to preserve historical accuracy, hence his indignant rejection of the government offer: 'My book won't be repaired by censors'. Thereafter, he had it printed at his own expense. Vinayak explains that his historically-minded father was dedicated to placing before his readers' eyes a true vision of the past; and that representing the beliefs of the time required reference to spirits and ghosts.

Vinayak was a recent member of the Indian Civil Services posted in Eastern United Provinces, what was once Awadh, when he wrote *NJC*. Constructed on the basis of remembered conversations and anecdotes, Vinayak treats his father as part of a larger community located at a particular moment in historical time. Looking beyond Nandshankar's achievements and the immediate events in his life, he embeds his subject in the political and cultural life of eighteenth and nineteenth-century Gujarat. The region had witnessed political and cultural rupture as Mughal and Maratha rule gave way to rule by the East India Company. An important concern of the biographer is to trace how members of Surat's elite experienced the transition from the Nawabi to British rule. 'A person is tied primarily to the cultures of the clan, then of the region and finally of caste', writes Vinayak, implying that social history is implicit in the writing of a life.

Vinayak's is a many-layered approach to the social life of Surat and its upper-caste inhabitants. Literary allusions—often going back to ancient times, women's songs and Farsi poetry—morph into an analysis of the changing social structures while cameo portraits of a generation of men and women of the period recreate the life-world of each historical period.

Surat was once the pre-eminent Mughal port, a gateway to the spice islands of the East and, through the Arab lands of the West, to Asia Minor. Portuguese, Dutch, French, Austrian, Swedish, and English traders first came to Surat before spreading inland. Surat, like Venice on the Adriatic, was a splendid city. For the Muslims of India it was the Gateway to Mecca. A pilgrim from north India arriving in Surat covered with dust could, after bathing in the Tapi river, be heard exclaiming, 'We are in the courtyard of the Holy Land!'

The bridal songs sung by the women of the city bespoke the geographical stretch of their imagination and the wealth at their command: 'Fetch her pearls from the Fort at Hormuz; tiny pearls from Singapore. Only gold from Sri Lanka will do'. Songs allude to wealth gained from migration: 'He who travels to Java does not return; if he does, he feeds three generations to come' (p. 22).

Even when Surat ceased to be a Mughal port, an afterglow of Nawabi culture remained. Brahmin and kayasth administrators competed to display their command over Farsi: Nagars translated their *sandhya* ritual hymn into the court language and called themselves by Persianised titles, such as Sahebrai and Mijlasarai. Humorous anecdotes recreate the social ambience of a city peopled with pretentious courtiers, inept physicians, brutal schoolmasters and pious wives.

For Vinayak, men of this period lacked vision; though drowning in debt they indulged an ostentatious love of grand displays: 'In this way your name attains immortality; what else then is the purpose of life?' (p. 59). Organising an elaborate parade for the bridegroom's party was a business enterprise requiring professional skills. So was the art of dressing the hair of young girls accompanying the bridegroom's horse in the parade, or of 'painting *tilaks* on women's foreheads, and of adjusting ornaments, often borrowed, to hang just so. ..."You have to have an eye for it, and not everyone does!"' (p. 59). These event managers earned themselves the official name of *Varghodia*; families across caste lines engaged *Varghodia* services.

By the beginning of nineteenth century, Surat had become part of the Bombay Presidency. The imposition of a new governing order at this stage did not alter people's thinking in any significant way, according to Vinayak. As if to illustrate the point, he holds up to ridicule an alcoholic English judge, trained at Haileybury College, being manipulated in court by his shrewd Gujarati assisting clerks.

A sea-change occurred, however, when in the wake of the new regime 'came English education, with its myriad cultural streams'. A new world of literature and culture, shaped by the European Enlightenment, was now open to the elite of Surat. Irish, Scottish and English schoolmasters swelled the ranks of the newcomers to become catalysts of change. Vinayak recreates Nandshankar's portraits of several of his teachers. His most affectionate and respectful one is of Henry Green, the first principal of the English School in Surat. Green Saheb treated his students effusively, without condescension. According to Nandshankar, 'distinctions of colour cast no shadow on our daily interactions'.

He introduced his students to his well-stocked library, inspired them to borrow books, and did his utmost to prevent religious influence from taking hold of the educational system. After the 1857 Uprising ended, Henry Green wrote a book under the pen name Indophile, in which he pleaded for a just treatment of the rebels.

A defining moment in Nandshankar's life was when Green Saheb introduced him to his friend Scott Saheb, a naval officer stationed in Surat. In words Vinayak attributes to Nandshankar, 'There were a variety of telescopes arranged on his terrace; looking through them at the skies, I glimpsed the universe. I cannot even begin to describe the joy that filled me then. ...I am a child of the universe—these were my feelings at the time' (p. 37).

The experience carried the student beyond the narrow margins of caste identity to a wider vision of what it means to be human. Nandshankar's subsequent career as a reformer, administrator and novelist is marked by a modest and generous sensibility.

❧

Chapter Two of *NJC* begins on a very different note. In language that is often figurative, occasionally dramatic but also good-humoured, the author reaches out to abstract questions regarding the conflict between tradition and modernity, relations between individuals and social groups, the treatment of women, and how an alien but more dynamic culture affects individual lives.

The chapter is set in the two decades between 1860 and 1880. Modern historians of Gujarati literature describe this period as 'The Age of Reform', a time when a group of writers and educators sought to transform their social world—they publicly denounced Tantriks and sorcerers who preyed on a superstitious people, actively preached against image worship, organised movements in support of a widow's right to remarry, and defied the dictates of caste.

Vinayak approaches the reformers' conflict with orthodoxy and the ensuing tumult in society within the framework of a famous myth from the *Vishnu Purana*. Arrayed on opposite sides, churning a cosmic ocean of milk are the gods (*deva*) and the anti-gods (*danava*), competing for the treasures that will surface. Transposed to mid-nineteenth century Surat, the gods are symbols of the 'new energy, subtlety and light of modernity', the anti-gods 'of all the old and inert forces of tradition'. Later in the chapter, he examines each of the 'gems' in the light of contemporary social divisions.

Vinayak held that conflict between tradition and modernity courses through individual lives. His declared purpose in the biography is to paint 'a clear portrait of the age', and to furnish his 'picture with the figures whose thought and actions left a mark on it' (p. 71). And so, based on stories that his father told him, he creates brief biographies of the three major literary figures, the three 'N's (*nanna*) of Gujarat's literature: Narmadashankar, Navalram and Nandshankar—all active advocates of social reform. The life stories, however, cover two additional subjects, Mahipatram Rupram and Durgaram Manchharam Mehta. In commenting on these figures, Vinayak merges his voice with his father Nandshankar's.

Rationality (*buddhivad*)[†] was the major influence on the group of reformers. Their manifesto was marked by zeal expressed in dramatic imperatives: '"Unite, brothers unite!" "Lift up the lowest rung of the caste ladder until it reaches the very top, so that the distance between high and low collapses, caste hierarchies disappear and society is united!" "Lift, brothers lift!"…"Dare to act!" is what we taught' (p. 85).

The poet Samaldas' is a counter voice speaking on behalf of tradition against these dangerous adventurers: 'Destruction awaits men who are adventurous' (p. 85). Vinayak's response to the poet's charge evokes a larger purpose, that reform of the existing hierarchical social order is necessary, as both unity and equality are prerequisites of national governance. The fruits of reform will transform Gujarat society: new methods of education will take hold and modern education will end superstition; men

---

[†] *Buddhivad* also refers to the seventeenth-century European Enlightenment.

will no longer worship images; women will be treated with dignity; and widows allowed the right to remarry, if only rationality is rightly understood.

Mahipatram and Narmadashankar were the most radical of those seeking reform of the existing social order. Mahipatram was the more intrepid, travelling to Europe in defiance of caste rules that banished from its folds all those who crossed the boundaries of India. Nandshankar, initially offered the opportunity to travel, had turned it down due to pressure from the family. In London and Paris, Mahipatram studied newly established methods of education and returned to India to become part of the educational reform in Ahmedabad. He turned iconoclast, daring to promote stern views against the worship of idols in a region where passionate devotees worshipped Lord Krishna's image in paintings and statues. With the zeal of a seventeenth-century English Puritan, he would hold aloft representations of baby Krishna and declaim, 'Watch! Your god is powerless. He cannot harm me' (p. 80). He viewed the world through entirely rationalist lenses and, says Vinayak, 'had not Keshab Chandra Sen sounded his clarion call, drawing him to the Brahmo Samaj and its reforms, Mahipatram might well have leaned towards atheism of the Charvaka school' of materialists (p. 83).

Narmadashankar was different. In him, lyricism sat side by side with heroism. Cast in the Byronic mould, he was Gujarat's swashbuckling hero and her best loved poet. Ever ready to fight injustice, he railed against the condition of widows and supported progressive reform, including widow remarriage. He was endowed with charisma and qualities of sound political leadership: the ability to speak hard words ('Speak, you who have taken vows of silence!' [p. 72]) and still, like a magnet, attract people. 'If an association was to be formed, a lecture given, people's consciousness raised or society reformed, he was there'."[‡] Vinayak draws attention to Narmad's essay 'Unity', which argued against caste on the ground that it prevented national unity.

Fortune was not kind to the poet; his life was, in fact, tragic. He married young and was obliged to set up house very early in

---

[‡] Labhshankar 1912[1933]: 4; translation mine.

life. The age lacked discerning patrons who, Vinayak suggests, might have supported the poet. Besides, poets are not meant by instinct to fit into society and, like the oil-presser's ox, go round and round in circles eking out a livelihood.

Narmadashankar was impatient, eager for radical change, and when it did not come, he retreated to launch a full-scale attack against those very forces that had freed him from the strangulating grip of tradition: 'Go back to your roots,' he declared; 'Unless you become as a seed, you won't ever experience the stately canopy of maturity' (p. 75). The embrace of modernity without a proper understanding of its underlying rational spirit was dangerous. To Vinayak, Narmadashankar's life was a symbol of modernity gone wrong.

Nandshankar admired Navalram above all his other contemporaries. As a literary critic, Navalram, he believed, wielded his pen with compassion. As a social critic, he was farsighted and predicted that 'the intoxicated passion' for reform would not last. As a liberal reformer, with faith in the power of education to bring about gradual change, he, like Nandshankar, 'favoured the Aristotelian Middle Path, a predilection that had its source in his calm and truthful character' (p. 30).

Having sketched cameo portraits of the major intellectuals and poets of the period, Vinayak returns to the myth of the churned ocean to examine the influence of each surfacing 'jewel' on the social world. Claiming that Nandshankar undertook the interpretation facetiously, Vinayak's own part-serious, part-pedestrian, but on the whole didactic reinterpretation of what at first glance appears merely to be a random list of objects takes on deeper meaning.

The moralising tone accompanying the analysis is justified because not all the fourteen jewels that emerged from the churned ocean were beneficent; there is poison, which threatens to annihilate the world and alcohol (*sura*), which leads men astray. There is also nectar. The value of a gem depends on how it is used. Human nature has two sides, the celestial and the earthly. Beyond the reach of reform, and even beyond rationality, there is human nature. 'Father,' adds Vinayak, 'put it this way: Ariel walks hand in hand with Caliban. In an age when the individual self is being churned, poison is infused with nectar in our temperament. To destroy darkness and spread light is the work of the gods' (p. 88).

His comments on Kamadhenu, the cow who grants whatever you ask of her, are interesting; they capture the ambiguities of the 'gifts' from the ocean. Father and son identify Kamadhenu with rationality (*buddhivad*). Kamadhenu will give you what you ask for, but 'you do not know what to ask of her, are disgusted with what you receive, and so push her away' (p. 87). The second-person usage here directly addresses the poet Narmadashankar, who understood modernity only partially, led an undisciplined life and, in the end, retreated into the past, dying an impoverished man.

The chapter, which began with the gods and anti-gods churning the cosmic ocean, ends with a seafaring metaphor. This time round, the conflict is between the collective voice of tradition and individual voices of modernity. The scene opens in real space and time: in Surat between the 1860s and 1880s, a large vessel sets sail on an open, uncharted sea, carrying intrepid seafarers willing to navigate an unknown future. Each has a unique rallying cry, but together the voices create a harmonious chorus.

At the helm sits the 'intoxicated poet' Narmadashankar, singing songs of heroism and love:

> Come together to forge new bonds,
> aboard a vessel of our own native land,
> flying the flag of reform. [p. 119]

Navalram adds in a gentle voice: 'Education is the death of superstition. Prepare yourself to serve the nation. Draw strength from the armour of intelligence. Listen to the poet's song and move forward' (p. 119).

Mahipatram proclaims: 'Be industrious! Persevere! Believe in the true God. Give up the worship of graven images! Listen, as I relate the tales of my travel' (p. 119).

And Nandshankar with great passion advises: 'Be radiant. Cultivate joy and the love of wisdom. In the process, beware of becoming a loudmouth or a swollen head, lest you become a laughing stock. Listen, I will read you a novel. At the very least, it will teach you a love of your land. Come below deck into the ship's treasure hold—the waves strike less violently there' (p. 119).

From the shore, conservative upholders of the traditional order call out, 'Come back! Come back, whilst there is yet time!' The three answer together: 'We have slid the boat into the waters. Whatever will happen is right' (p. 120).

❧

Vinayak becomes literary critic in Chapter Four of *NJC*. He analyses the sources of his father's book, explores its language, and describes the development of character and plot. Vinayak describes how he hears the musical echoes of the *charan*s and the *bhat*s, the Rajasthani and Gujarati bards whose songs preserved the story on which *Karan Ghelo* is based. In its use of metaphor, a typical mark of oral recitations, Nandshankar's prose becomes 'a daughter of narrative poetry'. Vinayak himself carries forward the bardic tradition: he speaks directly to Karan, and pleads with his audience to pity the king. He appeals to his readers to examine the nuances of Muslim speech, and to appreciate how metaphor is always within reach of what they want to say.

'Should you, dear Reader, wish to become versed in speech that is effusive, in words that have the power to please and to flatter, besides being lyrical', then listen to Allauddin Khilji's emissary speak, urges Vinayak (p. 182). Sent to persuade a defeated Raja Karan to surrender his daughter to her mother, the messenger's metaphors are eloquent:

> As long as she remains with you, Devaldevi will be like a deer separated from its herd. Like a fish removed from water, she will surely die struggling unless you return her to water. You have distanced a moth from light; away from the light how will she regain her joyful calm? You have uprooted a flowering plant from the garden and planted it in the desert sands of Marwad. How do you expect it to grow there without water? [*KG* 13.370; translation mine]§

§ All translations of passages from *Karan Ghelo* (Nandshankar Mehta 1866[1935]) used in this volume are mine, and cited as *KG*.

To contemporary critics of the novel who frowned upon the use of Farsi words ('iron filings served in a plate of gold'), Vinayak retorts with irony. He uses *gira* (speech), the arcane Sanskrit word for 'language', which most Gujarati speakers would not understand, let alone use, to highlight the role of everyday speech. '*Gira*', he categorically states,

> is no one's ancestral property; it belongs to the native speakers who inhabit a country or region (*mulak*); it must bear the stamp of their ways, their customs, their religious beliefs and so on. Should one pretend that Muslims never did enter Hindustan and that their language, their ideas and their ways have in no way influenced Gujarati speech (*Gurjargira*)? This kind of talk is pure illusion, perhaps realised only in the imagination. [p. 179–180]

In a stout-hearted retort to complaints that the writing, especially the debate in *Karan Ghelo* between Jains and Shaivite brahmins, appears difficult, Vinayak asserts that the 'fault lies in the reader's imperfect command' and ignorance of appropriate vocabulary, 'not in the language used' (p. 179).

Having thus turned aside the critics, but before concluding that the language in *Karan Ghelo* is 'straightforward and simple, yet expressive, passionate and effortlessly ornamented' (p. 179), Vinayak quotes his own favourite metaphorical passage from the text. The passage describes Raja Karan's two daughters nursing their wounded father back to health:

> Observing Karan's suffering, the ever-compassionate God was moved to pity. Like faint rain in the forest wilderness, like a ray of light in darkness, amid all his sorrow, joy and peace appear. Comfort, like drops of dew on parched earth, fills this doomed vessel as two ministering angels descend from the sky to replace the evil spirits who torment Karan. [*KG* 11.297–298]

Nandshankar, according to Vinayak, had a philosophical and writerly interest in the study of individual character; he portrays his protagonists with empathy for he believed that 'the least of a poet's or novelist's responsibilities is to ensure that his characters retain their appeal until the very last' (p. 178). Unlike bardic lore, which condemns Karan Raja as a coward, the Karan of the novel does not turn tail and abandon the battlefield. He is a brave but impulsive warrior, 'more impetuous than a child, always eager to act…he does not fear the consequences of his actions', and in short, he is a picture of 'thoughtless and reckless humanity' (p. 167). Recklessness is Karan's fatal flaw, not cowardice, argues Vinayak. 'We see him live to regret his actions, and yet his humanity imprints itself on our minds. He suffers, and we, the readers, in turn suffer with him' (p. 168).

After he loses the battle, and his passion for Roopasundari, his first minister Madhav's abducted wife, cools, the Karan in *Karan Ghelo* consoles himself by saying, 'It was all fated'. At this point the author intervenes to observe that, 'The truth is however that in life, he was hostage to his own deeds' (p. 167), not to fate. The modernist believer in free will and choice declares, 'When the events described above occurred in Karan's life, it was still in Karan's hands to alter the course of his future' (p. 167).

But then, by the very same token, does it not follow that Raja Karan's minister, Madhav—a fellow Nagar, who travelled to Delhi to seek Muslim emperor Allauddin Khilji's help in order to avenge his wife's abduction and his brother's murder—is responsible for the fall of Gujarat? 'Shall we make Madhav responsible for Gujarat's fall?' Vinayak poses this question directly to his father, and records Nandshankar's defence of Madhav: 'Father said that the advent of the foreigner on the soil of Gujarat was occasioned by the goddess' anger, and that therefore, our view of Madhav should not be entirely negative' (p. 173).

Clearly dissatisfied with his father's explanation, Vinayak tries to improve upon it by attributing chance and necessity as additional powers of the goddess. Necessity and Chance are Greek goddesses, Ananke and Tyche, but as accidental event and inevitable consequence, they are also secular concepts with currency in the everyday world. The goddess in her many guises attends Madhav throughout his journey to Delhi. In her vengeful form as Ambabhavani, the goddess prevents him from attempting suicide, so he can fulfil his quest for revenge against the king.

By chance, a fire breaks out just as he enters Delhi, and he is mysteriously presented with an opportunity to save the crown prince Khizr Khan. The prince's rescue paves the way to Madhav's audience with Allauddin. After all, as Vinayak argues or rather observes, there is no causal connection between Allauddin's ascent to the throne and Karan's humiliation of Madhav. Moreover, is it not mere chance that Madhav's audience with Allauddin happens at an opportune moment, just when the emperor is dreaming of becoming a second Alexander?

Events and actions in the present are driven by collective as well as individual actions of the past. This unseen force is accumulated *karma*—the idea that individuals, over time, collectively create and fall victim to a force which drives them. In this way, the past catches up with the present. 'Neither Karan nor Madhav lack the will to act', Vinayak reasons, 'But it is as though some unseen force pushes them, as though a tidal wave from the past is sweeping them away in its wake' (p. 175). No single human being has willed the loss of Gujarat; the loss is a result of historical necessity and chance. Contingency, in the person of the goddess, is the agent of Gujarat's conquest, and Madhav is merely 'an instrument of historical forces' (p. 174).

This idea translates into an aesthetic demand that novelists 'work towards a sense of historical inevitability, which then takes on the appearance of fate'. This aesthetic principle is shaped in the framework of collective karma. In this way, an old idea is conceived anew in a secular idiom and rendered comprehensible to modern Gujarati readers.

Vinayak does not analyse Allauddin Khilji's character beyond stating that it is a far more vividly drawn portrait than any found in the annals of history. The Muslim emperor is no villain; 'Virtue and vice, like shadow and light, are drawn' into his portrait (p. 178). Khilji, though cruel, is a just king.

Roopasundari, Madhav's abducted young wife, is tender like a 'still unfolding bud'. Vinayak contrasts her with the strong-willed character of Bhramar in Bankimchandra's novel *Chandrakant's Will*. Bhramar has the strength to kill herself, while Roopasundari sits neglected in a corner after Karan Raja's passion for her is spent. She is 'not someone who, when pulled in one direction, pushes with equal force in the opposite' (p. 176).

Continuing his floral metaphors, Vinayak describes Raja Karan's queen Kaularani as a tall, robust and courageous figure, a 'sturdy lotus' to Roopasundari's 'delicate *champa* flower'. 'Kauladevi's lament at leaving Gujarat rends our hearts', says Vinayak, but she is fickle-hearted, dazzled by the glamour of Allauddin's court. While later nationalist writers like K. M. Munshi find the character of a Rajput queen presiding over a Muslim emperor's court unacceptable, Vinayak views her with a detached gaze and says, 'Kaularani forgets the past. Is a lotus able to stop blooming?' (p. 178).

In 1880, Gagabhai Samaldas, an elder statesman of Kathiawad, received a letter from Dadabhai Naoroji in which Dadabhai described the comparative advantages of native governance as follows: '…if administered carefully and honestly, [Princely States] should share a far greater degree of prosperity than the British Provinces can ever attain. Everything is in favour of Native States' (p. 158–159). Nandshankar—who had served the colonial government as well as the principalities of Devgarh Bariya, Lunawada, and Sunth, and was Diwan of Kutch when Dadabhai's letter arrived—supported Dadabhai's opinion with arguments of his own. Vinayak states his father's case as follows:

It is supremely important, he believed, to serve in the public administration of Princely States, lest our own administrative genius fall into disuse. Administering states according to native systems is far less expensive because the system does not require the long and hierarchical ladder of authority. Native governance is based on friendly understanding; for Indians realise where the shoe pinches, and provide easy remedies for the pain. However, our people must undoubtedly learn from the English that a sense of duty is all important, and must be venerated. Independent judgement must like a river's course be kept in check; if it is allowed to overflow, total destruction will result. Patronage must be rooted out, talent encouraged, flattery consigned to flames, and partisanship kept at arm's length. If we adhere to these principles, there will be no happier political body than the Princely State. [p. 159]

Nandshankar's views remained constant despite his tenure as Diwan of Kutch ending abruptly, mainly due to court intrigue, for the Queen Mother was anxious that her young son marry into her own Jadeja clan, while the British Resident Major Reeves was against granting the Queen's wishes. Both sides were adamant, and Nandshankar was caught in the middle.

The issue—of whether it would better serve the larger interest of the people of India to have the Native States administered by Indians or by the colonial government—continued to be debated in Nandshankar's extended family. Two of Nandshankar's sons took on administrative positions with both governments.

The Diwan of Kutch reverted to his position as Assistant Political Agent at Rewakantha in 1883. That his talents outranked his official status is expressed through the words of a Mr Spence, then Collector of Godhra: 'Mr Nandshankar has carried on the duties with marked ability, and there can be no doubt he is drawn away in such an appointment' (p. 155); and further, that, 'It would however be very desirable to find some other suitable post for this officer. The Commissioners of Central and Northern Division should be reminded of the case' (p. 153).

Even as Assistant Political Agent, much work however still lay ahead, including setting right the disarray in the Princely State of Rajpipla, where 'The treasury was empty, the people oppressed, and there was no concern for their welfare as the licentious Raja was completely absorbed in marrying one woman after another' (p. 154). All this entailed hard work, which took a toll on his health. He fell ill with cholera, and recovered, but only to have his eyesight fail.

At fifty-five, having reached *vanaprastha*, when men are meant to foreswear the worldly life and prepare to retreat into forest wilderness, Nandshankar retired to the quiet seashore of Dumas, on the outskirts of Surat. He died in 1905, while Vinayak was away as a student in England.

Nandshankar Jeevan Chitra is an idealised portrait of Nandshankar. The aspects of the biography which describe in great detail Nandshankar's advice on school education, on women, on companionate marriage, and on caste, are didactic, as biographies of the period were meant to be. At a basic level, it is the life story of a modest man born in a traditional middle-class brahmin family of Surat, making his way in the larger colonial world as a revered schoolteacher, an able administrator in colonial service, a social reformer, and as Gujarat's first novelist. At a more complex level, it is an erudite and literary biography of a fortunate man who embraced the values of the European Enlightenment and successfully navigated what he believed was a dangerous passage to modernity. Unlike Nandshankar, not all who set sail on the unmapped high seas came equipped either with a moral compass, or the tranquil and detached temper to reach the other shore safely. That Nandshankar succeeded was perhaps a legacy of his traditional Indian values, so Vinayak suggests in a snapshot image of his father—an enlightened man seated under a banyan tree, with his face turned to the world, blessing his progeny:

> Like a man who renounces the worldly life and sits meditating under the shade of an old banyan tree, gazing at the wonders of creation, detached from it all and yet in love with it, I saw him elated and gently smiling. My eldest brother had five children, my second brother four, my elder sister Harsiddhagauri six, and my second sister Sulochanagauri two—in this way, from the solitary homes of Amritram and Tuljashankar had sprung an extended clan. There is a belief in the Shinto faith that our invisible ancestors help their descendants. May our ancestral hosts care for us! [p. 197]

The original manuscript of *NJC* has not survived, nor is there a copy of the first edition of 1916. A second edition was published forty-five years later, in 1961. My translation is based on the third edition of 1979, edited by Bhupendra Trivedi.

As already mentioned, Vinayak refers to his father by means of an inflected reflexive pronoun, *poté*, *potané*, which I have substituted with 'Father'. He refers to his mother as *Matushri*, which I have rendered as 'revered mother'.

In my translation I have tried to remain as close to the original text as possible, occasionally reversing the order of sentences within a paragraph. I have rendered proper nouns according to their pronunciation in Gujarati, for example: *Ramayan*, *Mahabharat*, and Kumbhakaran, and not *Ramayana*, *Mahabharata*, and Kumbhakarna; saheb, and not sahib.

All translations of other (or secondary) texts from the Gujarati, Sanskrit, Hindi, and Marathi—quoted by Vinayak Mehta in the original—are mine, except where otherwise cited. My translations of Farsi and Urdu quotations are based on their Gujarati renderings by the author.

My translations of passages from *Karan Ghelo*, quoted by Vinayak Mehta in the original, are from the ninth edition of *Karan Ghelo*, published in 1935 by Manubhai Mehta to mark the centenary of Nandshankar's birth. Besides Nandshankar's original preface, it also includes prefaces by his two elder sons: Markandrao Mehta's preface to the third, fourth and fifth editions, and Manubhai Mehta's preface to the ninth edition.

AUTHOR'S PREFACE

My hope is that in the absence of written records, the form I have adopted for a biography of my greatly revered father, Nandshankar Tuljashankar, will be acceptable to my readers.

I finished the present work in September 1913, and sent the manuscript to my elder brother Markandrao, to add to or subtract from it. A severely asthmatic condition had rendered him quite weak, so the work of editing it proceeded slowly. Then, of a sudden, on the 3rd of September of this year, my supremely beloved brother met his end. I did not refashion the manuscript any further and sent it to the printer as it was. I am very grateful to my good friends Mangaldas Pakvasa and Manilal Iccharam Desai for their help.

Vinayak Nandshankar Mehta
Baharich

Chapter I

DAWN

My father was born in Surat, on the fourth day of the rising moon of the month of Chaitra, in the year 1891 of the Samvat Era, or 21 April 1835 of the Christian Calendar. His noble eyes first beheld the Gujarat earth in a rented house located across from the Vaishnav temple at the edge of Shaitanphalia, in Gopipura Mohalla. My father's maternal grandfather, Surajlal Desai, lived in Olpad. He was a well-to-do man, respected in the community. However, being a widower, he was unable to bring his only daughter home for her child's birth. So, Father was born in his father's house instead of the maternal home, as was customary.

A person is tied primarily to the cultures of the clan, then of the region, and finally of caste. An individual may choose the direction in which his life will soar; he is responsible for the face he turns to the future. He is not responsible for the circumstance of his birth. Indeed, why is such a backward glance at all necessary? Once the arrow leaves the bow, what is to be gained by tracing its course? The initial thrust determines where it will land; why then worry about the path? We, in India, do not preserve our ancestral history.

Save for his name, nothing significant is known of Shobharam Mehta's son Mayaram, who counts among our ancestors. Did he create any ripples in the ocean of life? Did he try to reform society? We do not know. Like a bubble he rose above the surface of flowing water, and subsided. Only the steadfast stars watching from above are witness to his life. Someone, no doubt, is aware of his past but, if so, his mouth is sealed. Naturally, in times gone by, Mayaram would have interacted with individual men and women—but, like '*mugo ko sapano bhayo*, the dreams of the mute', the past is silent.

Many stories are still told in our community about Father's grandfather, Amritram Mehta, who was born around 1776. The flags of both the English and the Mughals flew over the port of Surat in those days when Ali Nawaz Khan was Nawab. Amritram was a jocular man, given to telling tall tales. He was shrewd, and either a clerk, or aspiring to be one. Having been bestowed with an enthusiasm for wealth, rather than its reality, his daring knew no bounds. He died young, at age twenty-six, leaving behind a small son and a spirited young widow.

The following story is told about him. On one occasion, a friend jokingly remarked, 'Hey pal, you've risen high, but I don't see you ride a palanquin'. 'So? Wait here and you will see me pass by, enthroned in one', Amritram swaggered.

In those days the Nagars and the Kayasths of the city enjoyed powerful positions in the Nawab's administration; since Kirparam Mehta was Diwan, the Nagar community in particular enjoyed special standing. Today, a man doffing his hat signifies his elevated status; in those days a young dandy donned colourful turbans in the Mughal style, and long *jama*s or robes with dangling scarves to proclaim his station in society.

Finely attired in this manner, Amritram proceeded to the palanquin shop and ordered a fancy sedan chair. No sooner was the order placed than the shopkeeper executed it. Convinced that Amritram was certainly the major domo of a wealthy household with some standing in the community, and in anticipation of a generous tip, the shopkeeper decided to humour him, saying, 'Why should you walk home pray, when our palanquin is at your disposal?' The invitation was just the ticket. Seated in his palanquin, wearing a pleased expression on his face, Amritram salaamed his friends, who had been waiting for him at an appointed spot, shuffling their feet. He next alighted at the doorsteps of Sheth Bhukanwala's house, where grand wedding celebrations were in progress. He entered through the front door and immediately exited through the back. Tired of waiting for him, the palanquin bearers probably departed. The impetuous Amritram must have ignored their grumbling—why should barking dogs bother an elephant? The hosts probably paid off the palanquin bearers, presuming that there had been some misunderstanding, and Amritram's friends must have complimented him for enjoying life gratis, without paying for its pleasures.

Amritram Mehta died in 1801. According to the traditions of the Nagar caste, a woman is bound to spend the first year of her widowed life in her husband's home. The widow Umiyakunvar was unwilling to spend a whole year with her husband's people. First of all, she was the daughter of a landowning Desai; she was in addition obstinate and, on top of that, she had tasted the independence given to women in Olpad. How could she tolerate being holed up in some corner of a small room in her husband's house, a place where she had neither family nor friend? Unfortunately for her, the husband's people were extremely orthodox, and they certainly would not allow her to flout custom. So, quietly one early morning, Umiyakunvar abandoned her husband's house and, with her child, left for her parental home. Before leaving, she wrote a message in charcoal on the front door: 'Do not look for me. I have gone to Olpad,' proving, at the very least, that the women of the time were literate.

There was no bridge across the Tapi river in those days. Umiyakunvar was of an impatient temper—the ferry seemed to take too long to arrive. So, strapping her young child to her back, she decided to swim across the river to the other bank. Fortunately for the young widow, it was the beginning of summer, so the waters were low, and she swam across to her parental home well before noon. She was probably greeted with cries of, 'Alas Umiya, you here?' Father knew his spirited grandmother, for he was ten years old when she died.

Father's father, Tuljashankar, spent his childhood in Olpad, where a substantial number of residents in the Nagar quarter of town were Desais. Across from Umiyakunvar's house was Surajlal Desai's seat. Umiyakunvar herself was a Desai, and she was determined to find for her only son a bride belonging to the Desai clan. It did not matter to her that she herself had married far from the immediate support of family and clan into an impoverished Mehta household. That her only son should obtain as wife Surajlal's only daughter seemed quite proper to Umiyakunvar. The considerable difference in age between Surajlal's little girl and her son was of no concern to her. For Surajlal was childless, although around twenty-seven at the time of Umiyakunvar's return to Olpad. Then, at the age of forty-two, a daughter was born to him and shortly thereafter, Surajlal lost his wife.

The betrothal of Surajlal's daughter to Umiyakunvar's son was arranged, and in due course the two were married.

From Acheson's account, a peace treaty known as the Treaty of Vasai was signed on 31 December 1802. According to the terms of the treaty, Raghoba the Peshwa was to surrender the *taluk*s of Olpad, Valsad, the Jalalpur districts, parts of Bardoli and Pardi, and the three villages of the 84th district—Katargam, Kumbhariya and Phoolpada—in return for the help the English troops rendered him. Since the Peshwa was against ceding Olpad, the town remained in possession of Narsimh Khanderao Vinchurkar, who held on to it, ceding in exchange parts of Bundelkhand through a treaty signed in 1803.[1]

The Maratha Sardar Gaekwad in turn had revenue rights over the town of Surat. He additionally controlled several villages of the Mahal district. The southern region of Gujarat had borne the brunt of Peshwa rule. The people of the district were aware that rather than annexing conquered territories, the Marathas' core strategy was to extract as much tribute from the region as possible. As a result the farmers were reduced to penury, and the land turned barren; agriculture almost disappeared.

At this point, the Peshwa was finally obliged to act. He gathered together the upper classes from every village and turned them into landlords or Desais who, in exchange for fixed revenue, enjoyed absolute power over the peasantry. Schemes related to the resettlement of villages, distribution of farmland, digging of wells, and revival of wastelands were vested in their hands. The

---

[1] The Treaty of Vasai, also known as the Treaty of Bassein, was signed between the East India Company and Peshwa Baji Rao II. Vitthal Narsing Vinchurkar, a Sardar of the Maratha confederacy, was present when it was signed (see Deshpande 1987: 151).

Desais held a great deal of power; unfortunately for them, it did not last long.

In 1817, when Peshwa Baji Rao sought refuge with the English, the Treaty of Poona was signed. And because Vinchurkar had acted against their interests, the English abrogated the previous treaty and seized Olpad from the Marathas. By this time, the English were acquainted with the ways of north Indian zamindars, and entirely convinced that the Desais were not doing what was necessary for the people's welfare. Besides, their loyalty was suspect. So the English abolished the authority that the Marathas had vested in the Desais and converted their revenue rights into cash transactions.

Even though Surajlal Desai was witness to the rise and fall of the Desais, he and the whole Desai clan believed themselves superior to the Mehtas. Which accords with the popular saying, 'The snakes are gone, but their marks are in the sand'; in other words, old habits die hard.

Tuljashankar and his bride Gangalakshmi set up house in Surat. According to Father, his father was employed in the Customs Department. The position carried a salary of five rupees a month, which rose to fifteen rupees at the time of his father's death.

In those days, to supplement one's salary by way of bribes was considered routine. Instead of being praised, a person who refused a bribe was regarded as otherworldly or eccentric. The distinction between right and wrong was so blurred that even the thought that it was a corrupt practice did not cross anyone's mind. You got your salary in cash, and your rightful 'extras' in kind. Only when the demand was excessive would it be regarded as dishonest. Otherwise things went on just as usual. That is why, in those days, salaries were deliberately kept low.

Fellow caste members considered Tuljabhai, as he was known, a principled man—a gentle sort, unassuming, straightforward, and fond of telling jokes. He was not arrogant. Though he did not have much money, he had no debts either and the household ran smoothly. His eldest daughter Jashodagauri was born in 1829. One or two sons conceived thereafter did not survive, so when Father was born, in 1835, the family's joy could not be contained. A younger sister, Kailashgauri, was born three years later.

Appointed specifically to stop the theft of grain, Tuljabhai's work required travelling from village to village. Of a sudden, one day, he found himself promoted, and transferred from Surat to Bagwada. Unfortunately, it was the wedding season in the Nagar community in Surat, and a series of sumptuous feasts with all manner of sweets in progress. Besides, the climate in the Mandavi air was considered noxious. A popular saying goes:

> If you are not dead by the time you visit Maldha, Limadha, or Motiphal, then come with me to Devgadh,
> 'I'll turn you green, I'll turn you yellow. What more can I do if you don't die?' says Devgadh.

Also,

> Bagwada will leave you only half dead, but Mandavi will certainly finish you off.

To have to abandon festive meals, and on top of that to suffer fetid waters, is that fair? True, you have worked hard, and your salary is raised by two rupees a month; even so, to be sent into the jungles was a cruel blow. Tuljabhai tried his best to have the transfer order revoked, but in vain.

The thought that he might feign illness then crossed his mind. To mimic the symptoms of jaundice is easy, so Tuljabhai rubbed turmeric all over his body until his eyes reflected the yellowish tinge of his skin. He drank salted water to induce vomits, and then proceeded to see the doctor. Knowledge of tropical diseases was in its infancy at this time; moreover, an English doctor had few occasions to treat this disease. Upon observing Tuljabhai's distended belly and his yellowed body, the doctor immediately recommended a two-month furlough; he further added a note stating that if his patient were to be transferred to an area where malaria was rampant, he was certain to die. With this doctor's certificate in hand, Tuljabhai got his leave sanctioned. Feasting on the sweets served at caste meals, Tuljabhai built up his stamina and, many mouthfuls of food later, prepared to do battle with the evil waters of Paliya.

Two major vices afflicting the men of his time were absent in Tuljabhai. He was neither ostentatious, nor did he have a vicious temper. Jocular he certainly was, impatient, too. You might even have seen him strike a person, but closer observation would have revealed the affectionately teasing speech that followed. Laughing, he would make others laugh; he would mock, but without a desire to hurt—like a bird alighting momentarily on a flat surface, pecking at it and then taking off. On occasion his equanimity would be slightly disturbed, but before it registered, he would be back to his old cheerful self. My maternal grandfather related a thousand tales about Tuljabhai that made us laugh.

Our great-great-grandfather on my mother's side, Himmatrai, died when he was old. It was the custom on returning from the cremation grounds to gather in front of the house where the fellow caste member had died, and to weep loudly; it was believed that the louder one's lamentation, the greater your attachment to the dead. With this in mind, Tuljabhai caught hold of my great-granduncle's hand and said, 'Jamiyatram! I'm going to howl at the top of my voice if the portions of *kheer* they serve at the ceremonial meal are niggardly'. Who would not laugh to hear this even on such a sombre occasion?

In those days it was considered very fortunate to die old, so what was there to mourn? Once, seeing Amritkunvar, a woman hardened by widowhood, wandering about hither and thither in anger, Tuljabhai asked, 'What are these offerings of food for your departed husband?' Her immediate response was, 'I have been searching for the damned man for such a long time now, without any luck. And why should he want to meet me anyway? Once the wedding season begins, with its torches and umbrellas, who would bother about a widow!'

Tuljabhai was widowed in his old age, so he had perforce to cook his own meals. On one occasion, he climbed down the staircase leading to his son's room and stood there, trembling. 'What's the matter?' asked the son. The laughter-filled answer was, 'Don't you see the flood descending? The *kadhi* is boiling over; I fear I will be swept away in the deluge!'

This broad-shouldered, well-built man worked until the very end of his days, even after his son had begun earning a decent salary, and there was no need for additional income. He lived to see his son's income grow to a hundred rupees, and a daughter-in-law—a veritable goddess of prosperity—light up the household. There was joy; there was comfort.

Lotuses swayed with joy in gentle breezes when, of a sudden, a killing frost descended—a fatal cancer attacked his throat. He might even have uttered the words, 'Death, oh wait a while, if but a moment longer. There is great joy in my life!' But how can you arrest the inevitable? A man filled with joy, a man whose joyous laughter infected all those whose lives he touched, was now face to face with death. Calling his young daughter-in-law to his bedside, he told her, 'Don't be afraid. I will stand guard by this doorway and finish off anyone who dares to harass you.' She was nursing him with care; his son was away at school as usual, teaching— his father had not been especially unwell that day—when news arrived that he had taken a turn for the worse. Father left school and hurried homeward. On reaching the vicinity of Dhola Kuva, he heard that Tuljabhai was no more. 'It was destined', people consoled him. So close, yet so far away.

When it was decided that I was to go to Europe, Father's old friends were concerned that he, already so aged, was willing to be parted from his son. Father's response was prompt: 'I hadn't gone out of town nor in any way parted from my father, and yet, I wasn't there by his deathbed. So what difference does it make if my son is nearby or not?' Recalling this incident, I am reminded of Father's calm, serious and radiant face. Even in my dreams I did not anticipate that a similar fate awaited me.

I have seen Tuljabhai's writing; it is mature and humorous. He was full of jokes, and he also happened to be a first-rate mimic. A dark-skinned man, he wore a tie-and-dyed turban wound around his head. 'Tuljabhai is a good man', this view held by his fellow caste members was indeed true. Intolerant of pretence, affectionate, straightforward, he was in every way both earthy and humane. Tuljashankar Mehta died, reposing absolute faith in his son's future wellbeing.

According to the standards of the time, Father's maternal grandfather Surajlal Desai's estate was a respectable one. Apart from the cash settlement he received as landlord, Surajlal had substantial land holdings. He also had the reputation of being serious and distinguished, whereas actually he was quite flamboyant, and, in his youth, extremely fond of racing bullock carts. It is universally acknowledged that, at a time when racing was fashionable, no one would have heard of a Surati driving his bullock cart at a slow pace. Once, while driving at high speed, Surajlal's cart overturned and his arm broke, despite which he continued his bad habit of driving at breakneck speed.

Whenever Father visited Olpad, his father would seat him by his side and drive him around the many villages on his estate. His aim was to extract rent from tenant farmers, using the four customary tactics of persuasion (*sama*), bribery (*dama*), punishment (*danda*) and division (*bheda*): 'Tame their addiction to indebtedness. Respond to their hundred lies with a thousand warnings. Live by the saying, "let witches devour pity's mother". Never allow tender feelings to surface'. This was Father's childhood experience, and from then on, he developed contempt for zamindari systems set up for the sole purpose of collecting rent.

The general belief that for a town-dweller to tie up all his money in land is to invite trouble can be traced to this period. The landlord's instinct is to maximise his revenue; the tenant farmer wants to minimise it. Moreover, there exists such solidarity among the peasantry that when a peasant's land is up for auction, no other peasant would bid for it. With the peasant wanting to demonstrate that the land is not fertile, farming declines. In short, there is none more deceived and, in turn, more deceiving than the peasant.

'My maternal grandfather, Surajlal Desai, had blocked a great deal of money in land deals, which he subsequently lost. After that he left instructions in his will that his moneys should not be invested in land', recalls Father. Surajlal Desai died at the age of eighty-four, in 1857, shortly after his son-in-law Tuljabhai's death.

Having travelled with his grandfather through the many small villages bordering Olpad, Father was well-acquainted with village life. His sensibilities were tuned to nature's playful ways. Having closely observed nature in her myriad forms, her mystery, her energy, her fury, and her tender ways remained engraved on his mind. In this respect, he was unlike his fellow townsmen, for Suratis are in general deficient in their appreciation of the natural world.

Readers of *Karan Ghelo* would have clearly seen that Father's descriptions of nature were not merely a product of the imagination, but born of eyes that had a friendly acquaintance with the natural world, as if nature had revealed her innermost secrets to him. Later, when, recalling this picture to imagination, the writer recreates it in words, his readers would have responded, amazed: 'Aha! Surely this is nature come to life!' The great poet Kalidasa, through a euphonic combination of word and meaning, suggests a mood of peace—you may even call it the ashram's essential spirit or its unique character—'*Naṣṭaśankā hariṇaśiśavo mandamandam charanti*: 'Slowly, ever so slowly the fawns move, their fear gone' (Kale 1969: I.1.15).[2] No poet, however learned, who lacks this intimate perception of nature is capable of such poetry. Vivid descriptions of nature's beauty found in *Karan Ghelo* are a direct reflection of Father's childhood experiences. How accurately he describes an evening in the village in Chapter Fifteen of *Karan Ghelo*!:

> Playfully kicking up dust in every direction cows and bulls wended their way back to the village after grazing all day; exhausted farmers, walking slowly, returned from their fields. With rolling gait, their horns swaying to the sound of bells hanging from their neck, returning oxen look forward to a night's rest. It is a beautiful time of day. The sun appears ready to exit from its western doorway. The scent from the surrounding trees and flowers gently envelops the air. Occasionally, the scent mingles with stench produced by the careless and lazy ways of men. A rubbish heap stands in front of every village house. Year after year, layers of cow dung and other waste accumulate in it, and from this poisonous pit, damaging particles waft in the air, which eventually cut short the villagers' life. But these poor creatures, like animals, were oblivious to the dangers. They reposed faith in destiny—what happens is the will of God. In this way, they spend their days in a state of happy ignorance. (*KG* 15.437)

---

[2] My translation accords with the author's Gujarati rendering of the Sanskrit in his footnote in the original text.

The beauty of nature mixed with the filth of human lives! Innocent images of the goddess overlaid with the fierce form of a malignant witch! All this was the product of Father's experience of the time. We will explore this subject later.

Father had witnessed the Dance of Creation in its myriad forms, and the experience had left a stamp on his mind. His graphic account in Chapter Sixteen of *Karan Ghelo* derives from the direct experience of his many pilgrimages to the Siddharaj Mahadev temple.

A renunciant and a brahmin, seated in a *dharamshala* smoking hemp, hear the sound of Karan's body falling into the water. The renunciant abruptly stops smoking his pipe, for it had begun to taste of poison.

> 'In the dead of night, who is this unfortunate creature fallen into the water? At this hour, it can't possibly be a man; it must be a dog or some such animal. Whatever it is, the creature has destroyed the rhythm of my smoke. The intoxicant no longer takes hold. This beastly creature has ruined my entire day. It is possible that I set eyes on a pariah first thing this morning, which staunches the opiate's flow. Let the man die, I am not going to save him.' However, when the corpse was discovered, the renunciant, who is supposed to have 'transcended all attachments',[3] was filled with the fear of being summoned before a law court. In due course, on recovering his senses, he remained eager once more to communicate his wisdom, and says, 'I am Brahman, the supreme spirit'. (*KG* 16.480–483)

Gangalakshmi, my grandmother, was a stay-at-home, entirely devoted to her household. She minded her own business and had no time for small talk or gossip. Dark-skinned, with a heavy-set body, she had a distinguished face that reflected her sincere, tender, affectionate, and self-confident temper. Which mother does not feel affection for her children? But Gangalakshmi's heart, finding no other channel for her talent, flowed uninterrupted into caring for her son and two daughters.

There was no pretence about Gangalakshmi. True to her nature, she worked ceaselessly, for it is not easy to keep order in

---

[3] A reference to *Bhagvad-Gita* (2.56): '*vīta-rāga bhayah krodhah*'.

a relatively poor household. Nor did she ever communicate the sense that she came from a grander home than her husband's. Under the circumstances, she, a Desai's daughter—moreover, the only daughter of a Desai with an income of six hundred rupees a year, a Desai not drowning in debt—who married into a poor Mehta family, was gentle and unassuming. Someone had composed a couplet to describe her:

> Gangalakshmi is sedate and of tranquil mood,
> Like the pure waters of the sacred month of Poash.

There is always great affection for an only son, but whether to publicly display such affection depends entirely on a person's temperament. Father writes, 'My mother shied away from displaying affection. For one thing, she was self-effacing; for another, there was the hidden fear lest embracing or kissing a delicate flower might crush it, cause it to wilt or even attract the god's envy, and the joys of the defenceless be snatched away. Many a mother when asked, "Whose children are these?" replied, "River Tapi is their mother". There were even mothers who refused to count the number of children they had. The Greek idea of *Pthonos* is based on a similar belief.'[4]

Mothers in India seldom have occasion to play with dolls in their childhood years. Even when they do, the joy of free play, and of imitating their elders which gives a child a subtle foretaste of the adult world, is all too brief. Denied this natural expression, women who give birth before they are twenty years of age, play with their children. Father recounts, 'I was my mother's toy. When I was barely four years old, I was engaged to marry the mother of my future niece. The young girl might even have been a few years older than I was. My mother's face beamed with joy when her tiny future daughter-in-law visited our home. The thought that a daughter-in-law was so soon to be part of her poor household filled her heart with pride.'

---

[4] According to Aristotle, *pthonos* is envy generated by someone else's good fortune (see Johnson 2019).

At play, children arrange their dolls' nuptials. Following the same pattern, Father's elder sister Jashodagauri was married to Manmathram.

The following family tree is interesting, even from a historical point of view.

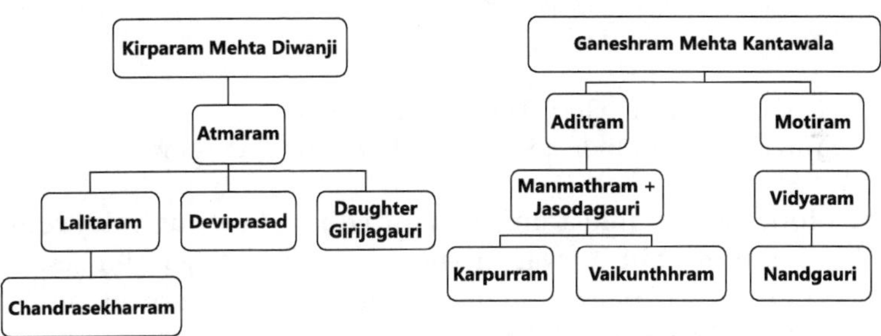

The Mehta family tree

Ganeshram Mehta was the deputy Diwan in the Nawab's court. When Kirparam Mehta accepted a pension of three hundred rupees from the English in 1800, Ganeshram, at the age of twenty-five, pitted himself against the temper of the time and pronounced, 'to accept monetary rewards from the English at a time when power is being snatched away from your former masters is perfidious'. Ethical standards of a high order did little to alleviate the poverty of his household. Ganeshram lost a pension of a hundred rupees, to which he was entitled, and died at the young age of twenty-seven.

Kirparam Mehta, on the other hand, was extremely shrewd; his conduct rested on an understanding of his times. Anticipating that the downfall of the Nawabi was imminent, he held that faithful service to the Nawab lay not in propping up the institution, but in obtaining the best possible settlement for his master. From what Governor Duncan[5] writes, it appears that Kirparam Mehta

---

[5] Jonathan Duncan was Governor of the Bombay Presidency, 1795–1811. His policy of recognising any petty chieftain as a sovereign prince accounts for the innumerable small states of the Presidency. See: https://en.wikisource.org/wiki/Dictionary_of_National_Biography,_1885-1900/Duncan,_Jonathan_(1756-1811) (accessed 1 August 2021).

negotiated the best terms for the Nawab, and was not particularly interested in securing a pension for himself. Before accepting the pension, his acquaintance with Farsi may have brought to mind the following stanza:

> *Aii zar! Tu khudānīst va lekin bakhudā*
> *Sattāre uyūb o kāzi ul hājātī*

> Gold, you aren't God. Though in His name
> You are able to hide all faults and do away with want.[6]

The blood of this able administrator coursed through the veins of Manmatram, but he was unable to advance beyond a clerk's salary of twenty rupees. The next generation of his progeny did not inherit Kirparam Mehta's sharp intellect, which illustrates what Father jokingly called a 'principle', that 'The goddess of wisdom skips every alternate step on the generational ladder'.

That Jashodagauri was extremely fond of her 'young brother' (which is how she addressed Father) is not surprising. My father, too, doted on his sister. This aunt played a leading role in arranging the marriage between Father and my dear mother.

In 1867, at the young age of thirty-seven, Jashodagauri succumbed to the dreaded cholera. This kind and sincere woman with a zest for life despaired at the thought of leaving behind two small children and so abruptly bidding goodbye to her worldly attachments. Father fervently promised her at the time that he would take care of his nephews. Devastated by her illness, she died in his arms. It is generally acknowledged that Father was not lukewarm in fulfilling his responsibilities to his nephews. Indeed, he ardently facilitated the education of both his able nephews; my mother, with equal enthusiasm, later arranged their marriages and helped set up their households.

Gangalakshmi, my grandmother, suffered greatly when Father was ten years old. Her intended daughter-in-law was growing older, and the Mehta household wasn't particularly well-to-do. True, they were not in debt, but following the adage that 'only

---

[6] My translation accords with the author's Gujarati rendering in his footnote.

those with staying power incur debts', the girl's family broke off the engagement, and married her into a Munshi household. Gangalakshmi feared that her son would forever remain unmarried. She probably undertook many vows and performed many austerities to propitiate the stars.

Father clearly recalled how very hurt his parents were on that occasion. 'Being a mere boy, I myself felt no pain. Looking back, I consider it fortunate that the matter was nipped in the bud. Had I wed the lady, I'd have been obliged to get a job right away; I wouldn't have continued my education and, like the proverbial oil-presser's ox, might have spent my life going round and round in the oil presses of the world. Spending my entire life as a clerk, I would then have joined the chorus singing Navalram's song: "We're not educated but we're married. Misfortune strikes us on every side."'

Father believed that Indian men should never marry women of the same age as themselves. Men ought to marry when they are between twenty and twenty-six; women should marry between the ages of fourteen and eighteen, because Indian women age faster than India's men. Moreover, he believed that one should not marry until one reaches a fuller understanding of the householder's life. For, if one marries too early, then the desire for that stage in life isn't sharply felt; and, what one does not fully appreciate one does not value.

Before too long, a new bride was found for Father. From the family tree given earlier, the reader would have noticed that his sister, Jashodagauri, was married into the Kantawala family. Father's gaze was already fixed on Vidyaram Mehta's daughter—his elder brother-in-law's brother's daughter. The girl's grandfather wanted her affianced to the family of the Diwan. That was because Motiram Mehta, my maternal great-grandfather, had at one time ostentatiously borrowed money to raise bail for Diwan Atmaram. Motiram was certain that the money would not be returned; if he were to give his granddaughter in marriage to the Atmaram family, she at least could enjoy the benefits of the pension—such was the scheme he entertained.

On the other hand, my maternal grandmother Occhavlakshmi was the daughter of Occhavlal Desai. The family was considered among the most prosperous in Gujarat. It was my grandmother's ardent wish that her own granddaughter marry Surajlal Desai's grandson, that is, Father. Motiram Mehta raised a thousand objections to the match: 'Tuljabhai's lineage is not particularly distinguished. Nandshankar studies English; does he conduct himself in accordance with the ordains of the scriptures?' In Gujarat, the mother's family owns half the rights in arranging nuptials; but in this case, it turned out that they owned all the rights. And so, at age four, my future mother became engaged to Father.

Father was sixteen at the time of the engagement. His mother Gangalakshmi's joy could not be contained. She worshipped the daughter-in-law as if she were the veritable goddess of good fortune, and played with her as if with a doll. 'On my first visit to my revered mother-in-law's, she sat me on her hip and, with smiling face and overflowing heart, showed off her little daughter-in-law to the neighbours', my mother recalled. The marriage was celebrated when Father was twenty-one and his young bride almost ten. My maternal grandfather supported the marriage, but was so dominated by his own father that he preferred to remain mute during the negotiations. Father's friend Dolatraiji had put in a good word on his behalf: 'He is by no means an atheist; it is just that in place of reciting the *sandhya* mantra, he studies his books. It is not that he has disdain for the prayer to the sun; please note that I intend teaching it to him'. Many years later, Dolatraiji would laughingly recall: 'Master (for that was what my father was always called) had begun the *sandhya* mantra, but recited it for only five minutes. Nonetheless, that reassured the grandfather-in-law to be'.

After Father told me about his own marriage, I often wondered whether his description of Devaldevi in Chapter Eleven of *Karan Ghelo* was based on personal experience. The writing is imbued with passion, but is at the same time chaste. I myself really admire this part of the book, which advocates marriage at an older age. If the same subject is broached by some other writer, I doubt whether the best of its kind even approaches what Father writes here.

> History tells us that in cultures where child marriage does not exist, where girls do not willingly allow themselves to be given

away like cattle to whomsoever their parents choose, where a sacred relationship like marriage between a man and a woman is not reduced to a commercial transaction between buyers and sellers, where an irrevocable knot like marriage is not tied between individuals without regard to their upbringing, qualities, or character, where the man and the woman are to a certain extent acquainted with each other's temperament and are compatible, and, being so acquainted, marry with the consent of their parents—in cultures such as these, it occasionally happens that an impoverished youth falls in love with a woman either belonging to a more prominent or to a wealthier family. It is also true that so long as he is poor, however deep the girl's love for the youth, he does not entertain the hope of ever marrying her. The girl's parents, either on the basis of practical considerations or pride, refuse consent. Nor does the young man, given his own status, wish to drown the girl to his own sadly impoverished depths. His love for her is so strong that he sets aside his self-interest and the immediate satisfaction of his desires and, instead, comforts her, 'I shall work tirelessly to acquire a high occupation and by the strength of my intellect win renown, acquire wealth, and only then ask your father for your hand in marriage. Years may flow by before this auspicious moment arrives, so, then, why be anxious?' When he sits burning the midnight oil engrossed in studies, his beloved's face appears before him; and when, tired of his studies, short of money, and troubled by all manner of difficulties, he considers abandoning his purpose, then, he sees her image filled with love, admonishing him with sweet words, 'Patience, Patience'. The difficulties that beset him, however insurmountable and frightening they seem, fly away when he conjures up the image of the beloved enthroned within his heart with the mantra of love. (*KG* 11.306–307)

His friend the poet Narmadashankar was unhappy in this regard. He was married at a very young age and, even before finishing his education, was forced to set up house in Surat. He had been at odds with his wife before she died. For seven years he remained a widower, during which period he fell into evil habits.

> To be fit in body is the first happiness,
> To have sons at home is the next,
> To have gold is the third,
> And an excellent wife is the fourth.

Measured against the above, Father had acquired bodily health, progeny, money, and, perhaps best of all, an excellent wife.

His doting mother's joy ended soon after her son's marriage. This straightforward, somewhat superstitious woman would often exclaim, 'Does a woman like me deserve so much happiness?' One day, as it happened, she fell in the veranda of her house. It was during the monsoon, when the floor was naturally slippery. There was a small cut on her foot. The cut bled. She bandaged it. When the pain became unbearable, the physician was summoned.

Deenabhai's eyesight was dim, whether by day or by night. But what is the need for an Ayurvedic physician to see? Diagnoses, after all, are based on examining the pulse, which requires a well-developed tactile sense, and, what the pulse communicates is heard by the ear. Deenabhai prescribed an ointment and bandaged the wound. The wound wasn't washed because the touch of water was forbidden. For seven days the bandage was not to be removed; in four days the wound began to fester. What could Deenabhai do? He washed his hands of the matter, and sat back as an ill odour pervaded everything. Father was told to give up hope for his mother's recovery—she had contacted tetanus, a fatal disease.

With trembling voice, Father recalled the event: 'My sturdy mother suffered severe convulsions, which twisted her body into a bow. I feared that her sinews and muscles would burst. I sat by her bedside hour after hour, but all our efforts proved in vain. At the age of thirty-six she left us; her calm, affectionate being was gone, her potential unfulfilled. Such abject hopelessness, such terror, such grief, such anguish seized me that I might have sunk into permanent depression, a deep emptiness on the verge of breakdown. Anger swept through my entire body—that blind doctor took my mother's life! It was this anger that kept me from brooding kite-like forever. I was able to weep out my grief, and it was the weeping that brought me back to humanity. Our household was truly broken; my mind received a tremendous blow—the sheer injustice of it all! I could neither read nor study. But time heals all wounds, and in time, mine, too, healed'.

After this period, Father lost faith in our commonly used Ayurvedic and Yunani cures. In times when antiseptic ointments were not used, the threat to life was very great. My maternal grandfather's mother, too, had died of tetanus at the age of twenty-four.

I recall Father saying, 'Deenabhai's vision was failing. As a doctor of standing, he would trot down the streets of Surat riding a pony, a groom accompanying him. The groom was instructed to tug the shawl in the direction of any distinguished gentleman about to cross the doctor's path so that Deenabhai could instantly greet the "elder brother, revered saheb, or sheth".' Deenabhai was well-respected, but not particularly skilled; moreover, whatever skills he may have once possessed were lost to failing eyesight. My grandfather used Farsi to allude to Deenabhai's incompetence: '*Nīm hakīm khatare jān*, the incompetent physician is an invitation to death'. The doctor was a gregarious man, not greedy; and Father would perhaps admit to having been unjust in his assessment—the doctor's assistant was even worse than the doctor.

The *Charaka Samhita* describes the qualities of an ideal physician:

> He should have complete faith in medical science, he should be experienced, capable, compassionate; he should wear clean clothes, be a first-rate surgeon, equip himself with appropriate surgical instruments, be good at diagnostics; he should be acquainted with human nature and the ways of the world; he should be without envy, without anger, able to cope with frustration; he should be affectionate with his pupils; and all his senses should be intact.

Since Deenabhai possessed not even a single quality listed above, the goddess of healing abandoned his side and sulked; in the words of a Farsi couplet, 'The hand that heals (*dasto śafā*) became the hand that kills (*dasto kaz*)'. A similar thought is expressed in the Sanskrit *shloka*:

> *Chitām prajvalitām dṛstvā vaidyo vismayam-āgatah* |
> *Nāham gato na me bhrātā kasyedam hastalāghavam* ||

> The physician saw the blazing funeral pyre and stood amazed,
> Whose skilled handiwork is that? Neither my brother nor I
> attended him.[7]

❧

Having described the culture of the clan in which Father was born, I shall now say something about the region to which he belonged.

Father used to say that Surat district is shaped like an inverted triangle, with its base enclosed by Gaekwad territory. At the apex lie Valsad and Paradi; the western corner comprises the fertile region of Olpad; the forests of Mandavi lie in the east. The land in the north-eastern and south-eastern corners is forested; so the pressure of population is towards the western end of the triangle, in the villages settled along the sea's edge. When the population grew, people tended to migrate seaward, crossing the ocean to other lands.

If you cast a glance at the western coast of Gujarat, you will see the rivers Kim, Sena, Tena, Tapi, Mindola, Purna, Ambika, Auranga, Par, Kolak and Damanganga flowing southward from east to west. The flowing river waters are like fingers pointing to the ocean. It's as if they were saying, 'Your destiny hinges on this great watery element. Your future achievements lie along its path'. In places such as this, seafaring sciences are born. Men become merchants when manufacture flourishes; the give and take of bargain becomes basic instinct.

Traditionally, when girls were married, the merry women of the household would sing of distant lands: 'Fetch her pearls from the Fort at Hormuz, tiny pearls from Singapore'; 'and only gold from Sri Lanka will do'; 'He who travels to Java does not return; if he does, he feeds three generations to come'.

---

[7] The verse is part of a collection of popular Sanskrit didactic and humorous verses. See https://sanskritdocuments.org/doc_z_misc_ subhaashita/subhash.html?lang=sa (accessed 17 March 2021). My translation accords with the author's Gujarati rendering in his footnote.

Achin was a major port in Sumatra; spices were bought from there and textiles sold. The volume of trade between Iran and Gujarat was so great it was as though a bridge made of ships connected the Persian Gulf with the Gulf of Khambat. Goods from India to the continent of Europe went via Asia Minor. It is not surprising that a loiterer from this very province of Gujarat showed Vasco Da Gama the route to Calicut. In short, the people of Surat were intrepid, enthusiastic, skilled at whatever they did, energetic and full of enterprise.

Only an earth such as this creates the intrepid warrior who thrusts his way forward, singing 'Plunge into battle, for victory lies ahead!' and plants the flag of his country. Even today Delhi Gate reminds us: '*Agarche Dillī dūr ast dushvār nīst*—Delhi may be distant but not beyond reach'.[8] And the markets of Barhanpur show the trade routes connecting Gujarat to the north. The mere mention of the holy city of Mecca brings to mind an image of pilgrims embarking for the holy lands from Surat.

What the port of Jedda is to Arabs, Surat was to Muslims in this region, for it was the port from which pilgrims set sail for the holy city. A Muslim pilgrim from north India would arrive in Surat covered with dust. After bathing in the Tapi river, clad in fresh attire, he would exclaim, 'We are in the courtyard of the Holy Land!'; only a channel of water divides Surat from Mecca. There is an ancient maxim which proclaims: 'Land divides, water unites'. For instance, the Greeks considered the Phoenician coast to be a mere suburb of their own cities, but Epirus—which was connected to Greece by land—a distant and uncivilised country. Similarly, for Muslims from the north arriving after an arduous journey by land, the sea voyage out of Surat signified speed and safety.

Surat, the largest port in the Mughal Empire, was known as the 'Gateway to Mecca', and also the 'Gateway to Trade'. Portuguese, Dutch, French, Austrian, Swedish, and English traders all first came to Surat. After building their emporia, they began to take steps to extend their hegemony over the land through trade. 'This

---

[8] My translation accords with the author's Gujarati rendering in his footnote.

is the garden where birds sing their own song, then fly away': what is said about Delhi is equally true of Surat.

The Mughals and the Marathas occupied Surat; but eventually, the English held sway. Just as the inebriated cobra sways to the snake charmer's pipe, so also the people of India danced longest to English tunes.

Suratis were the first to meet foreign traders, and become partners in their gains and losses. Brokers were involved in the packing and loading of goods, and in selling imported items. As a result, the brokers grew wealthy, began cultivating expensive tastes and seeking expensive pleasure, which added to Surat's splendour. 'The good life is better than a long life' is how people dismissed these stylish men, but those who say this fail utterly to recognise that their very words honour the courageous spirit of Surat's entrepreneurs.

About twelve years ago, Surat's Nagar Association invited Govardhanrambhai[9] to lecture on some inspiring subject of his choice. Father chaired that assembly. The honoured litterateur gave an exposition of the religious customs of the different castes of Surat, and likened Surat to Venice—Venice played in the celestial waves of the Adriatic; Venice was the gateway through which trade flowed; Venice became the intrepid spirit of youth and beauty. Such, too, was the splendour of Surat.

Father believed that a poor brahmin woman planted the seeds of trust when she returned, after several years, an object entrusted to her. Trust is the true basis of trade; so right conduct was the solid rock on which the castle of Surat's prosperity stood. As long as Surat remained true to these values, she remained unvanquished. Sparks flew as minds came in contact with other minds, and the resulting light opened up new perspectives. A sharpness of intellect emerged; sluggishness disappeared; the self-important frog-in-the-well mentality was annihilated. In the same way that a child looks with wide-eyed curiosity at the world, the people of Surat saw a new world open

---

[9] Govardhanram Madhavram Tripathi (1855–1907), the author of *Sarasvatichandra*, *Navalram Nu Kavijivan* and *Lilavati Jivankala*, among others.

up before them. They were the first to scrutinise this novelty and satisfy their curiosity.

The days were past when the sharp-tongued folk of Kathiawad would sarcastically ask the heavy-set villagers who lived near Surat, 'Hey, you! How far is the sea?' Just as salt is said to contain all taste, just as it preserves all, it brings an altogether different quality to the blood. When the Emperor of Germany had said of the Prussians: '*Sie Sind das Salz der Erde*—You are the Salt of the Earth', he may well have been referring to the proud people of Surat.

Surat had also experienced many political upheavals, but it is not necessary to elaborate upon them here. The reader will find all this chronicled in the *Gazetteer of Surat*, in Adelji Patel's *Surat ni Tawarif* (*Annals of Surat*), or in an essay on Surat in Narmad's *Collected Prose*. Suratis were expert ship builders; Surati vessels capable of carrying thousands of pounds of cargo aroused the amazement of Europeans. The Parsi community was considered the best in the field. The interested reader may consult a book written by Mookerji on Indian shipping.[10]

We now set aside this subject to explore incidents which influenced Father's personal life.

Father's memory of the earliest and most vividly recalled events in his life go back to the Great Fire of 1838. The fire began on Monday, the 24th of April, at five in the morning, in a Parsi trader's house where tar was being heated. Whether it was deliberately fanned by someone who envied the trader's wealth or whether it was the Zoroastrian taboo against putting out fires, no one knows; but the Fire God, not controlled at the start, quickly spread around a three-mile radius. At night, bursts of flames could be seen fifty miles away. The following morning, that is, on Tuesday, a wind started blowing from the north-easterly direction. Perhaps the people living in the area had insulted Goddess Amba—a foolish priest actually saw her abandon her throne and walk away. How can one describe those flying balls of fire? By Tuesday afternoon, the Fire God's sport reached its peak. He danced and skipped and played, and then, as if satisfied, softened his blaze. On Wednesday, the fearful fire

---

[10] See Radhakumud Mookerji 1912.

subsided. Many women burned to death in their own homes. Others who came to rescue lives lost their own. Those who lost their lives attempting to rescue valuables received no sympathy. Those who placed a higher value on property than life lost both life and property.

In his expressive style, my maternal grandfather described the event so vividly that we felt we were in the very presence of that destructive conflagration. The wreckage extended for ten miles around Surat. The terrifying tongues of that great inferno lapped up whatever little splendour Time's Wheel had spared Surat. Tall, beautifully decorated buildings standing close together and palatial stone mansions were uniformly reduced to ash. The fire destroyed the Gopipura temple and stopped just short of the textile printers' quarters. 'Look, half of Abhiram's mansion is burned down!' were the words of a *garba* that the women sang. This ruined mansion can still be seen standing next to late Motabhai Desai's house.

It was the fourth day of the waning moon in the month of Chaitra, Father's birthdate.

Later, Father recalled that when Navalram, Narmadashankar and he were preparing to consign orthodox beliefs and customs to flames, he would jokingly tell them that it was on his third birthday that the Great Fire had broken out. My maternal grandfather told us that on that day, their large family had filled a cart with furniture, left Sanghadiawad and driven towards Raghunathpura: 'We dropped our utensils and clothes into a well, covered it, and carrying our valuables with us, we left; nothing remained in the house except the rubbish. Of our misery there is little to add'.

Keshavram Mehta was considered an important member of our caste. Having worked at an official agency all his life he earned a very respectable salary. One by one, the very large houses that he owned in Gopipura burned down. It is said that before the fire, he walked with a straight back, but the shock of losing property was so great that thereafter he could no longer get up from his chair. 'Get me a cane,' he called out to his son Bhauji—and from that moment on, he was unable to walk without support.

If the fire broke the back of so prosperous a man, how do you think the poor fared? The condition of those belonging to the middle classes, with their pretensions to respectability, can hardly be described. Vishnusharma, in the *Panchatantra*, has correctly said that so long as the mouse Hiranyaka had the comfort of treasures in his hole, he could jump up and get at the food that the hermit Tamrachud hung from the ceiling, but when his store of food was stolen, he was unable to jump so high.[11]

Many adventurous young men died trying to retrieve utensils dumped in wells; the wells were filled with carbolic gas, and those who entered them fell silent. Many women of the Bohra sect sought shelter in mosques thinking they would be proof against the fire, but in vain and they, too, were charred in the fiery mosques. Many women died while giving birth.

The fear of theft, which had faded under the police chief Ardeshar Kotwal's watch, once again swelled in that ruined city. Large numbers of snakes surfaced from their holes. The worst, however, was how fear spread; hundreds of stories, of encounters with spectres, ghosts, witches and enchantresses—*shankhanis* and *yakshinis*—sprang from people's superstitious imaginations: 'a pregnant woman, now a *shankhani*, harasses the credulous people of the locality'; 'screams of people jumping to their deaths are heard here'; 'a spectre dances in that corner'; 'a ghost now wanders around guarding the treasure buried there'.

Father and my grandfather told me many stories about the fire, some of which I still remember. My grandfather's cousin lived next to what is now the cemetery. This happened one night when he was returning home. I shall relate the incident in his own words.

'Around ten o'clock one monsoon night I was walking from Khapatiya, by way of the Havadiya Square, on the Amliran Road towards Sanghadiawad. It was dark. Holding a lantern and walking along an unpaved road, I found myself outside municipal limits. I was sixteen years old at the time.

'My own half-acknowledged superstitions and the stories floating around me made me fearful; but how could a young man give in to fear? I was making my way swiftly through these welter of thoughts, holding on to whatever courage I could summon,

---

[11] See Mishra 1910: 27.

when a voice behind me called, "Wait a moment, please". They were words clearly spoken by a *shankhani* with a bewitching voice. It happened to be the very spot where the pregnant woman had died. My innards trembled, but I thought: what is there for a brahmin to fear?

'Mumbling the *Gayatri Mantra*, I walked in the direction of the voice. A young woman stood on the threshold of her house, holding an oil lamp close to her body. Her flame has gone out, I thought. In those days there were no matches and fire was lit with flints or sticks of cane tipped with sulphur. "My lamp has lost its flame, help me light it," she said. I walked up to the oil lamp that she still held close to her body, opened my lantern and lit her lamp with it. Just then a gust of wind arose and extinguished the flame in my lantern as well as her oil lamp. My heart was already in my mouth, and now this fresh misfortune! I almost screamed. How did this wind blow of a sudden when there was none before? Is it possible that a respectable householder's wife would stand on her threshold at such an hour? The woman spoke some words of relief and fell silent. I gathered my strength somehow and ran forward, bumped into a watchman, and automatically asked, "What time is it?" It was only when he answered that my fears finally fled.'

Grandfather's cousin then jokingly added, 'I am still not sure if that woman was an earthbound creature or belonged to another realm altogether'. In those days, fire was always available in a goldsmith's house; goldsmiths could be seen carrying their camphor-lit flames to their patron's houses, where women would gather. Perhaps the woman was one attending some such gathering.

Another story. A friend of Father's was returning from Haripar after a *garba* concert. It was late night; only one watch remained. The Navaratri festivities had just ended, and the autumnal full moon of *Sharadpoornima* was awaited. In front of goddess Amba's temple, my friend beheld a rabbit. What is a rabbit doing in an urban neighbourhood? Even before this thought completed itself, he met a dog. Before he could weigh argument against counter argument, a cow appeared, and then a donkey. He was stopped in his tracks, could neither run nor walk. Then, a young woman walked past him. At night people feared meeting other people and they feared walking out alone, never knowing what they might encounter.

In Gopipura, there was a peepal tree standing next to a temple. At night people passing by heard sounds of 'Ram has come, Ram has come'. Ghosts dwell in peepal trees, so everyone was absolutely convinced that it was a ghost. Some sceptic suggested that 'Ram has come' could easily be a watchman's call, but of course this explanation pleased no one. In Mulla Khadki, there was an old well near a mosque. Even in the evening if one went there alone, he would hear a voice coming from the well, 'I drown!…I drown!'

A calamity has befallen Surat. The gods are angry—this was the general belief. These unearthly voices and fearsome apparitions, bound to leave a deep impression on a child's mind, are vividly described in *Karan Ghelo*.

In Chapter Seven of *Karan Ghelo*, for instance, Keshav is killed and Gunasundari becomes a *Sati*; after that comes the downfall of Patan. The description of that episode is surely derived from Father's own childhood experience. Three days after Keshav's death there is a great fire in Patan.

> No sooner was it subdued in one place than it spread to another, burning many houses. People were frightened; they believed it was the gods' anger. Some claimed to have seen men flying in the skies lighting fires. Some felt that large boulders were being flung at their windows at night. In some houses cooked food turned foul; well waters turned into blood; loud screams were heard at night. None dared stir out after the evening lamps were lit; in some houses women became possessed. (*KG* 7.168–169)

Father's description of the brawl between Harpal and Shakti resembles the experience of his friend who, returning from Haripura with his mind inebriated by *garbas*, sees a rabbit and then other animals on the way. I will discuss this in detail in another chapter.

Trade in half-burned timber can be dated to this period. Father believed that the surname *Katpatiya* [timber merchant] emerged after the fire. The amount of rubble, brick and mortar lying around the city was unbelievable. Moreover, that very year, floods inundated Surat, and the debris was swept away along with valuables; the loss of life and property were ruinous.

Trade had already shifted to Bombay; so to Surat's unemployed citizens, their eyes made feeble by loss, their city looked like a fearful cemetery; its splendour, its aesthetic sensibilities lay buried. Bombay had become the new centre of business. Well-established families, who had moved to Bombay but returned on holiday to rest, eat *barfi*, drink the sweet waters of tanks, or even to drink toddy, stopped coming after their houses were destroyed by the Great Fire. A wedge was driven into the brilliant jewel in Sheshnag's jewelled head.

Surat's origins can be traced to the fishermen's quarters. Similarly, Bombay had its beginnings in the fishing village of Salset. An old love bound the people of Surat to the sea, a love that they reclaimed even when they moved to Bombay. For it was the Surati Premchand Roychand who brought the sea, that stood eight miles away, to Bombay's shores.[12] But now, Bombay alone seduces!

> Hail to the saintly Sea, hail to the Ocean *Pir*,
> Pray give us plenty of sugar and *khir*.

Fire and flood! Losses without count! Ruin untold! The conception of a limit ought to be kept within bounds—only then can virtue exist. Overflowing passion itself is vice. A man remains virtuous only so long as he does not stray from the middle path. Nandshankar favoured the Aristotelian Middle Path, a predilection that had its source in his calm and truthful character. He drove his energetic self at full speed, but held the reins in skilled and balanced hands. His childhood experiences and the knowledge he gathered as an adult all drove him in a single direction.

The fear of dacoits grew during this period. All manner of people took to thievery inside the city; outside, on the high roads, the Garasiyas attacked, looted and harassed people.

---

[12] This is probably an allusion to Premchand Roychand's Reclamation Project in Bombay; see Sanyal 2017: 380–382.

Gangu Galiyaro was Surat's Robin Hood. He sent out notes which said: 'Bring a hundred rupees to the following address', or 'Send us five hundred rupees, else you will be harmed. This is a royal command'. Should you not obey these orders, your entire household might be plundered and receive a thrashing as bonus. Gangu gave freely to the poor; so they sheltered him, and he could not be caught.

The textile printers took to robbery. So entrenched was *Kaliyuga* that even men from the trading castes joined the ranks of dacoits. Ardeshar Kotwal had worked hard to rid the city of lawlessness, and before the Great Fire, robberies had almost stopped. However, after the fire, and the flood that followed, much of the city lay in ruins, which provided natural hiding places for thieves. After that, neither could the 'guardians of the city' safeguard its dwellers, nor could the 'guardians of the land' safeguard those outside it.

Piracy also grew in strength. Ghoghar Rana was the chief of pirates in places like Ghogha, Peeram and so on. The fear he inspired can be seen from the lullabies mothers sang to put their babies to sleep:

> Sleep, my child, sleep—the pirates have come!
> Their heads hidden under lids, concealed by winnowing fans,
> They bring sheaves of rice tall as bamboo, mounds of dal
> heavy as grinding stones,
> The world is their platter, the sea their drinking bowl,
> They sit down to eat, and soon begins a brawl.

Whose dinner plate is the world! Whose drinking cup is the ocean! What can't such men achieve! Where can they not go!

In the Punjab, the Khatri pirate Harisingh spread terror. Mothers even now warn their children to sleep: 'Hush child, the pirate is here!' In Surat, Police Chief Ardeshar Kotwal ended this reign of fear. The pirates, who used to raid the textile printers' quarters and loot their wares, were appeased when craftsmen agreed to consecrate an image of their chief, Ghoghar Rana, and worship it. Even now during the Navaratri festival, one sees children playing with tiny statues and propitiating them mockingly with an offering of leaves.

Just as the Marathas used to begin their annual raids after Dussera, so the pirates would take to the seas after Rakshabandhan. People worshipped the river Tapi on the full moon day with offerings of coconut in the same way as people everywhere pay obeisance to the sea. On that day, one can imagine a helmsman praying to God to save them from the pirates. Mokhdaji Gohel was the last and most dreaded pirate to become chief when Ardeshar Kotwal took over the police department. Ardeshar Kotwal received a gold medal with a testimonial specifically praising his services for putting down the pirate menace.

The English established their hegemony over Gujarat in 1800. However, mere imposition of English rule did not alter people's mentality in any significant way. It was reform in education that brought real change.

Children of the time were educated, if you can call it that, in informal schools or in Islamic institutions. Traditional Sanskrit schools had all but disappeared. As the need for men who could recite the Koran by heart grew less, so did the schools dedicated to teaching only the Koran. Hindu and Parsi children went to village schools as they would grow up to keep accounts, and so needed to master the times tables. A school of this kind, known as Naran Mehta's School, stands to this day.[13]

---

[13] Bhaiya Pratapchandra Mazumdar describes the school as follows:

We all squatted on the floor, each on his square mat, rugged, under a large straw shed in the middle of the courtyard. Each boy carried his earthen inkpot either in his hand or suspended from strings and his mat in a long roll under his arm, with the palm leaves, on which he practiced his alphabet, sticking out at one end. The very beginners like myself, wrote with bamboo pens on palm leaves; those who were older wrote on plantain leaves; only those who belonged to the highest order of scholarship were allowed to use paper. We were all very noisy, because whatever each boy wrote, whether it was a syllable or a sum, he proclaimed with nasal intonation, so that the master, who was always dozing or smoking his hookah, might make sure that we were hard at work, and the boy himself might feel a zest in his literary progress. We were all very inky, as a sign that we meant to do our business in earnest. But there was another reason for it. No

Naran Mehta belonged to the brahmin caste. He set up his school in a ruined cellar and carried a long stick. Whether he used it at home or not we don't know, but at school he certainly wielded it impartially, in accordance with the old saying: '*pancavarṣāṇi lāḍayet, daśavarṣāṇi tāḍayet*: indulge children for the first five years, use the rod for the next ten.'[14]

In those days when a boy reached the age of four, his hair was shorn; he was placed on a horse and, accompanied by much song and dance, sent to school. Father would say, 'On that one day alone the boy went to school happy'. The occasion was festive, a holiday was declared and sweets distributed. The schoolmasters made us sing a tune: 'Wrap Mehtaji in a silken shawl'. For the occasion required that Naran Mehta receive a shawl, a scarf and a turban as gifts owed to the guru.

We wished a new boy to be inducted every day; we did not enjoy school in the least. We had to remain constantly seated in the same place learning the same old thing by rote, with the rod all too frequently on our backs. 'Children at home are up to all kinds of mischief; they fall; they quarrel; they annoy and tease their mothers. At least at school they will learn some manners, and, if nothing else, learn to be submissive'—it was this mentality that packed village schools with students. On his first day, as the sum total of those relegated to hell's darkness grew, the oldest pupil would draw the newcomer to his side. And on that day, as a shareholder in the common suffering, a new boy was made to feel welcome. The welcome may have been due to the sense that as shareholders in common suffering, it is best to divide the sum of pain between two. Or, it may have been keeping in mind the maxim, '*dukhe dukhā dhikam paśya*: in times of sorrow watch out for additional pain'.

____

sooner had a boy made a blot in writing than he wiped out the ink with his fingers, rubbing the fingers on his head, which was a sort of universal blotting-pad and pen brush, or he licked out the ink with his tongue, if it felt distasteful, which it invariably did, and then he rubbed his tongue with his dhotie. So from head to foot he was full of ink. The *Pathshala* was a friendly gathering and suited everyone. [as quoted in the original text]

[14] From the *Garuda Purāṇa* 1.114.59; see: https://www.sanskritworld.in/public/assets/book/book_50dbe61e54139.txt (accessed 23 March 2021).

When the government opened its own schools, Naran Mehta's lost its standing. 'Naran Mehta is bitter gourd,' the children's contemptuous words now greeted the old brahmin schoolmaster.

The British government opened schools in 1826. The first government schools were in Gujarati.

Pranshankar was master in the school set up in Gopipura. Though he appeared short-tempered, he was fair-minded: even if one student misbehaved, the whole class was flogged, following the maxim: 'A single misdeed sinks the entire boat'. In his class, additions were never less than in figures of a hundred thousand billion, and multiplications reached up to sums of ten billion and beyond. As we worked our sums, our revered teacher told his prayer beads, and sought refuge in the goddess of sleep. Awaking bewildered to a roomful of students, he would pretend to be coming out of a meditative trance, and always took care not to look like a startled cow and make himself a laughing stock in the eyes of his pupils. A teacher is one who rules, he taught us with the help of his cane.

The next teacher was Tripurarishankar. His standards were high. The teaching of mathematics in Gujarati schools reached higher levels than is presently found in matriculation schools. His pedagogic methods were so good that a love of numbers became permanently imprinted in each of his student's minds. The foundations of Father's own love of mathematics were laid in Tripurarishankar's school. Years later, Father translated a trigonometry textbook for this very school.

In 1840, a Board of Education was created; and in 1842, an English school was established in Surat. Father was enrolled in the English institution when he was ten. He writes:

'My fellow students were much older, some even sported moustaches, and the most backward student was usually the father of two. Our first teacher was Naoroji Parekh; his competence in the English language was extraordinary. Dr Dhanjishah Parekh I.M.S. is his son. We were taught Macaulay's essays; our teacher read them out aloud with great flourish, and he gave us a thorough grounding in English, history and general philosophy. It is unfortunate that our beloved teacher's last days were unhappy.

'Green Saheb was the principal of our school at the time. Having skipped three classes in a single year, I was the youngest student in my class. That may be why Green Saheb was extremely fond of me. He recited from memory the following world-famous passage from "Gray's Elegy", and jokingly remarked, "This tiny, enthusiastic student will rule over you, the way Cromwell ruled over England".[15]

'I was greatly interested in arithmetic, history, and English literature. History and literature were not taught separately in those days; we read only the great historical tomes, and our knowledge of literature grew simultaneously. In this way, we learnt passages from Burke, Macaulay, Gibbon and Hallam, plus hundreds of lines of English poetry by heart. Years later, when we actually understood the meaning of what we had learnt, we were overjoyed, and our real interest was piqued.

'It was really unfortunate that in 1850 Green Saheb left us to take on the professorship of a college in Bombay. That the people of Surat have not written an account of this great man's services to their city is a sign of duty failed. Green Saheb was the man who introduced us to what was best in English literature. Churning the ocean of England's literature, he sheltered us from baser works and presented us with nectar. Nor did he teach us anything that would draw us to the Christian faith.

'I read *Pilgrim's Progress* when I was much older; I must confess that with the exception of Milton's *Paradise Lost*, my literary tastes tended to favour authors who could more or less be called atheists. In those days one had to be especially cautious in this regard.

'The learned Christian Padre Montgomery trapped a Parsi youth in his snares: he persuaded Nasarvanji Manekji to become a Christian. Uproar ensued, and even so intrepid a people as the Parsis grew fearful of English education; Hindu children ceased altogether to go to English schools.

---

[15] Some village Hampden that with dauntless breast
   The little tyrant of his fields withstood;
   Some mute inglorious Milton here may rest,
   Some Cromwell guiltless of his country's blood.
                    [quoted in author's footnote in the original text]

'Green Saheb realised that the very purpose of education was being lost by these attempts at conversion. He thus began his valiant Bhagirath-like efforts to move heaven and earth, and the nether regions as well, to prevent religious influences from taking hold of the educational system. He wrote several articles critical of Montgomery Saheb's proselytising ways. Green Saheb then joined with Rustomji Modi, Durgaram Mehta and Father in placating the youth, and pacifying members of the Parsi community; twenty days after which Nasarvanji re-entered the faith of his forefathers.'

Father claimed that within the Nagar community lay a deep fear of conversion. Nagars and the Kayasths were the two communities that possessed significant administrative talent. With the advent of British rule, it became necessary to recruit educated English-speaking youth as clerks. Difficulties arose for the communities at this juncture: if you learnt English there was the danger of losing your faith; if you did not learn English you did not earn your bread and butter. Father held that the inhabitants of Surat were indeed lucky to have had a man of so generous a temperament as Green Saheb to head its education department. He used his well-honed debating skills to write openly against the proselytising Christian Fathers in newspapers across the country.

'Green Saheb himself did not attend church, and even prevented his friends from doing so. This attitude agitated English society, and the more narrow-minded said he was caught in the clutches of "a Native Delilah". Only a man of courage like Green Saheb would for the sake of uplifting an alien people suffer the torment and rude behaviour of his own community.

'The eventual result of his efforts was that education ceased to be a vehicle for promoting religion in Gujarat; figures like Master Ramchundra in Punjab[16] and K. A. M. Banerji in Bengal did not appear in Gujarat.[17]

---

[16] Master Ramchundra was a noted mathematician, and a convert to Christianity. His book, *Treatise on Problems of Maxima and Minima,* was promoted by the prominent mathematician Augustus De Morgan. See https://en.wikipedia.org/wiki/Ramchundra (accessed 24 April 2021).

[17] Krishna Mohan Banerji (1813–1885) was converted to Christianity in 1832 and preached the Christian faith. He was held up as an example

'Green Saheb taught his students with solicitude; he invited us into his private rooms and gave us a taste of the books in his library. He would make us read a book, read it out himself, lend it, even gift it to us.

'At the time, Green Saheb lived in Surat. "Nand", he would so greet me at his doorstep, then fling the door wide open and welcome me in. No servant ushered me; as a matter of fact, his doors always remained open. He introduced me to his fast friend Captain Scott, who belonged to the naval forces, lived in Surat, had cultivated interests in history, geography, and was greatly fascinated by astronomy. There were a variety of telescopes arranged on his terrace; looking through them at the skies, I glimpsed the universe. I cannot even begin to describe the joy that filled me then. The German philosopher Kant saw the vastness of the sky in the eyes of a dead sparrow; the sentiments the philosopher expressed were mine: "Two things fill the mind with awe, the starry heavens above, and the moral law within." Row upon row of travel books and biographies arrayed his cupboard shelves. Like the legendary *chataka* bird, I beheld this treasure house of wisdom with eager, thirsty eyes, then, with equal impatience, I proceeded to read the books. "I am a child of the universe"—these were my feelings at the time.

'My association with these two men attracted me to English virtues. Even though they were teachers and I a student, distinctions of colour cast no shadow on our daily interactions. Green Saheb never made us feel that our touch could be contaminating. True, we were well-mannered; however, we had no idea as to what the English might consider civilised behaviour. These generous men understood that many different communities other than their own might also be civilised. The word "native", used with contemptuous overtones for the first time in Bengal, lost its sting when conjoined with the term "gentleman" (meaning a householder).'

After the 1857 Uprising, Green Saheb's writings began to be read once again. Under the pen name 'Indophile', he wrote a book

---

of what happens when Indians are educated in English schools (see Das 2008).

in defence of Indians. Father was extremely fond of this book. I myself read it in the Cambridge University library. Father would say, 'It is not surprising that the country which produces such jewels should dominate the world. Yet, a majority of Europeans whipped up emotions and passionately called out for revenge when the rebels of 1857 killed their countrymen with excessive cruelty. Green Saheb shot forth his verbal arrows in order to pacify this tumultuous storm surging all around us: "Punish those who are guilty after a fair trial, but don't condemn the innocent, don't thoughtlessly include those who are innocent." When the goddess of vengeance with eyes closed and dagger in hand danced a bloody dance, she was ordered: "Remove the bandage from your eyes, lest English justice flounder."

'Green Saheb's writing enraged the entire English community of Bombay. Christian priests already infuriated by his openly expressed atheism, were incensed by what he wrote. Now, it was their turn to retaliate. In addition to the charge of atheism, Green Saheb was charged with treason. His enemies published articles against him and led attacks on all other fronts.

'At this juncture, Green Saheb was transferred to Deccan College, in Poona. Having expended all his energy writing favourably about Indians, having strenuously tried to influence government policy along a straight path, he was worn out and fell prey to mental illness. This great man died while still in his middle years, like Lord Canning, who also died at the age of fifty due to the strain of hard work.[18] The inhuman and yet entirely natural elation of the Christian priests at his death was only matched by the great and inconsolable sorrow of educated Indians.

'Green Saheb was a thorough gentleman. He wasn't really an atheist; "agnostic" might be a more apt description of his beliefs. He would certainly have agreed with Shakespeare's Hamlet, who said: "There are more things in heaven and earth, Horatio, than are dreamt of in your philosophy." Perhaps for the creative

---

[18] Charles Canning (1812–1862) was Governor-General during the Uprising of 1857, and later, the first Viceroy of India. See: https://www.nndb.com/people/159/000101853/ (accessed 4 May 2021).

imagination Hamlet's words carry connotations of a transcendent joy, or whatever, but for those who want to live a rational life, the maxim: "Believe only what you see" should apply—that was Green Saheb's philosophy.

'At a public lecture held in Surat at this time, a speaker had Green Saheb in mind when he declaimed: "Students! Observe on one side the agony of the atheist Shelley's death, and on the other the peaceful end of an observant Christian like Edison."[19]

'Montgomery Saheb counted among the cleverest Christian priests of Surat. He was a learned man, a seeker of wisdom, and inclined to press theistic doctrines. But with regard to Green Saheb, the fair-mindedness and generosity of the Christian clergy was so blanketed by doctrine that not a single ray of justice could penetrate it. Montgomery Saheb offered to teach me, and said: "If you attend my lessons, I'll teach you logic and philosophy." But my feelings against the clergy at the time were so strong that I did not avail of the invitation. Later, I lived to regret my decision.'

Reading Trelawny's account of Shelley's death, Father was struck by how radiant his countenance was even in death; he remained unconvinced by the distinction the speaker had sought to draw between Edison and Shelley. Flanked on one side by a great dramatist and on the other by an English nightingale, Trelawny stood facing his Creator: 'Nothing of him that doth fade/But doth suffers a sea change/Into something rich and strange:'[20] Shelley's was no death; it was a transformation.

'Green Saheb did not resort to untruths nor did he ever exploit anyone; he did not swerve from the path of righteousness; he laboured hard; so how would it profit him either to attend church or to worship idols? A great many students modelled their lives on Green Saheb's, in the devotional spirit of the Sanskrit prayer: "*Yad yat karma karomi tad tadākhilam Śambho*

---

[19] Percy Bysshe Shelley had provocatively declared himself 'an atheist' in 1816, and inscribed in his famous statement that he was an atheist, a lover of humanity and a democrat (see Henderson 2016).

[20] These words from Shakespeare's play *The Tempest* were inscribed at Edward John Trelawny's instance on the tablet marking the place where Shelley's ashes lay buried (see Trelawny 1858[2011]).

tavārādhanam: Every act of mine is entirely dedicated to your service, Lord Shambhu".'

With respect to religion, Father maintained that he himself did not feel bound to the *sandhya* rituals, nor did his natural impulses draw him towards God: 'For me, caste reform and service to society are ways of worshipping the Creator. This determination of mine was drawn from Green Saheb's exemplary life.'

A Farsi couplet says:

> *Tarīkat bahuz khidmate khalk nīst*
> *Na tasbī ho sajjādo dalk nīst.*

Without service to mankind you don't acquire knowledge of God, Prayer beads and the practice of namaz avail you not.[21]

'Another great teacher in those days was Dadoba Pandurang. By caste he was a Parbhu. Just as in north India, under Muslim administrators the Kayasth and the Khatri castes were known for their administrative competence, so also the Parbhus entered government services in regions where the Marathas ruled under the saffron banner of the Peshwas. Indeed, they were so entrenched that the chief administrator, irrespective of his caste affiliation, was known as Parbhu. (In north India today the title Lala, because of its association with the Kayasth caste, is applied to all clerks.) However, after the Marathas ceased to govern Surat, the caste ceased to have any role, and this cultivated community disappeared from Surat.' In worldly matters everything depends on practical necessity—the Parbhus' departure happened to be my father's favourite example of this general principle.

Graham Saheb succeeded Green Saheb. He, too, greatly favoured Father, who, in 1849, was nominated monitor for students in lower grades; he was even allowed to teach classes. Graham Saheb was an extremely skilled teacher of arithmetic. Six feet tall, broad-shouldered, well-built, with an anger as great as sage Durvasa's, and a heart as soft as candle wax. Father never

---

[21] My translation accords with the author's Gujarati rendering in his footnote.

forgot his friendship with this generous Irishman. 'Graham Saheb shortened our names: I became Nand, Mahipatram was Mipe, Parvatishankar Porvety and Adelji Adel.'

'Graham Saheb would welcome us into his private room and entertain us, no matter what he was doing, even if he was at dinner, a whole chicken unflavoured by any *masala*, not even pepper, and a large bottle of alcohol standing close by on his table. The sight of him gobbling up his food reminded us of Kumbhakaran's gargantuan appetite. Graham Saheb did not invite us boys to dine with him; he was not in the business of converting people to Christianity. He never discussed religion but followed Socrates: "To each his own path, his own god".

'Graham Saheb was a hot-tempered man, kindly and unpretentious. Of modest means, he was nonetheless generous. We used to be shocked by his habit of erasing the blackboard with spit. "It's a bad childhood habit", he confessed one day. "Because we live in a cold climate we suffer from hydrophobia".'[22]

On 1 June 1852, Father obtained a clerk's position under the superintendent of schools. His prestige grew along with his salary as he advanced from being a student monitor to becoming a clerk. 'I bought myself a pony and toured the districts with Graham Saheb. He was naturally capricious; sometimes if he was in the mood he would speak in erudite ways; when he got his wires crossed, he was unable to add two and two. But an unbroken stream of affection oozed from him. Tears of regret would well up if he happened to be angry. His intention, on receiving his pension, was to live near the Niagara Falls. "Nand, I will welcome you with all my heart when you visit me," he assured me. After he left, he wrote at least twice. This god-fearing, simple man was determined to swim under the Niagara Falls; I fear that he died attempting this awesome feat.'

'One day, in the course of inspecting schools with Graham Saheb, we arrived close to the Parnera hill. After work ended that day, we decided to visit the Maratha fort on that hill. He peremptorily rejected my advice to take a guide. "What's the

---

[22] The word 'hydrophobia' is suggested by the author in the original text.

need?" he cried. The need, however, appeared very soon: the road was difficult, filled with thorny scrub, and by the time we reached, night had fallen. "Nand, the area is visited by the leopard after sunset and I have forgotten to bring my gun. I shan't return by the same path. I mean to slide straight down," he said. I warned him that his body would be badly lacerated if he did that; on the other hand, the possibility of encountering a leopard was remote. But the devil was astride his soul; he sat on the ground at the very edge and immediately began sliding down. I myself decided to return by the same path by which we had climbed. I sought the aid of a tribal from the forest to guide me for a short distance down the hill, and reached my destination very late at night. I was surprised to see small fires dotting the site. Spotting me in the distance, Graham Saheb came out of his tent. Apart from a pair of shorts, his torso was bare; his entire body appeared lacerated and his clothes torn. He greeted me with these words: "I had imagined that your tiny body was adorning the supper-table of the Parnera Leopard. And what was I going to say to your father?" He had lit fires to ward off leopards, but also to ensure that I would not lose my way. Even in the torrid heat of summer, he had fires lit for my safety. Would even real fathers be so concerned about their sons?

'I said, "You appear injured."

'"Rubbish," he replied. "It is of no consequence. Skins are like cloth; tears can be stitched back together."

'Before he could say anything further, a great hubbub arose—a tiger had stolen a calf from a nearby village. Tigers may roam the mountain, but to find that the great beast was seen roaming the plains at the bottom of the hill! Still, I had felt no great fear the entire time that I was walking back; I knew that until the animal becomes a man-eater, he does not attack humans.

'Graham Saheb taught me riding. He used to seat me on his thoroughbred horse Valour, and then twitch the reigns. Riding horses is similar to swimming; one learns naturally. You will soon learn to ride, perhaps after falling four-five times or so. "If you're afraid, fear won't ever leave you, and you won't learn to ride."' Till the very end, the habit of riding stayed with Father.

'Graham Saheb, who used to belittle one of our mathematics teachers, told me the following story: "The schoolmaster had once thoughtlessly remarked that riding a horse was easy: you just sit straight and maintain your centre of gravity; how then can you possibly fall? By and by, the pedantic fool learned the distinction between principle and practice. Unable to maintain his 'centre of gravity', he rolled in the mud."

'After examinations ended, Graham Saheb would gather the schoolmasters and lecture them on pedagogic methods. I myself did not lodge with the other teachers; I stayed with Patel or Desai families. People in the village were extremely hospitable; I was brahmin by caste and considered close to the Saheb, so they took good care of me. They served lavish meals, but I would not eat food cooked by others, so they sent me raw provisions. Anavil brahmin women are extremely welcoming hosts; they sent me *papaḍ* and other condiments. Nor did the poor things do it out of any ulterior motive; rather, it was a natural outflow of human kindness. I had great affection for the village folk; they were simple, straightforward, natural, unlettered people, with a fund of native intelligence. With minds totally made up, mixing fact and fiction in complete disregard of evidence, they spun tall tales—all of which delighted me.

'Once, a large crowd had gathered in our tent; the atmosphere was beginning to get rough. Suddenly, Graham Saheb stood up and ordered everyone out. He then caught hold of a fat barber and dragged him back into the tent. Graham Saheb forced open the trembling man's jaws and shoved a pill down his throat. I stared, wondering what had possessed him. Meeting my eyes, he smiled. I did not smile in return. Composing my childish eighteen-year-old countenance in a display of severity, I said, "Saheb, you are being disrespectful of these people to have thrown them out. Your inspection tour will fail." He replied, "Never fear, Nand. I don't care if I accomplish very little. My intention wasn't to throw them all out; I had thought to catch that impudent barber. To catch him I drove everyone out; in fact, he was the first to run. I thought a dose of laxative might do him some good. Go out and tell them that I gave the man a laxative; it wasn't poison." Basically, I am by temperament quite light-hearted; so I couldn't at that moment contain my laughter.

'I stepped outside and saw the following scene: the fat, well-fed barber lay prone on the ground, every effort being made to get him to vomit. The rascal's state was truly pitiful: his eyes were turned up, his limbs trembled, and streams of perspiration rolled down his temples. When I told them the truth, that what Graham Saheb had administered was not poison but a laxative, the barber suddenly got up and, pushing aside his helpers, shouted, "Get away you beggars! Move you witless fools!". All false pride now, he stood up straight, cleared his throat and proclaimed, "From the beginning I told them that Saheb was a prankster, but these cowards insisted he had poisoned me. How does it profit Saheb to be rid of me? Who else would take on the burden of carrying a flaming torch to light his way at night?" An incarnation of the eternal spirit of Jeevram Bhatt![23] Your power is everywhere refulgent! The barber arrived the very same night to light lamps in our locality. Graham Saheb gave him a rupee as reward.

'In time, I became well-acquainted with Irishmen. They are moody, full of jokes, obstinate, playful, shrewd, full of fun, authentic but also eccentric. They have a capacity to enter your hearts wherever they go. But beware! Never depend on them; beware of the surrounding shale should you anchor your boat on their shore.

'After inspecting schools, we returned from Billimora to Surat by sea in a large shore-hugging boat. Now came time for Graham Saheb to leave his job. He took a two-year furlough and bade us goodbye. Six months after his departure, he submitted his resignation. Tears filled his middle-aged eyes as he embraced me before leaving; in me affection and trust were unlimited. "Remember, you have to come to Niagara. You will truly taste my hospitality there." The mention of Niagara brings back memories of Graham Saheb, and my heart begins to overflow like the ocean at moonrise. That his leaving would enhance my prospects, that I might even become headmaster—these selfish thoughts did not

---

[23] Jeevram Bhatt is a comic character in Dalpatram's play *Mithyabhiman Natak*. See: https://archive.org/details/in.ernet.dli.2015.319124 (accessed 1 August 2021).

diminish my sadness at his departure, and I found tears running down both my eyes.'

One last anecdote about Graham Saheb remains to be told. One day, my father went for a walk with Graham Saheb, who happened to be carrying a large stick. Father writes: 'On the way we came upon a group of pallbearers returning from the cremation site; they were having a good time, smoking *bidi*s, chatting and gossiping. They appeared to belong to the lower orders of society. As we approached the bereaved home, unaware of the death in the family, the crowd of over hundred-odd people, who until a moment before had been so jovial, let out howls of false grief. Like lightning Graham Saheb flew into their midst, waving his cane. All ran for their lives. Afterwards an astonished Saheb asked me what it was all about. I explained to him the custom. "Disrespect of the dead isn't something I can countenance," he explained, justifying his Bhimsen-like ways.

'Graham Saheb was followed by Good Saheb.'

Until the time I left Surat to study at the college in Vadodara, I would accompany my father and maternal grandfather on their evening walks, and ask them about the past. They would recount, and I would listen with sharp attention and later reflect on what they had said. 'We wore turbans and long *angarkha*s (tunics) to school, and so were greatly embarrassed when we were punished and made to stand on a stool. Graham Saheb was not above thrashing us for behaving badly, but never for any fault in our work.

'Of my fellow students, Adelji Manjibhai was considered the most proper. "This is too much, it is far too hot for me," he would delicately say. We would laugh. How should heat be a problem for young men our age? Adelji was greatly interested in astronomy. He had complete knowledge of the placement of stars, of sunrises and sunsets. His sideburns—in those days Parsi men kept the rest of their heads tonsured—were always well-combed, his clothes without wrinkles, his slate clean, his books covered in good cardboard—everything about him was "superfine".[24]

---

[24] The word 'superfine' is in English in the original.

'Mahipatram was as disorderly as Adelji was finicky. His work habits were helter-skelter, but his mind was precise, with an obstinacy of purpose evident even then. He was also affectionate, straightforward and simple in his ways. We were friends to the very end.

'Lala Ratanlal (Kayasths lived in our neighbourhood) was a free spirit. He was clever but put in no effort at school. In fact, the naughtiness of the entire world seemed to lodge in him. Early in the morning, before school began, he would go about removing the wooden ladders that led down from the top storeys of shopkeepers' homes to their shops below. The 'blessings' issuing forth from the mouths of these barely awake, hardworking men as they enthusiastically stepped down onto the roadside must certainly have borne bitter fruit.'

'Graham Saheb was in the habit of poking half-asleep boys with the point of a penknife. "Ratan," he would order, "go fetch that penknife from the office." Barely had the order been issued than Ratanlal would rise, taking his own sweet time to go to the office, and return empty-handed: "Saheb, there are no signs of any penknife. I have looked everywhere." Dozens of Graham Saheb's penknives were lost this way.

'Jagjivandas was ahead of our batch. Mukundbhai was considered to be very proper. His mind, too, was inclined that way—he neither laughed nor did he mingle with the rest of us. He was by nature very serious; one could even say he was wise as the words issuing from his lips were unusually wise. He was the only one in our class whom we addressed in the formal *tamé*, not *tu*. He wore his *dhoti* meticulously, layer upon perfectly folded layer, and never joined in our rowdy play.

'Parvatishankar was poor, but of resolute mind. He saved his coins, and was extremely clever with numbers. Parvati—adventurous Parvati—he was my true friend!

'Jebhai was about average in studies, but he became the bright spark of our student life. Boundlessly joyous! Others laughed and made others laugh, but not Jebhai. Keeping a straight face, he would choose an appropriate moment to shoot his witty arrow, and I would find myself bent double with convulsed laughter. Once Graham Saheb caught hold of Jebhai and forced him to drink a glass of port wine. It was either the lad's fair skin or his slightly plump physique that probably attracted the teacher's attention. Jebhai was not in the least bit pleased, but putting on a brave front, he laughed and said to me, "Pal, don't please mention this to anyone else." I kept the matter to myself. Jebhai had, however, related the story to each of his friends, exhorting each one to keep the matter quiet. Eventually, the story came out and everyone became aware of what had happened, and so began a round of accusations: "I might have let out the secret, but why did you?" At that point Jebhai confessed that he himself had told the story to each one of us. How we laughed.'

Jebhai was a man of character. He had risen to a high position in the Department of Education. At the time of my elder brother Markand's wedding, I came down to Surat from Kutch, and found Jebhai ill. I went to see him. There was the usual satisfaction felt when in-laws meet, but my old friend, though ailing, stood up with difficulty and as we clung to each other with remembered affection, tears filled our eyes.

An extraordinary age was ending. The Nawabi was in decline; but even in decline an afterglow remained. The Sanskrit language accompanied Saraswati, the goddess of learning, into forest exile and remained immured there. Men learnéd in that language found no patrons; the study of Sanskrit no longer served any purpose, and so the institutions connected with it broke up in parts of Gujarat ruled by the Nawabs. But the language continued to flourish with Peshwa support in regions under their sway.

Farsi was the official language and widely used. In fact, speaking the language was such a craze in Surat that members of the Raiji family, who counted among the most able administrators, even gave themselves fancy Persianised titles, such as Mijlasarai and Sahebrai. Sahebrai used to recite his *sandhya* in Farsi, and angrily ordered even his family priest to converse in that tongue. Poetry contests were the rage. The assembly of poets is known in northern Indian cities of Delhi and Lucknow as *mushaira*. Likewise, members of the Nagar and Kayasth castes met and recited their Farsi compositions in Surat.

Abheram, a Kayasth who was exceedingly proud of his Farsi, once presented the Nawab with the following question: '*Hazure vala!* Your Majesty, should the name Adityaram be spelt with the initial *ain* or *alif?*'

The Nawab's intellect matched his thick body, so he replied, '*Bilasak,* without doubt with *ain.* In my Diwan's home the common *alif* would never be used.'

'*Khudavande nevamat!* Protector of the Faith! Consult Aditramji. His name Adityaram, being a Hindi word for sun, must surely begin with an *alif.*'

Adityaram arrived. The Nawab Saheb addressed the question to him. The clever Adityaram guessed that the question rose from a wrangle and that the Nawab's preference was for the name to begin with *ain.* The outcome reminded Father of Saadi's and Vishnusharma's almost identical sentiment: '*Darog maslahat āmez biha az rāstiye fitnāngez.* A sweet untruth is superior to a bitter truth', says Saadi, and Vishnusharma offers the same: '*Satyam bruyāt priyam bruyān, na bruyāt satyamapriyam.* Speak what is true; speak what pleases others. What is true but bitter don't ever speak'.[25] And Saadi says,

> *Agar roha ruzrā goyad sabast-ī |*
> *Bibāyād guft inak māho parvīn ||*

Should the emperor say, 'it is day,' say it is day; if he says, 'it is night,' say, 'it is night—I see the shining moon and stars'.[26]

And so Adityaram replied, '*Baja farmate hain Jahanpanah! Bande ka nam ain se shuru hota hai.* Oh Protector of the World, what you say is true. Your captive's name begins with an *ain.*' The Nawab, twirling his moustache with pleasure, said, 'Well-spoken, Chopdar. Topple this fool from his seat'. Abheram fled, and never again did he boast about his command over Farsi, or show his face at court.

Such fruitless parrying did make the mind quick and the wit sharp, but added naught either to human welfare or to good governance. Similarly in classical India, a grammarian's joy in reducing his metrical rule even by a single syllable was compared

---

[25] The translation accords with the author's Gujarati rendering.
[26] Ibid.

to the joy of a son's birth.[27] To say the right thing at the right moment, to illustrate the point with the help of some poet's well-known verse, to be quick at repartee, preferably embellished with figures of speech and balanced syntax—all these were special skills of the time. Appropriate use of words and well-constructed sentences added a lyricism to the speech of the period. Men clung to their verbal inventions, repeated them from time to time, and revelled in the audience's response, 'Bravo! Well done! Fabulous!' They were like the sculptor who makes a beautiful marble image and then seeks to embrace it.

Certainly, poets' gatherings found support, but is truth nourished in this manner? When Babar entered India, he wrote: 'Among this uncivilised folk, there are no assemblies, no custom of sitting together in council. They have no awareness of how to speak or how to behave.' All these 'defects' pointed out by Babar had by this time been eliminated.

The aberrations associated with erotic love, and sanctioned by those in high office, gained new currency. Men who considered alcohol taboo, who believed in a Muslim's defiling touch, now felt honoured to accept a bidi from the hands of a courtesan. Should the woman be a musician and salaam the man, it was, to use my grandfather's wry words, 'as if the viceroy had shaken hands with him, there was such pleasure and pride in the recognition so conferred'. And beyond all that, if ever the lady laughed, then the lotus of his heart verily blossomed, with smiles overspreading his face.

How is it that most courtesans usually belong to the Shia sect? This question has not been properly investigated. The Sunnis are rather strict in their ways, but the Shias, with their heart-rending laments for 'Hassan-Hussein', compose their funeral dirges in procession. Singing these dirges, new members enter the same eternal round. The Shia path is indeed quite unique.

---

[27] *Ardhamātrālāghavena putrotsavam manyante vaiyākaraṇāh* alludes to a principle of simplicity in Sanskrit grammar, sometimes termed Panini's Razor, after Occam's Razor. A modern restatement of the principle is: 'Select the theory that introduces the fewest assumptions and postulates the fewest entities' (see Kiparsky 2007).

In Surat, overflowing crowds fill the entire distance from the Mirza Chakla right up to Lakdipol to watch the mourners. Courtesans don fakir's robes and join the mourners, singing dirges. Men with a taste for music stand and watch the dramatic rendition with encouraging cries of 'Bravo! Bravo!' They comment on the fakir style of the women's clothing, 'How wondrously well it suits her!' Some even become fakirs and, attired in green, join their real or fancied mistresses to weep by the side of their weeping companions. The women at home were illiterate; the men natural connoisseurs of beauty. 'I am intoxicated with beauty; you are empty of such feeling. How can we, then, come together?'—with these thoughts the men would wander in search of what was unavailable at home.

The very same people who at one time believed that 'the gods delight [in homes] where women are revered—*yatra nāryas tu pūjante ramante tatra devatā*,'[28] also wrote:

> *Yadi svāc śītalo vahniś ca candramā dahanātmakah |*
> *susvādah sāgarah strīṇām tat satītvam prajāyate ||*

> Only if fire were to turn cold, the moon fiery,
> and sea-water sweet, will women be true.

Once-brilliant precepts from the Vedas were eclipsed; the beauty of worldly life was thought to turn men away from the path of virtue; false ideologies gained ground; instead of transformation of the material realm, it was thought wiser to eradicate the material world altogether. Torture of the body was considered superior to cultivating the body and the senses. 'Birth itself is the fruit of sin' expressed a widely held belief. With the loss of independent thought, dependence grew. Woman ceased to be the mother of the clan, and became a mere object of pleasure; instead of enthusiastic involvement in statesmanship, she was eager to throw tantrums. Is it any wonder that she is the way she is today? The Universal Mother, Universal Sustainer is the source

---

28 One of Vinayak Mehta's favourite verses from the *Manusmṛti* 3.56 (see *Manusmṛti* n.d.).

of all spirituality. It is she who, with the quality of her thought and her conduct, teaches the transformation of the material world into the spiritual realm. Because we disregarded her, demonic sexuality took hold, intellectual liveliness was destroyed, and dark ignorance pervaded all.

In Shelley's poetic rendition of Plato's *Symposium*, Agathon, in a similar spirit, speaks words redolent with sarcasm and contempt: 'Oh you dancers and singers! Go inside to entertain the womenfolk, while we debate philosophical issues.'[29] There is speculation that in ancient Greece, women were veiled. The poet Shelley's comment is relevant here:

> The women thus degraded, became such as it was expected they would become. They had the habits and qualities of slaves. They were devoid of that moral and intellectual liveliness with which the acquisition of knowledge and the cultivation of sentiment, animate as if with another life of overpowering grace, the lineaments and the gestures of every form which they inhabit. Their eyes would not have been deep and intricate from the workings of the mind and could have entangled no heart in soul-woven labyrinth.[30]

Just as Pericles fell victim to Aspasia's intrigues, scores of moths plunged into this half-light.[31] The first example that comes to mind is that of Charudatt and Vasantasena.[32] Thereafter, the texts seem to suggest that to be considered worthy, a man must be instructed in a courtesan's household. Only a courtesan is endowed with the graceful arts of beauty and has the capacity to make men drink of its potion. The *Daśakumāracarita* describes the education of girls, but only for those who will grow up to be courtesans:

---

[29] From Shelley's translation of Plato's *Symposium*. Vinayak's quotation is not exact (see Shelley 1915).

[30] From Shelley's 'Essay on the Literature, the Arts, and the Manners of the Athenians' (see Shelley 1906).

[31] See 'Pericles and Aspasia', http://www.classicalathensgoldenage.com/pericles_aspasia.htm (accessed 4 May 2021).

[32] The reference is to *Mṛcchakatikā* of Shudraka (see Ryder 1905).

Kamamanjari's mother, keen that her daughter set up with Marichi, lectures her wards on the systematic methods of educating courtesans: 'She should be instructed in all the arts associated with the body—dancing, reciting, singing, painting, preparing perfumes, making tasty foods, flower arrangement, calligraphy, witty conversation, grammar, philosophy, logic; she was taught the game of cockfighting and chess and the seductive art of gambling.'[33]

Is there a single word here relating to the education of an ordinary householder's daughter?

This was the state of society when the Muslims arrived. That Muslims consider women inferior to men is well-known. Even ordinary men are allowed to marry more than one wife. As a result, from the very beginning young girls are moulded to be attractive, even seductive; those qualities were cultivated in a girl that would enable her to take precedence over her husband's other wives.

In *Karan Ghelo*, Father wrote:

> The rights to move around freely that women enjoyed during the reign of the Rajput kings, now disappeared. Muslims considered vile any woman walking freely on the street. By and large even women of dignity faced insults if they walked unveiled on the street. As a consequence, women's carefree days ended. Everywhere they were locked up like prisoners. Even in respectable homes the need to curtain off women's quarters in *purdah* emerged, adversely affecting their lives, their manners and their conduct. (*KG* 13.381)

George Meredith in his essay on comedy quotes the French essayist M. Saint-Marc Girardin's conversation with an Arab gentleman. Referring to women, the Arab man is reported to have said:

> 'YOU can look on them without perturbation—but WE!'... And after this profoundly comic interjection, he added, in deep tones, 'The very face of a woman!' Our representative of temperate notions demurely consented that the Arab's pride

---

[33] From *Dandin's Dasakumaracharitam* (see Jacob 1873).

of inflammability should insist on the prudery of the veil as the civilizing medium of his race.[34]

How can such respect owed to women, so evident in the *Ramayan,* emerge within the ranks of Muslims?

Nāham jānāmi keyure nāham jānāmi kuṇḍale |
Nupūre tvabhijānāmi nityam pādābhvandanā ǁ 4.6.22 ǁ[35]

I know not her armlets nor her earrings/I truly recognize only her anklets, because out of respect time and again I bent down to touch her feet.

This is Lakshman's response, in the *Kishkindha Kand* of the *Ramayan,* as Ram wanders along a path strewn with ornaments, indicating the direction in which Sita's abductor fled, and asks Lakshman whether he recognises these jewels.

In those days there was no purdah. However, out of respect for women, men set natural limits to their baser instincts. Vasantasena and Kamamanjari replaced Sitadevi in due course. 'Springtime is where my beloved dwells'—Ram's sentiments here express the innately pure aspects of love in that period when the *Ramayan* was composed. And who is not filled with joy when he hears the words Bhavabhuti places in Ram's mouth?

Āvivāhsamayād gṛhe vane śaiśave tadanu yauvane punah |
Svāpahetur anupāśrito'nyayā Rāmabāhur upadhānam eva ǁ 1.37 ǁ

From the moment we were married, at home, in the forest, in childhood and following that in youth/Rama's arms unaided and without design were her cushioned shelter.[36]

---

[34] See Meredith 1897.

[35] From *Valmiki's Ramayana* 4.6.22; see https://sanskritdocuments.org/sites/valmikiramayan/kish/sarga6/kishkindha_6_frame.htm (accessed 4 May 2021). The verse is not part of the critical edition of *Ramayana* published by the Oriental Institute, Baroda; see: https://sanskritdocuments.org/mirrors/ramayana/valmiki.htm (accessed 4 May 2021).

[36] From *The Uttara-Ramacharita of Bhavabhuti* (see Aiyar and Parab 1903).

The men of that age were able to express these sentiments with pride. Now they read Farsi poets, and wrote poems in praise of the mistress' curled and coifed hair. A poet writes,

Tuze aṭkheliyān (ādāi) kahān suzi men bezār baiṭhā hun ||

Whence your obstinacy? I sit bewildered by your side.

All verses belonging to this genre of versification passed off as great poetry. Courtesans took part in the joys and sorrows of the family. If there was a death, courtesans beat their breasts in the house of the deceased. During Holi, they were invited to sing songs, they threw colour and inquired about the wellbeing of the women of the household. Passers-by looked up with blazing eyes to watch those privileged by fortune to stand in a courtesan's balcony, their eyes lit not by righteous passion, but blatant envy. Their feelings for the unattainable fruit would spill over into the sarcastic cry, 'So, you're finally at your Aunt's doorstep!'

The madness had reached such proportions that when a certain man died, the relatives carrying his corpse to the cremation grounds passing by way of his mistress' house would be met with lamentations from within. Had his unfulfilled spirit been wandering about unseen, the cries would instantly have saved him the descent into hell, or even won him liberation from the cycle of life and death.

I shall relate one last story before leaving this demeaning subject. A man addicted to sensual pleasures left his house one evening. His better half certainly knew where this gay blade was headed; even so, she demanded, 'Whereabouts are you going?' Receiving the disdainful reply, 'I'll go wherever I wish to. It's no one else's business,' the woman kept quiet. The libertine closed the door; stroking his moustache and chewing his *paan* he was building castles in the air when he heard the door behind him rattle. Looking back, he saw his better half leaving the house, a mattress under her arm! 'Where are you going?' the words promptly escaped his lips. 'What business is it of yours? I'll go wherever I wish to!' came the equally prompt answer. The man was deeply ashamed; moustache drooping, he turned around.

Our hope is that the marital vows between husband and wife have since been sufficiently restored.

It was also a time when men were greatly interested in fine cuisine. I have already mentioned how Tuljabhai, pretending to be ill with jaundice, had turned away from his new posting to feast on *kheer* and soft *rotli*s served at the death feast of Jamiatram's father. Whenever an elderly person died, ritual feasts, held on the thirteenth day after death, were ferociously attacked by all. Some old men sent out invitations to their own ritual death feasts even before they died, and their spirits partook enthusiastically of the meal.[37] If grand feasts were held for first pregnancy ceremonies, can you imagine the spectacular celebrations on the occasion of marriages and thread ceremony rituals? During a successful marriage season, the home fires remained unlit for months; you would be fed twenty-four hours of the day during these celebrations. And even though a great deal of food was poured into the belly, the digestive powers did not usually fail. And even when indigestion killed a few here and there, the saying '*amṛtam kṣīrbhojanam*: a meal made with milk is indeed the nectar of immortality' held sway. Indeed, nothing diminished the craze for a good meal.

Father writes, 'It used to upset us to see people derive so much joy from these unfeeling ceremonial feasts for the dead, so my friends' group refused to attend these meals. When a certain Mehta died, on the thirteenth day, *kheer* with *rotli*s were prepared for the entire caste. Unfortunately, his son had renounced *kheer* on the occasion of his first wife's death. Not consuming the food on the thirteenth day of his father's death meant that it would

---

[37] In Chapter Four of *Karan Ghelo*, he relates a story about an old man which illustrates the culture of Surat of Nandshankar's time: 'In the course of a pilgrimage, a certain sum is reserved for charity. It was his [the old man's] dearest wish that after allocating to charities, what remained should be served in the form of ghee to the entire caste. The prestige denied him during his lifetime he would enjoy in his afterlife when his caste members cried "Bravo!"—the thought transported him to heaven; indeed, he was certain he would enter the gates of Shiva's Paradise on the strains of their accolades' (*KG* 4.98).

not reach his ancestral spirit, so *basundi* was substituted for *kheer*. He drank a good deal of that sweet. We were extremely annoyed when the story reached our ears. Swami Dayanand, the author of *Satyartha-Prakash*, in the course of a lecture once truly asked, "*Baman kā pet kuch letter box hai ke usme kuch anna dālege vo kāgaz māfik pitr ke vahān pahunch jāyegā?* Is the brahmin's stomach a letter box that whatever food you put into it will duly be delivered to your ancestors' home?"

'Mixing vegetables was considered an art, serving them a craft. A well-served meal has to be composed of good food and artfully arranged speech. The meal was not set up to be a battlefield; rather, it was a stage set for drama. Just as an actor who fails to enact his role properly continues to repeat his lines over and over again until the end of his days, so also a badly conducted feast embarrasses the host for life.

'When Ochhavlal Desai peeled his bitter gourd, not only the Mehtas, but also the Desais, abandoning their rivalry on this one occasion, would run to watch him. One could even say, "*śākapriyāh Suratavāsinah*: Suratis love vegetables".'[38]

Indians of the time only seldom settled their disputes in court; tort actions were rare. But if by chance at the festival banquet the buttermilk turned out to be sour, not only was payment withheld, but a complaint was almost lodged in court for serving it! Oodo Dongerpara held a degree in the culinary arts! He was like Bhimsen, and could boast of his cooking prowess. People like him ate, drank and made merry, but they were also thoughtless, easygoing, and turned blind eyes to the future. Forever deep in debt, like moths they frittered away their lives.

My maternal great-grandfather, Motiram Mehta, was a sort of nineteenth-century Nagar bard. He would post bail for anyone and everyone. His grandiose ways saw him sunk in debt, which eventually led him to ruin. If there was a decree against Police Chief Ardeshar, the guarantor would be Motiram Mehta. If Diwanji sank into debt, it was Motiram Mehta's land that was put up as collateral. The gesture satisfied his hunger for status.

---

[38] A play on the Sanskrit adage, '*brahmano bhojanapriyah*: brahmins love food.'

Unfortunately, Mr Puffed Up would have to hide when the bailiff arrived at the door. With a monthly salary of a hundred and twenty-five rupees, he still left behind a debt. My mother says, 'When I was a young girl, we had standing orders to say that grandfather was not at home to strangers who came to the door asking for him.'

Then there was an extraordinary chap by the name Ratanram. He was an advocate, but all his earnings came from artful theft. He took commissions and set up a business supplying victims to advocates. One day, as he walked down the street carrying an expensive English umbrella, a friend carrying a Chinese umbrella approached him from the opposite direction. The friend could not help saying, 'Look friend, I paid one and a half rupees for this umbrella, a full twenty-four *annas*'. 'But have you seen this?' Ratanram retorted, showing off his own umbrella. With a cold look, the friend asked, 'Did you buy it, or was it stolen?' 'Steal it? No, my good sir, the trick is to borrow it,' replied the man who lived off borrowed sums. 'Indeed, when the time for settling my loan draws near, I shall enter the following note in my diary (we lawyers keep a record of public law suits): 'Child Ratan, you will stay away from a certain locality for six months. You will increase the size of your side burns and change the colour of your turban.'

Ratanram had other large debts. To escape creditors, he would change appearance and flee; he did not, however, always get away. When a creditor finally caught up with him, this pious fraud transformed himself into a devotee of Shiva, covered himself in holy ash and sat in a pose of such deep meditation that the creditor was taken aback. Questioned, Ratanram immediately went on the offensive, 'Scoundrel! Don't you dare annoy me! Just you watch my anger.' And then shaking himself, he allowed the ash rubbed on his body to billow as he threatened, 'With my inner fire I shall burn you and reduce you to ash'. At the time, brahmins were used to bullying others with threatened curses so the trembling petitioner left without collecting his debt within the stipulated time period.

Sau chuhe khake billa haj ko chala; like the proverbial cat who goes on a Haj pilgrimage having eaten a hundred rats, Ratanram went to Benaras as if to perform his final sacrificial rites. He arrived in great state and was warmly welcomed by the priest. When it came time to pay the priest his *dakshina*, Ratanram said, 'Look Maharaj, I will not reward you with a fleeting momentary gift. I am giving you these certified title deeds for two of my villages'. Greedy for more, the priest said, 'The scriptures ordain that there be a grand banquet for brahmins before the mantra, "thus ends the pilgrimage" is finally uttered'. Ratanram declared that he had no cash on hand to pay for such a celebratory meal. 'Am I not here, my patron?' offered the priest, proceeding to lend Ratanram the required three hundred rupees. Ratanram spent more than half on the meal, gave his *dakshina* from the remaining sum and said goodbye. The priest had probably swindled many a pilgrim, but in Ratanram he found a man who was more than his equal. Indeed, he had found an expert, a far greater guru. When the priest's servant arrived in Surat with the title deeds to lay claim to the property, they discovered that Ratanram had no connection to the villages he had 'gifted'.

Nagars and Kayasths everywhere were invariably in debt to an Atmaram Bhukhanwala, or a Chakawala, or a Bhansaliwala. When their eldest son reached marriageable age there were funds enough to provide the bride's dower, but for the marriage of the second son, a debt had most certainly to be incurred. Even the Desais found themselves sunk in debt. The colourful Turk may claim that gold means as little to him as the shoe on his foot, but when he approaches the moneylender, he prepares to wear those very shoes on top of his head. Can a debtor hold on to such false metaphors, that gold is like the dust of my feet, and still retain his dignity?

'He who has, gets'—this saying soon proved true enough. If the creditors' clerk did not shadow your doorsteps, you were not only considered not high born, but most certainly neither noble nor powerful—in fact, no one would want to marry their daughter to you; you were doomed to remain single. '*Koi din gāḍi koi din ghoḍā, ne koi din pāun se chalnā ji; koi din lāḍi, koi din vāḍi, koi din fakkam kaffā ji.* One day a carriage, another day a horse, and some days on bare shanks you walk; one day a beloved, another day a mansion, and some days nothing at all.' In the blink of an eye you could be transformed from wealth to beggary—such was the instability of the time. 'You who love freedom, eat and drink to your heart's content. Don't be anxious about the morrow' was the rule by which men lived.

On a salary of a thousand rupees a month, Police Chief Ardeshar had a debt of five lakhs! A thousand attempts were made to attach his property, some of which he hid at his rich friends' houses. Sadly, he usually recovered only half of what he hid. Ardeshar was charged with using force to recover his money; in due course, a not-guilty verdict was reached. A large crowd of well-wishers accompanied the sedan chair in which he was carried home. At home, my maternal grandfather recalled Ardeshar seated with two large bags full of tens of thousands of rupees, handing out fistfuls to people standing on all four sides. 'Up with Ardeshar! Down with his enemies!'—rose the cry. And Surat's imbeciles continued to imitate his extravagant practices. In order to heal a rift within the mendicant ranks of the Nagar community, my grandfather borrowed money to feed the entire caste and, in addition, presented ochre garments to all.

Any and every manner of person was bent on putting on a grand show. The bridegroom's procession, to give you an example, set out in great pomp, the front line led by a lavishly decorated child groom, the jewellery specially borrowed for the occasion to ensure that people hail the family's splendour. In this way your name attains immortality; what else then is the purpose of life? Organising the bridegroom's procession for weddings became such a specialised skill that these event managers earned themselves the name '*Varghodia*'. Families across caste and clan invited *Varghodia*s to organise events. Makubhai was considered the preeminent decorator of those who walked on the frontline of the procession. The art of dressing the hair of the young girls who accompanied the bridegroom's horse, or of painting *tilak*s on women's foreheads, and of adjusting ornaments, often borrowed, to hang just so were all his; he was the expert in all these areas. 'You have to have an eye for it, and not everyone does!' In the age of the Antonine Caesars, the Romans were brought to ruin by just such ostentatious displays. Similarly, Surat in its decline indulged in such lunacies. The condition of our Surati brothers was like the flame that burns brightest before it dies.

Even after that age ended, many would have observed Keshav Raiji, who remained ever the same. He had served his apprenticeship under Police Chief Ardeshar, and subsequently risen from a clerk to a manager. His wages did not add up to much, but he had many indirect and crooked ways of adding to his income. With Ardeshar's downfall and loss of position, someone suggested that Raiji look for a different job. 'A master is like a husband; you can serve only one. If I have to work, it'll only be at Ardeshar's, who has Nausherwan's sense of justice, Hatimtai's generosity and Yusuf's beauty', was his response.[39]

Raiji was large-hearted; the heart was indeed generous, but the head contained not a single thought for the future. 'Raiji, something has to be done!' Hardly were such beseeching words spoken than he'd say, 'Go child, take a rupee from that alcove, and buy yourself some *mava*.' Until the end, he owned a shop in the square, which he rented out. When he walked over to the shop to collect rent, people would applaud, 'Bravo, Raiji! Bravo!' The words flattered him, so he distributed an *anna* here and an *anna* there as reward. In negotiating deals he tended to haggle over the price, make a thousand pretences, but would finally settle for a price far higher than was warranted. 'This is happening because Ardeshar is no longer there to enforce the law,' he would say as he left the scene, all the while vigorously chewing paan.

The only watch Raiji wore was from Istanbul, a gift from Ardeshar. Wearing it, he would strut about, greeting everyone in style. On meeting an acquaintance, he would hold out his watch

---

[39] Nausherwan, Yusuf and Hatimtai are heroes of the Persian and Arabic world. Nausherwan was celebrated for his sense of justice and his wisdom. See 'King Nausherwan Adil', https://www.thesufi.com/nausherwan-adil/ (accessed 24 April 2021). Hatimtai was a pre-Islamic poet known for his generosity. See 'Story of Hatimtai 16', www.sacred-texts.com/isl/bus/bus06.htm (accessed 24 April 2021). Yusuf is Joseph of the Old Testament. According to Ustadh Abdullah Anik Misra, 'Yusuf "was indeed given half of beauty is a rigorously authenticated hadith found in Sahih Muslim, Ahmad, and others.' See: https://www.seekersguidance.org/answers/general-counsel/is-it-true-that-the-prophet-yusuf-was-given-half-of-beauty-and-the-prophet-muhammad-was-given-all-of-it/ (accessed 24 April 2021).

and say, 'Tell me the time.' How does so well-dressed a man not know how to tell the time? Perhaps he was offering others a glimpse of a beautiful object.

On Gudi Padva day, dressed in starched clothes, he mounted his ox cart and set out to visit Ardeshar. Crossing the Shetanphala locality on that day is like crossing the Khyber Pass—you can't take a step without becoming entirely covered in dust. Raiji's old father Amritlal happened to be sitting on his veranda. 'What are you waiting for?' he cried, ordering young men loitering on the street to rain dust on Keshav, who soon found himself enveloped in it. Sharp words were exchanged between father and son. 'Arrest the offenders,' Keshav Raiji in turn ordered his policemen. No sooner was the order given than several Nagar youths were rounded up and marched off to court. In a show of strength, the old man headed the procession.

As the arrested youth were presented in court, the popular Police Chief Keshav Raiji's eyes fell on the old man. 'This old man' he said, 'has lost his wits. Despite warning, and then in your honour's name, they threw dust at me.' The old man retorted, 'Yes son, we would have ruined the reputation of the Nagar and Kayasth youth had we not thrown dust at you on the Festival of Dust. He lies, your honour!' This particular Sohrab and Rustom did not fight it out to the end. The old man was pacified, and the deflated Keshav Raiji's moustache was seen to droop.[40]

There is another amusing story they tell about Keshav Raiji. Once a young friend of his said, 'You claim great friendship with Jagannath Sheth, but how does one know what you claim is true?' And Raiji retorted, 'You are deluded! Will you be convinced if I bring you a photograph of the man?'

This headstrong idler travelled to Bombay and proceeded to Vinayak Jagannath Shankarsheth's house. Arriving, he sent in word that a friend of the late master was waiting. He was welcomed with great honour. Hanging from the wall was a portrait of the

---

[40] The reference is to an epic tale of a father and son on opposing sides of a battle. Mathew Arnold rendered the original story from *Shahnameh* in the form of a tragic epic poem. See https://www.poetryfoundation.org/poems/43604/sohrab-and-rustum (accessed 24 April 2021).

Sheth's. Raiji gazed at the portrait for a few moments, and then broke into sobs.

'Why do you weep?' inquired the host.

'He loved me like a son,' Raiji explained. 'And though his image will lodge eternally in my heart, it will die with me, and no sign of him will survive thereafter in our home. How will my descendants remember him? He had agreed to give me a photograph, but alas the Sheth went to heaven before that could happen.'

'It is no big deal. You can have this portrait.' In this way Raiji obtained the picture, won the wager, and returned triumphant to Surat, twirling his moustache.

Keshav Raiji Saheb was everybody's protector and patron, but heir to only one. He was ever ready to meddle, even jump into, other people's business. If he succeeded and received credit for his work, he twirled his moustache; if he failed, he chewed his disappointment inwardly, always presenting a smiling face to the world.

Once his brother Sampatrai berated him, 'Brother, you are polluted, don't ever enter our kitchen'. Blinded by rage, the older man shouted, '*I* pollute you? Well then, take this!' And picking up a dog standing nearby by its hind legs, he flung it into the kitchen—that unpolluted space. The howling dog escaped; the rest kept the matter secret: what you don't know doesn't hurt.

Women of those days were used to physical work; they were robust, their bodies strong. Since there was no running tap water in the house, they single-handedly fetched water from tanks, cleaned the house, looked after children, cooked. As a result, their bodies were well-exercised. Beauty in the women of the Nagar community had not yet vanished. A collection of Dayaram's lyrical poems reveals his appreciation of Nagar women—they were strong, artistic, and endowed with a natural radiance. The well-known saying, 'You may get blouses made to order, but do you have the waists to wear them?' suggests that Nagar women set the fashion that women of other castes imitated. These women were certainly not soft!

My maternal grandfather with tremendous zest told us stories about the Diwan's household. 'When Mayaram Diwanji died, the ungrateful and wicked Nawab Tedhbakht Khan decided to take possession of his faithful Diwan's house. However, even before her husband Mayaram's corpse left for the burning grounds, his widow secretly drew valuable jewellery from the safe, and with her two sons, Kirparam and Kashiram, escaped to Olpad. The area was under the sway of the Peshwas, so she was able to settle down safely. Bearing the safety of her sons in mind, the lady allowed her home to be looted.'

Another time he told me the following story: 'A servant of the Nawab had eyed a young girl belonging to the Diwan's household. With evil intent, the Nawab told Mayaram, "A caparisoned palanquin will arrive at your house to fetch a certain woman I wish to meet." There was no sign of anxiety in the household when the Nawab Saheb's palanquin arrived. Arsenic had been brought to the house, and this sixteen-year-old celestial beauty dressed to travel to the Nawab's was instead transported sleeping to meet her Lord of Death. The palanquin bearers remained waiting while members of the clan prepared the funeral bier for her departure to the cremation grounds. Honour was thus saved.'

Oh women of Surat, you have slender bodies, heroic spirits, and are capable of great work, and yet, you retain your seductive powers! You stand by your own views in public and discuss caste issues, plying passers-by with verbal shafts: 'Why do you sit, pray? Why do you stand?' Then, as questions pile upon questions, as your arrows gather speed, you most certainly retain glory in our midst. In the course of the wedding ceremony, you women instantly compose rhyming couplets; the *double entendres* in your wedding songs drive their targets up the wall. Indeed, the saying, 'Where four women gather, they quarrel' truly illuminates these occasions.

Among the Nagars every juncture in the life-cycle of a girl child is marked by a special ritual. The child bride, still in short *ghaghras*, is given the ritual bath; when she comes of age, her forehead is decorated with intricate designs; still in her teens, she walks between her house and her in-laws'; when she is with child, like some queen she enjoys being admired. Once she bears children, she loses herself in arranging and rearranging their nuptials; when widowed, she turns her face away from the world and, resigning herself to a bleak future, makes herself unattractive. The couplet says, 'In happy times joys remain; in times of sorrow tears rain'. But just as rain does not long remain upon the hot earth, so too the streaming tears on her cheek soon dry. The children of illusion, fallen into illusion, say:

> Let not joy and sorrow enter the mind; they are within the body incised,
> Sorrow of the sufferer never ends; all is in Lord Ram's custody.

Both joy and sorrow are products of the mind! This age, caught as it were in illusions, was a happy one: 'Where ignorance is bliss, 'tis folly to be wise,' they say. The poet Akho tells us: 'Life is a dark well, but nobody ever drowned without quarrelling.'[41] To repeat the words Father places in Gunasundari's mouth: 'The sin of searching for lasting happiness in this world is at the root of sorrow.'

In those days living was easy, things were inexpensive, salaries meagre, and because earnings could be supplemented in other ways, a person's real economic status remained hidden. Life was straightforward. Wavelets of joy quickened the routine tenor of a woman's everyday life; she managed to enjoy herself in many ways, not flinching even when the shadow of widowhood was closing in. Once in a while, and especially on festive occasions, she dressed up with ornaments to become the focus of admiring eyes. 'We'll learn how to cope as and when misfortunes strikes' was the guiding principle of her life.

Father described the effects of an ascendant Muslim power on the men in Chapter Thirteen of *Karan Ghelo*:

> They lost their vigour; their martial spirits went into decline, and their instruments of warfare rusted, like unused swords. Poor Hindus, like goats and cows, ate grass. Instead of taking up arms they took to words and spent time grumbling: the rustier the sword the sharper the tongue. And instead of fighting back they put up silently and slavishly with tyranny; so the faults of lying, pretence,

---

[41] Akha Rahiyadas Soni (1615–1674), also known as Akho, was a Gujarati spiritual poet with an acerbic tongue. See https://gu.wikisource. org/wiki/ (accessed 5 May 2021).

cheating, pettiness, weakness and laziness took hold. These habits have not been erased even though five hundred years have elapsed since the onset of Muslim rule. (*KG* 13.384)

My father's marriage to Motiram Mehta's son Vidyaram's daughter, Nandgauri, took place in the year 1855. At the time, my revered mother was only nine years old. Father recalled the occasion with overflowing joy: 'I was out inspecting schools in the districts with the Saheb. When I asked leave for the marriage ceremony, Saheb very reluctantly granted me seven days. Since the journey was difficult, a great deal of time was spent travelling. And because our resources were limited, we could afford only a short ceremony, but we managed to perform the rituals custom required.

'Even today, a garden made of paper flowers stands in the way of the horse astride which the bridegroom rides in procession to the ceremony. Just as the procession nears the pavilion where the bride's people await it, the garden is looted. This custom in all probability is borrowed from the Muslims. My horse got startled when the garden was looted and it reared up, and my turban fell to the ground. This was considered an extremely inauspicious beginning. Motiram Mehta was a superstitious man; to remove obstacles to the future success of our married life, he ordered me to appease Lord Ganesh.'

My mother began coming to her married home when she reached the age of ten. She cooked the morning and evening meal, and then returned to her parents'. Grandfather Tuljashankar was very fond of her. After he passed on, and there was no elder to watch over her in our home, a neighbour filled the need, so my mother kept up the practice of cooking meals at our home. Describing my mother's radiant countenance, her grandfather's chest swelled with pride: 'Nandgauri was of medium height. Her complexion was bright, the vitality of youth lent pinkish tones to the skin. She was lean of body, had a noble forehead, a proud, not too wide mouth, and magnetic eyes filled with affection. A liveliness ran through her willowy body, appeared in her every gesture and sparkled like occasional lightning in her eyes.'

From the moment this beauteous lady of good fortune, a veritable Lakshmi, entered our poor home, our star became ascendant—or so our neighbours believed. At the time, there was only one maidservant in our home, so most household chores fell to my mother; she had of necessity to work hard. (Today, she is old, and there are several servants in the house; nevertheless she doesn't sit idle.) 'One who works (*kām*) brings enchantment (*kāman*)'—such beliefs formed her character. Her enthusiasms were limitless; she was an enemy to all that is frivolous and crafty. Freed from the web of joint family relationships, she emerged a gently smiling bud from her father's house. Living unsupervised in the company of her protective and affectionate husband, the bud flowered into a mature and radiant woman. By God's grace, she retains her glow even now as I write this.

Motiram Mehta's family was not different from the general run of Hindu households in that it had little regard for girls. Who knows whom the girl will marry? Will she be happy or unhappy? The only fruit (*phal*) of her existence is for her to get married and leave (*jāy*) her parental home. In this respect, she is a *jāyphal*, the departing fruit. This pun on the word for nutmeg (*jāyphal*) was sometimes exaggerated to suggest that for a girl, a permanent departure from the world could be the best outcome. How could the gods play in the homes of people who think this way?[42] Indeed, only ghouls leap in households such as these.

Nandgauri entered the new environment longing for happiness. Like a tender vine around a mature tree, she wrapped herself around the older man, a humanist, and very soon became absorbed in the householder's life. Family is indeed an amazingly crafted fabric. The man is the warp, the woman the woof. If the weave is to last and the texture to remain smooth, then both threads have to join in an even weave. That is why women in India are called '*ardhangana*' (the other half).

Nandgauri used to say, 'We were poor, but we did not owe a single penny. As his salary grew we spent more freely, without changing our basic style of life. I did not turn an angry face when he extended a helping hand to his sisters. "The brother

---

[42] This harks back to the Sanskrit verse quoted earlier in this chapter: 'the gods delight [in homes] where women are revered' (*Manusmṛti* n.d.: 3.56).

has money, the sister is in need and asks for it, he has given it", were my thoughts. He fulfilled all my heart's desires. I was thrifty and began to save. Even when his salary reached two hundred and fifty rupees, we kept only one servant. We did own an ox-cart, but the man who drove it worked only part-time. He would teach at school in the morning, and I would go to my mother's and return in the evening. My association with him rid me of all fears. I placed my faith in my preferred god, who has done well by me.'

Father was the Assistant Master from 1854 to 1858; in 1858 he became Headmaster of the school he had first joined as a poor student. His salary, as the first Indian head of the English school, was two hundred and fifty rupees.

Since ancient days, the Mother Goddess was installed in our home during the Navaratri festival. For twelve years Father had himself observed the dietary restrictions, eating only fruit during the festival season, but my mother celebrated Navaratri with great pomp. The ceremonies that she first performed in Nandod, and later in Surat, were even more impressive than those described in Chapter One of *Karan Ghelo.*

The Nagars of Surat were greatly drawn to the goddess Amba. Rituals connected with the goddess imbibed Vaishnav elements and were free of blood sacrifice. Father believed that this was due to Jain influence.

The *garba*s composed and performed in Surat have been acclaimed since early times. Nor will you find such discerning and rapt audiences elsewhere. Even the unsophisticated rustic will flock to them, saying, 'A *garba* being performed by the Nagars! We have to see it!' Father probably drew on his childhood memories of the Dussera celebrations in *Karan Ghelo* when he described the celebrations Karan witnessed on his way to the War Council.

The people of Surat wrote *garba*s about noteworthy public events. A pirate once charged with kidnapping a goldsmith's wife, only to be freed by the courts, was rendered into a *garba* thus: 'Say Ram, Ram, say Ram once more/The pirate stole the goldsmith's wife from Navapora.' The women still sing the song, drumming on their mortared floor. Once a merchant killed his servant, and the incident was immediately written into a song: 'Townsmen, just look at Jagubhai's outrageous act/The son of Motiram he brutally hacked!' Travadiji has occasioned numerous such *ragas* and *raginis*.

The inhabitants of Surat are discerning, full of humour and witty. Even today they are that way, in joy as well as in sorrow.

My maternal grandfather was in the habit of repeating a saying: 'If you've been made to sit on a donkey, why get off outside city limits?' I once asked Father what the origin of this saying was. He said that in the old days, in fact, in his childhood, if you swore a false oath or broke a contract, you were sent to jail; but over and above the jail sentence, or sometimes instead of it, you were seated on a donkey and paraded around town to the sound of beaten drums. After which you were deposited outside city limits. During the Nawab's regime, one side of your head and half your moustache were shaved clean. Once, an incorrigible and obstinate convict was punished in this manner and set down on the outskirts of the city. He is supposed to have requested the man who drove the donkey, 'Brother, I have endured the punishment; now don't send me home on foot'. 'Aren't you ashamed?' asked the driver. The convict's response became the popular saying: 'If you've got a ride on a donkey, might as well get dropped at home'. So this merry fellow went home riding the very same donkey. In other words, if you do anything, do it to its very end, what's there to be ashamed of? If you have to abandon shame, do so completely.

Father made fun of the way justice was dispensed during this period. 'The magistrate's position was hereditary, so he became the butt of many jokes. Once a bullock belonging to an oil-presser fought with a bullock belonging to a Muslim and broke the latter's horn. A complaint was lodged with the magistrate. The magistrate turned the pages of the commentaries on law and uttered the following couplet:

> *Lāl kitāb me likhā yun* |
> *teli (ghānci) laḍāve kyun?* ||

> In their red book they duly write,
> Why did the oil-presser make the bullocks fight?

An exchange of bullocks was the final punishment imposed on the oil-presser.

Diwali festivals were gala affairs in those days. The following passage is from *Karan Ghelo*:

> The beautiful women of Patan with powders of many hues created intricate floor patterns either by hand or with stencils. Women competed with each other, asking passers-by which of the designs was best. With delight they adorned themselves with fine saris and jewellery, and were anxious to be admired; from time to time it would seem as if their joy broke out in spontaneous song. (*KG* 2.22–23)

If you substitute the word Surat for Patan, a picture of Diwali celebrated in the city of Surat flashes before your eyes.

Chapter II

MIDDAY
The Teacher

The life of a society in some sense mirrors individual lives. For, in every man's life there comes an occasion when the ocean in his being storms forth, its life-giving waters spill over, and foam-crested waves break against the shore; so it is with societies. The German poets call this time of life *Sturm und Drang*.

The stream of German poetry seemed to run thin during the reign of Friedrich the Great. Very occasionally, the rising tide of French poetry did flow into Germany's minor tributaries. True to the Sanskrit adage '*supūrā syāt kunadikā*: shallow rivulets may easily flood',[43] these rivulets soon overflowed, but no foam billowed; one noticed fresh winds driving the currents, but the waters remained sluggish. French influence changed sartorial styles, affected the German language, daily life was fashioned after French ways, and the culture of France, such as it was, became enthroned at the centre of Germany's intellectual life.

The picture changes, however, when we look at the poetry of Lessing (1729–1781), Schiller (1759–1805), Klopstock (1724–1803) and Goethe (1749–1832). With them, a strong universal current enters the stream of German culture; gigantic waves rise with such force that the culture's narrowed banks are unable to contain them. As 'great aspirations have a precipitous fall: *manorathānām-ataṭa-prapātah*',[44] earth falls into the river's surging

---

[43] The Sanskrit adage is from Vishnu Sharma's *Panchatantra* (see Mishra 1910: 1.26).

[44] The Sanskrit adage is from *Abhijnāna Śākuntalam of Kālidāsa* (see Kale 1969: 6.10).

waters and in several places the water turns muddy. Can a person who falls into such flooding rivers ever emerge unmuddied? Indeed, should a man step down even to dip his toes, and then, happen to get caught in the rushing turbulent waters, it is certain that he would not get out without getting muddied. The Sanskrit adage expresses the creative turmoil of a changing age.

A similar sea change occurred when British rule was established; in its wake came English education, with its myriad cultural streams. The influence entered Madras, Bengal, Maharashtra, and Gujarat somewhat early. Though a proper comparison between two such vastly different civilisations as Britain and India may be difficult to explicate logically, the contrast between them is, however, sharply stamped on the mind.

In a well-known myth, the gods and the anti-gods competed with each other to churn the cosmic ocean. On the one side were the anti-gods, meaning all the old, inert forces of tradition; on the other were the gods, meaning the new energy, subtlety and light of modernity. The two forces stood facing each other, churning the ocean that was Gujarat. Foaming butter occasionally swam to the top; sometimes even a rich jewel surfaced from the deep. Since the ocean kept being churned over a considerable period, sooner or later it coursed through the life-stream of those who stood in its midst. The churning continued throughout their lives for longer or shorter periods.

Narmadashankar (1833–1886), Navalram (1836–1888), and Father (1835–1905) experienced the churning as it rose and, sooner or later, as it subsided. In order to paint a clear portrait of the age, and to furnish my picture with the figures whose thought and actions left a mark on it, I shall narrate the stories that I heard directly from Father about these men.

Narmad was Gujarat's Byron, her swashbuckling warrior-hero equipped with armour and shield. He had seen it all—victimised widows, prejudice against darker races, flattery of the upwardly-mobile wealthy, arrogance of family status, and the unbearable tyranny of custom. With a Voltaire's (1694–1778) biting pen and the enthusiastic spear of Cervantes' (1547–1616) hero Don Quixote, he waged war against all. Like Byron's Childe Harold, Narmad displayed his pride in human nature, and his contempt for modern man's fallen status, in language that was by turns lyrical, bitter and acerbic. Flashes of Byron's Don Juan also appear here and there in his poetry.

Like a magnet, Narmad drew people to his views: 'Set up associations wherever possible. Give lectures. Enthuse the population! Reform society!' With eyes inebriated by ardour, he would proceed to enforce his views. His eyes did not exactly hold out an invitation; rather, they matched his words: 'Come out of your dark holes, you skulking wretches! Quit your choked wells. Soar into the skies! Get a life, you frigid lifeless statues! Speak, you who have taken vows of silence!' And so his passionate message spread like contagion, and people began to emerge from their holes. When pompous traditionalists and those against progress of any sort scoffed, saying, 'It's all very well that you come out of your holes into the open, but let a kitty cat cross your path and you will be destroyed', prompt came Narmad's reply, 'We intend to bell that kitty cat', which cut his critics short.

Frogs left their forefathers' homes—actually, they were mere puddles—and migrating towards lakes and streams, began to croak there. Selfishness shrank; magnanimity swelled. The character of Euphorion from Goethe's *Faust* suddenly stared us in the face. Narmad is Goethe's Euphorion, and so is Byron—Euphorion, the child born of the marriage between the gentle, civilised Greek, Helen and the ardent, handsome German, Faust. Euphorion never touches the earth; from the moment he is born he leaps and springs into the air. He soars high and he sings and sings, only sings.

True, there were some who soared high with Narmad. There were others who flew, but unable to keep up, resorted to short cuts, drank alcohol, and smoked hemp. Still others rose only to fall. The rest walked dragging their feet, imagining that they flew. Nonetheless, the self-worth of each individual grew, and with it an element of transcendence entered the minds of men.

On the banks of the Narmada, in Chanod, Dayaram Jivatri (1777–1852)[45] had created a tide of lyricism. So also, Narmad

---

[45] Dayaram Jivatri was one of the great lyrical Bhakti poets of Gujarat.

flooded Gujarat with poetry; the only difference between the two was that Narmad substituted social reform for Dayaram's leitmotif of erotic love. Narmad set up associations in several places to break the vow of silence that had taken hold of society. Father recalled that Narmad was never disappointed with the size of his audience; instead, he read and reread his essays and asked his audiences to debate social issues.

The following paragraph from Narmad's 1851 essay, 'The Advantage of Joining Associations', remains relevant to this day:

> Should four or five people get together, prattle, jabber or rant against government policy, the gathering cannot be termed an Association, even if the groups contain a few learned men. But even if four people were to get together, ponder over and discuss in a civil manner issues relating to wisdom, knowledge or some kind of gain, it could truly be said that an Association had met. The decline of India is primarily due to the fact that, 'our country has lost the practice of men familiar with political thought getting together with the educated public to discuss social issues.'

Narmad's essay 'On Unity' was written with a view to breaking down caste identities in order to forge a larger national unity. This stormy period of his life was marked by Narmad-Quixote, the iconoclast charging into the battleground to engage with idol worshippers and to joust with all four of Francis Bacon's 'Idols of the Mind'.[46] Thereafter, he neither noticed nor cared whether those confronting him were herds of sheep or mere windmills; in his determined imagination, the least object took on the adversarial form of the anti-gods he was out to battle.

We complete our description of Narmad here.

Narmad was true-hearted and remained faithful to his impulses—it was imperative for him that he practise the views he favoured. When a destitute widow faced difficulties, he invited her to his home, assuring her that she would fit into it with ease. He did not give a hoot about his reputation, acted in complete

---

[46] The reference is to 'Idols of the Tribe, Idols of the Cave, Idols of the Marketplace, and Idols of the Theater' (see Hall n.d.), from *Novum Organum* by Francis Bacon (1561–1626).

disregard of caste opinion, did not care whether his reputation rose or fell—even the thought did not enter his generous mind. The sanctimonious may say what they like about Narmad's relations with the widow Savitagauri. I myself maintain that what is said about his earlier actions is true; afterwards what was to happen happened, but he very definitely chose the best way to lift Savitagauri out of the tyranny of tradition and its anti-gods.[47]

There was a fair bit of bravado in Narmad's personality; it made him take upon himself sins for which he was not responsible. 'Go away! What are you anyway? Do what you want. Unlike you, I'm not a secret sinner', he would say. I am certain that not even a fraction of the ugly rumours spread about him is true.

Narmad, however, lacked a sense of humour; as a consequence, he exaggerated whatever he did and said. His writing occasionally lacked taste; it could even be considered coarse. But that was the fault of the times. With the historical sense missing, people believed that everything to do with the past was worthless, that everything from the West stood for progress, and that progressive measures must be implemented right away, not gradually over time. It was as if someone were to lay down a law that every Gujarati must dress in clothes of the same size, no matter that some are emaciated and others large.

The attitude Narmad expresses in his famous poem 'Plunge headlong into battle, victory lies ahead' is typical of the period. Unfortunately, his end was filled with grief.

What Macaulay wrote in his essay on Johnson regarding the period following Pope's death to Wordsworth's first work—that the period lacked great patrons who might have nurtured literary talent—also holds true of the Gujarat of this time.[48] Though

---

[47] See Narmad's autobiography *Marī Hakīkat* (Narmadashankar 1994); and Yagnik and Sheth (2005: 80).

[48] From *Macaulay's Life of Samuel Johnson*: 'Thus, at the time when Johnson commenced his literary career, a writer had little to hope from the patronage of powerful individuals. The patronage of the public did not yet furnish the means of comfortable subsistence. The prices paid by booksellers to authors were so low that a man of considerable talents and unremitting industry could do little more than provide for the day

Narmad lived in a stately home like Saraswati Mandir, his earnings came solely from his writing; hence his life was not less difficult than that of a half-starved, ill-dressed poet living in an attic on Grub Street. Just as the Germans, on seeing their motherland fall into the Austrian trap after having achieved independence in 1913, imagined a past when she was a bird in free flight, Narmad, too, fell prey to a similar mood. He grew despondent when he did not see immediate change, not realising that social change does not emerge within a single life span. Still, his rousing battle cry continues to ring in my ears:

> Let us march forth to victory, the bugle sounds, the bugle sounds.
> Let us plunge to battle, for further triumphs lie ahead.

At the present time in India, reform of the social order is an absolute necessity—only when reform is implemented will individual conduct improve. As of now, no individual is able to act against the dictates of society and, if he does, he is perforce distanced from it. Individual change depends on changes in social attitudes. Reform of society is therefore essential.

Narmad's was a colossal contribution. With the courage of love as his flag and the pen as his sword, he set out to battle. Within the wilderness of the world, our society was like a mature tree whose sap was being squeezed by the thorny undergrowth surrounding it. Narmad, to an extent, cut away this undergrowth. Unfortunately, in his later years, he launched a full-scale attack against the very tree that he had freed from the strangulating grip of tradition: 'Go back to your roots,' he declared. 'Unless you become as a seed, you won't ever experience the stately canopy of maturity.'[49]

---

which was passing over him. ...The season of rich harvests was over, and the period of famine had begun. All that is squalid and miserable might now be summed up in the word Poet' (Macaulay 1903).

[49] 'He [Narmad] denounced reformists and reform as well as the "European" world view for the last ten years of his life and became an ardent believer of Vedic religion. This U-turn left a deep mark on the intellectual life of Gujarat in the last quarter of the nineteenth century' (Yagnik and Sheth 2005: 81).

Ill luck struck down Narmad himself—a stately *saro* tree that stood tall, adorning the landscape. Misfortune brought about his downfall. Every inhabitant of Gujarat grieves to see the proud poet's head bowed low.

Had Narmad been endowed with a constructive temper, he might not have sunk into nihilism. In truth, men are instruments of a mysterious power that requires some to dig and others to fill. Like a multi-purpose spade, each individual has a rightful place. Indeed, which of our five fingers is without use?

Goethe describes Byron as the embodiment of the restless warrior spirit. When Byron adopts the thinker's constructive voice, he is a child, so Goethe maintained: *sobald er denkt, ist er ein kind.* Goethe's opinion of Byron applies exactly to Narmad. The productive work Narmad undertook during the latter part of his life added nought to the wisdom of the country; it did not result in any tangible good; in fact, it brought harm.

Father was a close associate of Durgaram Manchharam Mehta (1808–78),[50] the excellent schoolmaster at the Gujarati School in Surat. He was an iconoclast of all superstitious beliefs, in many ways a preceptor very much like Dayanand Saraswati, only that he lacked Dayanand's extraordinary constructive ability. In an age where there were hardly any men willing to share another's pain, Durgaram Mehtaji and Bhau Daji (1822–74)[51] were exceptions. Bhau Daji, who stood surety for a tailor in court and brought low a proud magistrate, is glorified even today in verse. Selflessness, empathy for the suffering, virtues hardly ever seen in our own age except among the Buddhists, were re-introduced into the country through English education.

-----

[50] Durgaram Mehta founded the Manav Dharma Sabha, an early society for religious and social reform, in 1844. See: https://ia801608. us.archive.org/32/items/in.ernet.dli.2015.537961/2015.537961.Durga-Ram.pdf (accessed 5 May 2021).

[51] Bhau Daji was one of the most public-spirited figures of nineteenth-century India. A distinguished Sanskritist, numismatist, and physician, he researched ancient medical texts in search of a cure for leprosy (see Mukhopadhyay 2018).

'How can goodness prevail over power?' we would hear this axiom repeated by weary old men. But not Durgaram Mehtaji, who would sit in the market place and town square, and if he saw a policeman lay forcible claim to a poor woman's merchandise, would intervene and march the offender straight to court. No policeman dared harass the poor in his presence. Should an orphan fall at his feet pleading for succour, Mehtaji would sacrifice all the means at his command to come to his aid. It was not out of self-regard or for the sake of his reputation that he acted so generously, for he was often reviled, and when in need himself, was unable to raise funds.

'Truth needs no defence' was a constant refrain of Mehtaji's. His friend Manekram Umiyaram once challenged him on this. Manekram, or Makubhai as he was known, was the chief pleader in the district court at the time. He said, 'Mehtaji, suppose I were to falsify your proposition that truth needs no defence, what then?' 'Try,' replied Mehtaji, and Makubhai took on the wager. Father recounts: 'In those days administrators of the East India Company secured their positions through patronage—no matter how incompetent they were. Before being posted to India, they were trained at Haileybury College in England.[52] The judge in the district court at the time happened to be an alcoholic; Makubhai worked while the judge doodled. One day Durgaram Mehtaji, wearing a green turban, was arguing the case on behalf of a rather unfortunate man. The judge was seated with his face to the wall and his back to the assembled audience. Makubhai slyly gestured to the judge, as if to say that this particular case lacked merit, and that, "You will reach a quick decision if you squeeze that fellow in the green turban." Thereupon the white man turned around to look at Mehtaji, who, with full faith in the

____

[52] From 1806 to 1857, Haileybury College trained young men nominated by the directors of East India Company to administer their territories in India; see 'The East India College', https://web.archive. org/web/20161222023519/https://www.haileybury.com/explore/ haileybury/heritage-archives/story-haileybury/east-india-college (accessed 25 May 2021).

English judicial system, was fearlessly arguing the case, and said, "You are hereby fined a hundred rupees!" "On what grounds, Saheb?" Mehtaji growled, bewildered. "A two-hundred rupee fine, then!" Before Mehtaji could respond, the judge saheb declared a four-hundred rupee fine.

'Mehtaji's salary was thirty rupees per month. To take on *pro bono* cases, even fight at the cost of one's own pocket and, instead of earning accolades, to have insults hurled at you! His eyes downcast, an infuriated Mehtaji turned pale. As the judge spun around to face the wall once more, Makubhai motioned to Mehtaji to come and sit next to him, and in an effort to calm him down whispered, "The final signature on the order has to be mine. Naught will come of this. You have nothing to fear. I was merely trying to break your obstinate belief that truth needs no protection." Not endowed to any great extent with the gift of humour, Mehtaji was furious; but in Makubhai there dwelt a gentleness of unlimited good humour, which enabled him eventually to pacify a fury that was like Lord Shiva's. That evening when our circle of friends met, Makubhai said, "I was afraid lest he open his third eye and reduce me to ashes, he looked so enraged!" Mehtaji laughed, and all of us soon forgot the incident.'

Father and Mehtaji would travel from market place to city square, discrediting the hocus-pocus of sorcerers, ascetics and Tantric practitioners of magic. 'Experiment on us,' they provocatively challenged the crowd. In the previous section, I have shown how superstitious the people in Surat had become, and how necessary it was to break this superstitious frame of mind.

Sculpting your enemy's likeness from a paste of *aḍad* dal and slashing it in order to finish off the intended enemy is a vivid example of a kind of sorcery that has been practised worldwide since time immemorial. There are plenty of mantras in the *Atharvaveda* meant to serve similar purposes. In Europe, Catherine de Medici (1519–1589), the dowager queen of France, was particularly keen on these magical rituals. She had Regnier, a grocer and resident of Florence, make wax models of her rivals, and experimented on these figurines with the help of spells. The belief was that these experiments on inanimate objects would affect the living person.[53]

With drum beaters announcing the event, Mehtaji and Father publicly sent word inviting well-known sorcerers to step up and do their worst. 'Don't be afraid', they promised, 'We won't seek alternate cures if your experiments are successful.' These demonstrations proved effective in influencing the more ignorant classes as well as those who were, in future, to seek services at princely courts. The latter were not really superstitious; however, their original scepticism was reinforced when with their own eyes they saw the magicians fail. There were a few Tantriks who accepted Mehtaji's dare, though none proved his case.

Father's vivid portrayal of attempts to exorcise the ghost lodged in Phoolarani in *Karan Ghelo* reflects his own times. 'Harpal, disguised as a Tantrik from Lucknow, announces his arrival: "I am expert at the black arts; I cast magical spells that kill, hypnotise, control, harass, render unconscious and seduce" (*KG* 7.189).' The author of *Karan Ghelo* wanted to prove that there was no such thing as fate; indeed, he believed that men suffer the consequences of their actions. He wanted to build public opinion around a principle that prods individuals to act rather than passively accept the trials that life thrusts on them.

In the manner of a Catholic padre, Durgaram Mehtaji stood in Havadia Square, declaiming in favour of widow remarriage. Referring to Mehtaji's widowed aunt, his wicked enemies would ask, 'Why haven't you arranged to get *her* married?' Mehtaji, not remotely angered by the question, responded coolly, 'I would not stand in her way if she were inclined to remarry'. Father took part in these public discussions; until the very end, he determinedly held to the view that no one had the right to keep widows locked up in the house to prevent them from marrying, if the widow wished to do so.

His friend Shri Dolatrai once asked Father, 'Master (that was how Father was addressed those days), having once given away your daughter, how can you give her away a second time?' 'If that

---

[53] See 'Catherine de Medici: Queen Mother of France' (Hughes 2010).

is the only difficulty standing in her way, let her give herself away!'
was Father's instant reply. The *Manusmṛti* says that if parents do
not arrange a marriage for their daughter, the maiden who is keen
to marry has the right to do so on her own.[54] A person's life ought
to flow like a stream, unrestrained: whatever a person considers
right, whatever accords with her own wishes, she is entitled to do,
so long as it does not harm another. Father believed that societies
in future would pass laws to enable individuals to live their lives
unfettered; in fulfilling his individual self-interest a person would
also fulfil the interests of the societal whole.

Durgaram Mehtaji preached tirelessly against idolatry. Vaishnav
sects at the time were so deeply grounded in this devotional form
that his efforts proved in vain. On the matter of image worship,
Father's views were very clear. He did not himself worship images,
but he did not believe in preventing others from doing so. He
did not even perform the *sandhya* ritual. My revered mother,
however, continues to celebrate the Navaratri festival, which has
been celebrated with pomp and pageantry in our home from the
time of our forefathers. Father himself had no faith in the 'Mother
Goddess made of pots', but he did not interfere in others' beliefs.[55]

In this matter, Father's opinion on idol worship differed
from Mahipatrambhai's; he held that Mahipatram's views on
this subject were similar to those of the Puritans. To put an end
to idol-worship, the Puritans of seventeenth-century England
ferreted out statues from every nook and corner of England's
churches, they tore down paintings, statuary, and stained-glass
windows. Similarly, Mahitpatrambhai used to hold aloft a statue
of the child Krishna and declaim, 'Watch! Your god is powerless.
He cannot harm me'. Dayanand Saraswati took an equally harsh
stand against the worship of idols.

---

[54] *trīṇi varshany udīkṣeta kumāry ṛtumaty api satī* |
ūrdhvam tu kālād etasmād vindeta sadṛśam patim || (*Manusmṛti* 9.90).
See: https://archive.org/details/ManuSmriti_201601/page/n193
(accessed 4 May 2021).

[55] The goddess is represented in the aniconic form of a pot. In the
Navaratri festival in Gujarat, she is represented in the form of a pot
containing newly sprouted grain (Jayakar 1980: 20).

Father on the other hand maintained that image worship did no harm so long as improprieties did not accompany the ritual. It is true that the worship of idols is a lower form of religiosity, but there isn't anything intrinsically wrong with the practice. More pragmatically, he maintained that by waging war against it, the rest of the social reformers' agenda becomes unacceptable to the general public. A certain class of people will always worship images; to fixate on the resulting harm is futile. The 'utility of error'[56] ought always to be kept in mind by social reformers: when you snatch away someone's doll, you have to think about what will replace it.

Durgaram Mehtaji earnestly endeavoured to heal fissures within his own caste and to do away with conflict across castes. On these issues, he and Father were in complete sympathy. He, in fact, believed that it was imperative to mend rifts with the Vaidik brahmins. Mehtaji himself wore his turban in the Nagar style. He told Father that should he have a son and Father a daughter, a marriage should be arranged between them. My parents were agreeable to this, and had there not been such a small age gap between my elder sister Harsiddhagauri and Mehtaji's elder son Ratilal, no one knows how things might have been. When Shobharam Mehta married his daughter to Somnarayan, Father took a leading role in the debate that followed and clearly indicated his strong support for caste unity. It was probably inevitable that their granddaughter should later marry a Nagar brahmin.

Durgaram Mehtaji remained the head teacher of the Gujarati School in Surat for a considerable period. Several young men passed out of school under his tutelage. All of them bore the stamp of his responsible, enthusiastic, ethical and reformist attitudes. He honed his students into skilled readers and writers and, beyond that, taught them to let knowledge govern their conduct. He also taught them arithmetic and inculcated habits of clear and meticulous thinking.

On returning from Kathiawad, Durgaram Mehtaji renounced the world. In a letter which began with the words, 'An old

---

[56] The phrase 'utility of error' is in English in the original text.

friend in new attire', Makubhai wrote to Father about Mehtaji's renunciation: 'I have assured Mehtaji Saheb that should his sons fail to perform his funerary rituals, we will do so ourselves. But Mehtaji himself is so anxious to achieve nirvana, a release from future births, that he has refused my offer'. Reading the letter tore Father's heart.

We have already mentioned Mahipatram, who held the front rank among those who opposed image worship. His greatest desire was to abolish idol worship, which at the time was the anchor of people's lives, firmly held in the captain's hand.[57] Mahipatram wanted to seize the anchor from the captain and replace it with a religious movement properly suited to the future needs of all the castes of Gujarat. So, he decked out the Brahmo Samaj, a religious reform movement from Bengal, named it Prarthana Samaj, and brought all his hard work and care to establishing the order in Gujarat.

Mahipatram was extremely assertive in this regard; his opponents called him obdurate. Smug traditionalists, angered by his reformist zeal, said all kinds of things about him. None of this talk affected Rao Saheb in the least. Having put aside superstition, he bid lyricism goodbye and viewed the world through the lens of his rationalist glasses; he acted in accordance with what he saw himself, what he recognised and had grown to admire. 'Who takes teachers by hand holds society in his palms'—quoting this maxim of Napoleon's, Father would say, 'The efforts made by Rao Saheb Mahipatram and Navalrambhai to educate an entire generation of teachers greatly benefited society. Indeed, Gujarat owes them a deep debt of gratitude'.

Travels through Europe had a positive influence on Mahipatram. Because the love of his own land was strong in him, he urged that only those European thoughts and modes of action well-suited

---

[57] The word 'captain' here possibly refers to the *goswamis* or priests of the Vallabhacharya Vaishnava sect, who were accused of 'corrupt, degraded, and licentious practices' by the journalist Karsandas Mulji in his weekly *Satya Prakash*. Subsequently, a case of libel was filed against him in the Bombay High Court, which he won (see Ranganathan 2008). In 1877, Mahipatram Rupram wrote a biography of Karsandas Mulji (see Yagnik and Sheth 2005: 76–79; also Rawal 2002).

to the Indian ethos be adopted. This is not merely empty praise for Rao Saheb's resolute character. In fact, had not the 'ballast'[58] of his mind been strong, had not Keshab Chandra Sen sounded his clarion call, drawing him to the Brahmo Samaj and its reforms, Mahipatram might well have leaned towards atheism of the Charvaka school.[59]

Navalram's outlook was of an altogether different sort. He was an effective reformer, but like the ripples on a lake, his mind constantly sparkled with new ideas. The purity of his character most certainly exemplified the axiom: 'a dye properly takes hold only on unblemished cloth'. His mind was endowed with sharp critical powers. Like a bee, he sucked whatever had an aesthetic flavour, and managed to convey a honeyed taste. Nor did he abandon compassion during his critical examination of someone else's work. Navalram set about his task like a surgeon who, during surgery, wields his scalpel with attention to the lungs, pulse and blood of his patient. Grasping the superior aspects of a text and criticising its shortcomings, taking care to express his judgement with grace, his was an extraordinary god-given talent.

Every critic sees through tinted lenses. Navalram's lens caught the virtues of the age: the beautiful benefits of sound education, the insights and transformative powers of rational thought, the efforts to forge human unity, and finally, the daring, intoxicated leaps of adventure. He was able to record all that he saw in youthful language.

Naval's style was indeed novel. He possessed the empathy so characteristic of Suratis; he wielded words like a delicate scalpel, not like a cruel axe. His writing sparkled with sharpness, shine and precision; of hardened vulgarity there wasn't a trace. Until the very end, Navalram remained a severe but compassionate critic. In their attitudes, he and Father were alike, except for the fact that Father did not keep an account of his thoughts in the form of a diary.

A daily newspaper called *Gujaratmitra* was an effective instrument for promoting ideas of pertinent reform. The late

---

[58] The word 'ballast' is in English in the original text.

[59] The Charvaka was an early philosophical school of Indian materialists.

Dinshawji Ardeshir Talyarkhan was the editor.[60] Both Navalram and Father wrote largely for this publication. But my father was not egotistical; indeed, so averse was he to any form of self-display that he tended not to disclose his contributions, nor did he keep a list of his publications.

The lens through which Navalram viewed the world had no need for telescopic sight—from the very beginning he entertained doubts as to whether the intoxicated passion for reform would last. Father consistently advised me to read Navalram's commentary on reform, and the writings of T. H. Huxley (1825–1895),[61] should I want to become a discerning critic. Navalram reviewed *Karan Ghelo* for *Gujaratmitra*; and when Navalram's play *Veeramati* was published, Father wrote a favourable review for the same periodical, pointing out just one of its shortcomings—that the religious debate featured in the play is better suited to novels than to drama; on stage, debates of this nature grow tedious. Navalram's work, throughout, reveals a vision that is coloured by contemporary events, as though he gleaned history from the ballads (*rāsaḍā*) of the period.

Father confessed that he preferred the play *Veeramati* to *Vanraj Chavda*, because Naval drew portraits of the characters of the period with more clarity and aesthetic delight in *Veeramati* than in *Vanraj Chavda*. 'When waves of poetry swelled in Naval's imagination, where was the wise prompter who could tell him, "Naval, you're making a mistake! Write novels, not plays!"' Drama leaves a more vivid impression on the audience, and that is why both Narmadashankar and Navalram went against their natural inclination and wrote plays.

The portraits sketched above recreate before our eyes the two decades between 1850 and 1870, when, according to Father, 'Rationalist philosophy was our mantra, our "Open Sesame". In the story "Alibaba and the Forty Thieves" from the *Arabian Nights*, Kasam forgets the mantra and instead calls out "Open Faith",

---

[60] *Gujaratmitra* published a column dedicated to literature called 'Akshar ni Aradhna' (see Datta 1988: 1875).

[61] Thomas Henry Huxley was a biologist, and an avid supporter of Charles Darwin.

"Open Love", "Open God". Kasam forgets the mantra whose true meaning is "Open Intelligence", and so he perishes.

'"Unite, brothers unite!" "Lift up the lowest rung of the caste ladder until it reaches the very top, so that the distance between high and low collapses, caste hierarchies disappear and society is united!" "Lift, brothers lift!"—such was our constant and principled philosophy. "Dare to act!" is what we taught.

> Destruction awaits men who are adventurous,
> Learn from the examples I give, so sings the poet Samaldas.

'We did not approve of the poet Samaldas' cautious way of thinking. Instead, "Leap! Rouse yourselves!" became our first principle. We were inspired by the very same spirit of adventure that in the sixteenth century led Francis Drake and Hawkins, in search of a passage to India, to sail west instead of east. This enterprising spirit inspired—indeed, thrust—us to think about the governance of our country.'

Even as a teacher, Father's methods were to draw out and cultivate the inner strength of each student so that he flowers. He would say: 'Don't pack your student's minds with useless information. The storeroom of the brain will spring leaks, or overflow if you do so; in either case, what you teach will remain unabsorbed'. He firmly believed this, and refused to allow his own students to learn exclusively by rote. 'Read extensively; grasp the substance of what you read; go beyond mere words to attend to the emotional tone; cultivate a habit of consulting dictionaries; translate English in simple and expressive language,' Father instructed his students.

'Devote extra space for arithmetic in the timetable, and if you pair arithmetical principles with diagrams from a young age, your mental capacities will grow stronger and more stable. Moreover, even your conduct will acquire a certain steadiness due to extended acquaintance with these principles. I did not allow the mistaken view that history and mathematics stand in opposition, or that those who are accomplished at one subject are incapable of handling the other to take root.' Knowledge of mathematics is the body's form; history is the animating universal spirit. Civilisation is born only when the two become united—this was one of Father's first principles.

My mother reports that he left for school after finishing his morning meal at half past nine. Before that, at the break of dawn, he devotedly attended to the needs of the many students who arrived at his doorstep. In this way, impoverished students, those without means, became educated and he, in turn, received their deeply felt blessings. Shri Tapiprasad Desai's sons, Shri Veerprasad and Manidharprasad, were among those who came in the morning. Even though he stood squarely against the current reform movement, Tapiprasad had no qualms about his sons interacting with Father. This was because he had faith in Father; according to him, Father was 'a jewel in the rubbish heap of reform. Does a jewel lose value even if it falls into a dung heap?' Tapiprasad Desai was Mukundrai's maternal uncle, and was known even among friends as Tapimama.

I will now turn to the new faith that inspired this age. The myth of the gods and the anti-gods churning the great ocean to bring forth fourteen treasures is well known. One must not immediately assume that these gems are wholly beneficial; they either do good or prove harmful, depending on the uses to which they are put. Occasionally, Father explored this myth in a humorous vein in the context of his time. Dhanvantari, the physician of the gods; Lakshmi, the goddess of good fortune; the conch; Rambha, a celestial damsel; the *parijat* tree; Airavat, Indra's white elephant; Kamadhenu, the cow which fulfils all your desires; *amrit* or nectar; *sura* or wine; *Kaustubh*, the jewel close to Vishnu's heart; the seven-headed horse; and the celestial damsel Urvashi were the treasures to emerge from the churning.

Dhanvantari, the physician of the gods, has to be identified with the new science of medicine. To abandon the modern and seek shelter in the traditional would most certainly bring you to Death's door!

When Lakshmi, the goddess of good fortune, knocks on your door, calling, '*Ko jāgarti, ko jāgati*: Who awakens? Who is awake?'

and then intends to place a *tilak* on your forehead, you don't say, 'Wait until I wash my face and return'. Lakshmi weds the man who labours, who is alert and all attention, not one who is half asleep.

Narmad blew the new conch very hard to teach his people: 'Learn brothers, learn. Move forward. Be adventurous'. And yet, the very same conch, in due course, became the instrument announcing death on the battlefield.

Rambha is the celestial damsel, the untouched image of the beauty of creation. Who hasn't tried to win her?

The Moon inspires the tide of aesthetic joy overflowing in men's hearts.

The *parijat* tree is a model of the ideal man: it showers with scented flowers even those who shake it violently. Without asking, it bestows its all to even those who leave it alone.

Airavat, Indra's white elephant, symbolises wealth. Who hasn't sought additional wealth to rebuild Indra's paradise on earth?

The philosophy of the European Enlightenment is Kamadhenu, the cow which fulfils all your desires. But you do not know what to ask of her, are disgusted with what you receive, and so push her away. '*Kim tayā krīyate dhenvā yā na sūte na dugdhadā*: What use is a cow that neither calves nor gives milk?'[62] This is what Narmad claimed afterwards. In Navalram's words, Narmad committed himself to the doctrine that truth is beyond human understanding.

Amrit or nectar is universal knowledge. Drink of it. Share it with others. Don't keep it locked up to seek liberation for yourself alone.

Sura is not used metaphorically; it is alcohol or 'red water'. The poet Akha has said: 'Men are apes, and on top of that they drink, and so Akho fears all their ilk'.[63] In this adventurous age, monkey-mindedness took hold, the mischievous age became associated with alcohol and then, because certain ruin lay ahead, there was damage to the reformer's cause. Men without restraint insisted on 'red water'; they could do without everything, but

---

[62] From the *Panchatantra* 0.5 (Mishra 1910); see: https://archive.org/details/PanchatantraSanskritHindi-JpMishra1910/page/n17 (accessed 5 May 2021).

[63] Akha Soni (1615–1674); see p. 64, note 41.

not liquor. The unregulated life, a truly irrational way to live, is poison. The truth is that anything can become nectar or poison, depending on whether it is used in a measured way or not. Where there is nectar there has to be poison: what has no balance is poison.

Kaustubh is the jewel close to Vishnu's heart; the jewel reflects the state of the world as it is. This means that the social reformer should restrict himself to uplifting society, not creating a new social order or destroying the existing one. His duty is to usher change that accords with the temper of contemporary times, and also to ensure that reform does not lapse, but remains constant.

The seven-headed horse stands for the power of the poetic imagination. '*Bhargo devasya dhīmahi*: We meditate on the sun god's radiance'[64]—these words from the Vedic hymn addressed to the sun god, who rides across the sky in a chariot drawn by the seven-headed horse, are true. The word *bharga* in the mantra is apt in that it suggests poetic brilliance as well as the intoxication of youth, 'the twenty-five donkey years' (*gadhdhapachisi*).

There is a story in the *Arabian Nights* about a dervish who flies into the sky seated on a bronze horse. He becomes agitated as the horse continues to rise higher and higher in the air. He has forgotten the right mantra and is unable to restrain the horse. The horse lashes him with his tail, blinds him in one eye and tosses him to the ground; similarly, to rein in one's creative powers is not easy. In this world a man must engage in some kind of livelihood in order to fill his stomach; he cannot and will never survive on his poetic powers alone. If his creative capacities are real, he cannot but fly high; but without the means to control it, he will lack the ability to rein in his horse.

Human nature has two sides, the celestial and the earthly; one sees this duality everywhere. Father put it this way: 'Ariel walks hand in hand with Caliban. In an age when the individual self is being churned, poison is infused with nectar in our temperament. To destroy darkness and spread light is the work of the gods'. The period between sixteen and twenty-five years of age in a

---

[64] From the *Gāyatrī Mantra* of the *Ṛgveda Mandala* 3.62.10 ; see: http://www.sacred-texts.com/hin/rvsan/index.htm (accessed 5 May 2021).

man's life is referred to by several names. Kabir Saheb speaks of the period as 'the cunning delusions of the twenty-five-year old'. These years are usually referred to as 'the twenty-five donkey years' (*gadhdhapachisi*). German poets honour the period and call it a vain search for the passion fruit (the black lotus), while others describe it as a period of *Sturm und Drang*. The world-famous German writer Goethe has drawn a beautiful and accurate portrait of his earlier youthful passions. One could even describe the period as stormy, resentful and full of fancies.

At the end of student life, a short opportunity for gathering newer experience presents itself. At the end of this stormy period comes the tranquil life of the householder. The sooner this tiny tattered boat, flung from shore to shore, finds shelter from the ocean's storm, the better it is. The turbid waters of life then clear, and he is indeed fortunate who reaches the safer bank early.

> *Mohenāntarvaratanur iyam dṛśyate muktakalpā |*
> *Gangārodhapatanakaluṣā gṛṇhatīva prasādam ||*

> This beauty appears gradually to recover her senses,
> like the Ganga once muddied by her tumbling banks
> reaches clarity.[65]

The traveller emerging from the pit of the first twenty-five years is like the celestial damsel Urvashi escaping from the grips of the demi-gods and gradually growing into radiant serenity. Navalrambhai had effectively dwelt on this subject when he wrote about Narmadashankar:

> It is not true that sexual attraction for women is the only impulse born at this juncture in life. A great many desires arise in the self, each seeking expression. The desire for women, an equally strong desire for adventure, or passion to make a name, roil the soul. Both love and valour sprout fast and free, like bamboo shoots; one's entire self is stirred by this sudden onrush of energy. A

---

[65] From Kalidasa's *Vikramorvasiyam* 1.8, available at: https://archive. org/details/VikramorvasiyamByKalidasa1879/page/n21/mode/2up (accessed 29 June 2021).

man's natural propensities then shape these impulses. In men of a certain type the desire for women flowers into pure selflessness, a surrender that has an aspect of divinity to it. In some, the impulse stops at mere pleasure; in others, societal norms set limits to the urge; still others descend into knavery and behave like animals. In a similar fashion, the desire for fame leads to vain and boastful strutting; some concentrate on acquiring wealth; some want to win honour and dignity, while in others it inspires a quest for knowledge, for virtue or valour in battle. Among the highest ranks of men, noble impulses born at this age endure for the rest of life, finding their highest good in the worship of wisdom, of virtue and love of country. (Pandya 1891[1911]: 256–257)

Fortunately, my father obtained the state of serenity early in life. The reader would have learnt from the last chapter that his experience of the householder's life was refined and bonded in affection. He himself had acquired learning, and sought enthusiastically to educate his students in order that they emerge as modest and dutiful patriots. He was eminently successful in this endeavour—that is what dozens of his grateful students maintain. A teacher totally dedicated to wisdom, abiding in absolute truth, living a life of purity, with achievements that are grounded in a quiet beauty will most certainly draw students onto the right path, and ensure that they do not stray away from it.

A mere glance at the young men who passed through his hands in Surat reveals treasures; they grew up to be men who proved their mettle in the trials of the world. Among Father's numerous students, the following come easily to mind: Veeraprasad, Karpurram, Manidharprasad, Mansukhram, Adelji Dorabji, Talati, Dorabji Gimi, Jamshedji Dalal, Harisukhram, Madhuvacram, Bhimbhai, Krishnamukhram, Sumukhram Motabhai Desai, Lallubhai Gordhandas, Dahyabhai Harjeevandas, Professor Tapidas, Bamanji Adelji Modi, Kekhushru Modi, Khanderao Bedekar. You will hardly find anyone from this list who would not have praised his teacher's learning, his virtuous character, and his friendliness, or failed to display affection for his 'Master Saheb'!

His pupils would describe in detail the routines of their master's life: if you visited his house in the mornings, you would find him helping students; even at school he would be ready to tutor them in his free time. Father's chief aim as a teacher was to awaken a love of learning in his students, to spark their curiosity, and to encourage enterprise. Look before you leap was his motto, and 'base your beliefs on closely examined evidence'. To reflect on your actions was an essential aspect of the practices at his school.

'Macaulay was our Bible', Father said, and claimed that contemporary writers were so enamoured of Macaulay that his literary style has left a deep impression on the Gujarati language. Mark Pattison (1813–1884) writes that 'if an uneducated person wants to acquire culture in a short span of time, he could do no better than to seriously read Macaulay's books'. A large number of people read Locke and Berkeley. Of poets, they read Shakespeare, Milton, and Byron; a few read Shelley, Pope, Grey, Goldsmith and Scott. Among English prose writers, Burke, Macaulay, Mill, Locke, and Darwin were read with great interest. Bulwer Lytton (1803–1873) was favoured over Scott. The dazzling grace of Lytton's prose plus his rendition of events covering diverse periods of time and space attracted readers. If one really wants to appreciate Scott's novels, you have to savour the fragrance of the Scottish heath and partake of a simple meal of barley and oats! Dickens and Thackeray were well-loved. In addition, travel books, which provided a great deal of information about the world, were extensively read; indeed, books on America, Africa, Central Asia, Iran, Arabia and China were read the way novels are read today. The limits of the world stretched far and wide and, at that time, factual reports about exotic places proved more wondrous than novels.

Father worked for fifteen years as teacher, first at the English School, then as headmaster of the same school, and finally as headmaster of the Teacher Training College. 'The man who works makes magic'—in his case this principle was founded in reality. From Navalrambhai's biography we know that in the May of 1867, Father was transferred to the Licence Tax Department, and Navalram, this critic of Gujarati poetry, became headmaster of the Training College. Since both Father and the poet Narmadashankar have drawn fine pictures of the age, it is not necessary to write about the subject again.

According to Father, it was a general belief at the time that poets live completely unregulated lives. Thomas Moore's famous biography of Byron reveals how the poet conducted himself very differently from ordinary men; he even became addicted to narcotics.[66] People of the time usually drank *bhang*, alcohol and smoked tobacco. 'An unregulated life is a complete life'—the idea is not entirely false. Unregulated lives will not lead astray those bred in cultures that are whole, and therefore stable. With neither an old, experienced sailor to show the way, nor an English sailor with a compass to guide it, the tiny raft of culture in Gujarat was pushed out to the high seas, far from the shelter of its harbour. If the raft then is not steered properly, it is bound to flounder and sink. 'The influence of the time has left a mark on me,' and so confessing, my laughing father showed me his snuffbox.

Apart from inhaling snuff, he had no other vice. He did not eat paan, smoke bidis or chew tobacco. He touched neither alcohol nor any opiate. In seeking to avoid its artificial and vulgar forms, even classical music was being abandoned in Surat. In Emperor Aurangzeb's puritanical reign, the *sitar*, *sarangi* and other musical instruments were consigned to flames; vocal music became exclusively associated with courtesan houses; because music violated what was considered proper, it was shunned. However, Father's circle of friends was very fond of classical music. On festive occasions, they invited musicians to perform the *mujra*; for them, the performers were true artistes. In my own time, the *mujra* had reached the zenith of dry, un-aesthetic formalism; I would burst out laughing when I listened to it. Father then told me the story of Uttam (The Best) and Jhagmag (Razzle Dazzle).

'Uttam was an old woman who suffered from dropsy, so her stomach was enormously distended. A veritable personification of ugliness—with a voice that was divine. Her high notes played on the listeners' heartstrings with such verve that gave birth to an inner music, an unending stream upon which one's life seemed to float. Jhagmag was equally ugly. Like the witches in *Macbeth*, she had grown a beard. But I have myself never heard a voice so deep, so resonant, so mature. They were not dancers, so their singing remained untouched by artificial blandishments. We, ourselves

---

[66] See Moore 1839.

connoisseurs of good music, used to arrange performances of *mujra* in complete disregard of distinctions of caste and creed. We cared only for the music, the music that swells like a slowly rising tide upon whose crest joy is borne.

'Of the pair, Uttam was the first to die. In the early hours of one morning, around three or four o'clock, Jhagmag began singing *Rag Bihag*. We recalled Jhagmag striking the old familiar musical note, expecting Uttam's voice to join her in singing the high ones. But when no response came, Jhagmag's inner music ceased, so the outer voice came to a halt, and with a cry of distress she collapsed. The expectations of her inner being suddenly thwarted, the strings of the *sarangi* broke, and she fell unconscious.'

Talking about his earlier life, Father recalled that with the passage of time, few people remembered Jhagmag and Uttam. But they remain supreme exponents of the classical style of their time.

My maternal grandfather Vidyaram, Mukundraiji, Bholanathbhai, Dolatram, Makubhai, Father, and a few others were great patrons of music. Their friends and acquaintances attended musical soirées held on the occasion of religious festivals. Father spoke expansively about these soirées. 'On all sides Surat was surrounded by beautiful gardens. They seemed to invite people to enter and partake of beauty. The garden laid out by Tehbakht Khan in Salabatpura had by then lost its lustre, but in Begumpura there was a garden laid out by Aurangzeb's sister; outside the gates of Katargam was Hafizuddin's garden. With the fading of Mughal grandeur, it had become wilderness. In earlier times it was known as the Tyrant's Garden, because many local houses were razed to create it. In addition, on the way to Katargam there were about four or five private gardens. Each Monday in the month of Shravan and on festival days we would go there. Sometimes we organised musical performances; on other days we chatted. Makubhai's sharp piercing words, Keshavbhai's openly ridiculing ways, Jaibhai's pompous erudition, my own uninhibited laughter, Mukundbhai's smile—as if he were afraid to show his teeth—and Vidyarambhai's habit of repeating the same story a hundred times, each time with new and wonderful overtones…I shall never forget the experience.'

Makubhai and Vidyaramji regaled us with tales of Haileybury's civilians. As senior law clerks, the two ran a flourishing practice and, given their sharp wit, could make Englishmen from Haileybury dance to their tunes. Nothing was too hard for them to fix—they could do it with their left hands. A forgetful English judge was once sent out to Surat. Having imposed the death penalty in a case, he baulked when the moment to sign the warrant arrived. 'I have most certainly not imposed the death penalty; why, then, would I now take a man's life?' he asked. 'Saheb, do remind yourself,' replied Makubhai, and then began spinning a yarn: 'Saheb, don't you remember, the peon was snoozing and you yelled at him. On suddenly being awakened, his turban dropped to the ground; you laughed. On the balcony a sparrow was chirping, *chi-chi*; you flung a ruler at the bird. And seeing the witness yawn, you ground your teeth'.

'Without doubt, Manekram, without doubt,' responded the judge saheb, 'I did sentence the man to death', and then went on to initial the death warrant presented to him.

There was a story about another judge saheb who drank a 'peg' every hour. When they wanted the plaintiff to win the case, Makubhai and Vidyaramji would ensure that there was no delay in serving up the 'peg': clerks would be sent off to the judge saheb's manservant to hurry him up. When the two intended the plaint to be defeated, the servant would tarry, the effect of alcohol would wear thin; the irritated judge saheb would start finding fault, and proceed to dismiss the case.

There is the story of Romer Saheb, a miserly man given to counting his pennies, and his servant Najar. About to depart for England, Romer Saheb turned towards Najar and asked, 'Well, Najar, what should I bring back for you?' Najar scratched his head and replied, 'A bolt of longcloth'. Other stories about Romer Saheb and the devout Herbert Saheb were also current at the time.[67]

My maternal grandfather Vidyaram told us about Pinney Saheb, who was very friendly with Indians and insisted that they

---

[67] John Romer, a long-time resident of Gujarat, was the magistrate of Surat (see Heber 1830: 300).

dine with Europeans. 'He would invite anyone and everyone to sit at his table in his bungalow. Except for the late Kalabhai Vakil, no Hindu had the courage to accept his invitation. Pinney Saheb loved grand entrances. Once, the sessions court was being held in Bharuch during the wedding season in the wealthy merchant community. A merchant, believing that seven generations of his descendants would prosper if the judge saheb were to grace the occasion, sent out an invitation to Pinney Saheb. He accepted. Arranging for the visit fell to my maternal grandfather. 'Pinney Saheb said, "If we have to go, we will go in great pomp." Accordingly, a retinue of horsemen arrived with great fanfare to fetch him. All of us accompanied Saheb to the celebrations.

'The evening's entertainment had begun, so the bride and bridegroom were summoned to meet the Saheb. The bride was around twelve or thirteen years of age. She bent down to touch Pinney Saheb's feet. Pinney Saheb was taken aback, worried that he might have to give her a present. He turned to me (Vidyaram) and asked, "What am I required to do?" I replied, "Give her a token; if not a flower, bestow a petal." Promptly and with great presence of mind, Saheb placed in the maiden's hand a cardamom seed that the host had given him, adding his blessings to the gift: "May your wedded life be as filled with fragrance and flavour as this sweet seed."

'After the maiden departed, the groom was summoned. We saw a child arrive, rubbing his kohl-lined eyes. The face, now smeared all over with kohl, gave the boy a dreadful look. An oversized turban hung loose on his head. A dark face, and a dark body covered in a dazzling brocade jacket! Continuing to rub his eyes, he bleated "*meh-eh-eh,*" like a little goat, protesting, "Father, why did you wake me?" Seeing the child in such a state, I gestured to the host to take him away. Fortunately, Pinney Saheb was completely engrossed in the dance being performed.

'Pinney Saheb was keen to establish close relations with us Indians. He brought his own new born child to me, and said, "Make him into a brahmin." "Saheb, forgive my incivility," I replied. "The child can become a brahmin only if you burn a *seer* of sesame seeds on his head!" Pinney Saheb laughed, "That can't be done." "Nor is it so easy to make a brahmin," I replied.

'In those days the position of the chief judge in civil courts was reserved for members of the aristocratic landowning classes. A householder named Meerza was an aspirant for the position. Pinney Saheb ordered Meerza to present himself at court at ten o'clock in the morning. We waited till eleven o'clock, but Mianji did not appear. So, a candidate below him was nominated to fill the position. Finally, at noon, a tired looking man was seen roaming around the courthouse. "Mian, why so late? The position has already been assigned to someone else."

'"I don't care," replied the dandy. "Am I a serpent that I should change my skin! I did set out from Begumpura at half past nine this morning, and have just arrived. Had I the money to hire a carriage, why would I want the position? *Kyā muzāyakā! Kyā yah muzīkī māfak men meri chāl bigāḍatā! Begumpāre se saḍe-nav mein chalā, abhī ā pahunchā. Kirāye ki gāḍi kā dām hotā to umedvāri kyun kartā?*"[68] I looked down at his feet and noticed that there were high heels attached to shoes so narrow that I am amazed the fool got here at all!'

My grandfather Vidyaram told us this story over and over again. He would strike his forehead, and remark, 'False pride has lost these Musalmans all they had. "Why should we change our ways?!" is their constant refrain. These obstinate men don't know how to change and adapt to changing times'.

Just as the Haileybury College civilians obtained positions in India through family connections, so also high court judges in the country were selected only on the basis of family status.[69] Since a high social status does not necessarily come endowed with intelligence, injustice was rife. A high court judge on inspection duty in Surat once arrived to scrutinise the local judges, and caught a Muslim judge nodding off in court. As the saheb sat watching, wondering how long his slumber would last, about four minutes went by and then, the gentleman's nodding head came crashing onto the table. He woke up with a start and his eyes met the saheb's, who was seated next to him. Their gaze

---

[68] The English translation is based on the author's Gujarati rendering.
[69] For more on Haileybury College, see p. 77, note 52.

held, and before the Englishman could question him, the judge turned a piteous face to him and with folded hands cried, "Your servant has two wives, Your Lordship!" I don't see how the saheb kept a straight face. However, within the week an order arrived, and the judge was pensioned off.

A Nagar brahmin from Veesnagar, also a district judge, refused to fill the logbooks of the day's proceedings himself, but would let his head clerk, a shrewd kayasth, write them. Later, with all good intentions of checking the log, the Nagar would begin, 'Child, let me see how you've recorded the day's proceedings…?' and the rest of his words ended in snores. Waking up, the judge resumed checking the log with flattering words, 'How shrewd you are, my son! How well you imitate my style! A great man's assistant, too, is bound to be great!' and then would proceed to sign the log. The clerk had recorded the day's proceedings keeping his own interests in mind. This judge, in due course of time, lost his position and was made to sit at home.

With men such as these heading the courts, bribery was rife. If a litigant offered the judge a meal of *shira* and *puri*s, his opponent would counter the offer with, 'What would you know about serving good food? I myself serve *basundi* with *puri*s, and savouries made with *val*!' The bidding would ultimately descend to competing offers of chutney. Arguments in a court of law would proceed thus: if the judge liked a particular kind of sweet, the litigant praised it, and the judgement favoured the person who made the best offer. 'There is only one God in the universe,' a plaintiff would declare, raising one finger, 'and I place my trust in Him'. His opponent would raise three fingers and in response declare, 'I believe in a trinity of gods'. The head clerk would then announce, 'In this Kali Yug, judgements are given by the five-member council (*panchayat*)'. Reduced to an auction, justice could not have been further degraded. Seeing the judges behave this way, the rest of the administration ceased to have any regard whatsoever for justice or for the people's welfare.

Keshavraiji, whom we have mentioned earlier, had seen ballroom dances. Since no one before had witnessed the English dance, Raiji regaled his audiences with his account. 'Oh brother, first they strangle her, then they make her hop, they make her run, they twirl her round, then they feed her, make her drink—this is called a dance! Tell me brothers, is it not easier to train a mare and dance with her? While stroking her you fit the reins, then you make her jump and run; to calm her down you walk her around in circles; and finally, you feed her hay and give her some water to drink.'

'Our friend Jaibhai would sermonise against idol worship, in Sanskrit: "Hé, hé *Lambakarṇa!*"[70] Apart from this phrase, he knew not a word of the language. But all those who themselves knew no Sanskrit believed that Jaibhai spoke in the exalted language of the gods. During Moharram, Jaibhai would seat himself on a wooden platform spread with mattresses and, with a straight face, preach in Arabic, having instructed some persons in the audience to say *amin* "when you hear the word *Khuda*" and sob when the Karbala is mentioned. Jaibhai was a great mimic, and even fierce Muslims seated right in front of him could be seen nodding their heads in sincere appreciation and commenting, "What an able Maulvi Saheb we have here!"'

Bathing in the Ashvinikumar was a fashion as agreeable as picnics. According to Father, the death ceremony rituals required young men of the caste to bathe in the Ashwinikumar, so most of them knew how to swim. Even though he was wildly enthusiastic about bathing in open water, Father did not know how to swim. He would enviously watch his maternal grandfather, his friends Mukundbhai and Dolatbhai swim in a variety of styles, even in their old age—flat on their backs, on their stomachs, and with their legs crossed underwater like frogs.

Father once told me the following story: 'Once, my friend Mukundbhai and I were bathing at the *ghat* near the Fort, when the fancy took us to play games. He turned a summersault under the *ghat*, and then I myself jumped in after him. Suddenly, we found ourselves caught in a whirlpool. To this day I am amazed how we managed to escape with our lives'.

---

[70] In Sanskrit it literally means, 'O' Long-ears or Elephant-ears!' and is possibly a humorous reference to the elephant-headed god, Ganesh.

Father also mentioned a member of our caste named Keshavram, who was an able swimmer. 'He would plunge headlong into the Tapi river when it was in flood. Having reached the middle of the river, he would shout: "I drown! I drown! Save me!" When fishermen hurried to reach him in their boats, Keshavram would greet them with laughter, making fools of them. Once, as fate would have it, he was swept into fast moving waters of the river and got caught in a whirlpool. This time, when he truly needed help, no one responded, so holding up his solid gold ornaments, he cried, "Whoever rescues me will have these as reward." But no one dared enter such churning waters. Keshavram drowned. His body was found on the side of the Ramnath Mahadev temple. Afterwards, the gold ornaments he was wearing were sold and the money spent in building a *ghat*, which exists to this day.'

Wrestling and other Indian sports happened to be very popular in the period. Every locality had its own wrestling pit—Karunashankar's being the most famous. My maternal grandfather Vidyaram claimed that the fingers of expert wrestlers were like sharp scissors. Father did not himself enjoy the sport. 'I find a certain coarseness in it,' he pronounced, and 'one's wrestling companions were not well-bred. Then again, you work ceaselessly to build your muscles, but the moment you fail to exercise you gain weight—that I disliked. I enjoyed walking and horse riding instead, and so my body was somewhat weaker than those of my friends.'

I learnt how strong my seventy-year-old maternal grandfather's body was when he was teaching me physical exercises. Though he was nearly eight years older than my father, he appeared the younger man. He could toss half a *maund* of puffed *moong* beans in the air as if they were flowers and, with open mouth, proceed to devour them.

The men folk of that period had prodigious appetites. Daulatraiji's physique was like a wrestler's; each day he consumed more than a quarter seer of heavy *dahl*. A delicately-built Desai, watching a cook from Dungerpura making thick *roti*s, once inquired, 'Hey man, what is this you make?' 'A hundred-layered *roti*,' replied the cook. The Desai was curious, 'What exactly is that, my man?' 'Sir, it is made by folding the dough over in many, many layers.' The Desai was horrified, 'But consuming those could kill you!' The cook replied, 'Not eating them would kill you, too, sir.' The Desai fell silent. The way men exercised in those days gave them a digestive system that was like fire in the belly; the fire consumed whatever reached it.

At the time, relations between men and women were not always cultivated. It was indeed difficult to find couples who understood each other and fulfilled each other's mutual obligations. There would hardly be any difference in age between husband and wife, so a helpless youth of between sixteen and eighteen years of age entering the householder's life would try a thousand strategies to dominate his wife. Eventually, however, the husband, notwithstanding his uncivil behaviour, would fail to cope with his wife's oblique resistance. So, in accordance with the saying, '*durbā kuśtan baroze avval*: kill the cat on the first day',[71] he would try to enforce his will upon her. Thereafter, some would twirl their moustaches and boast, 'How well we control our wives!' while others hid their humiliation in the same way as men hide their bald spots. Seldom was there a situation where,

> Complementing the other's needs, reciprocating each other's feelings,
> heart blending with heart, the well-matched couple becomes a complete whole.

A typical scene of domestic life is conveyed by the relationship between Manchatur and Dharmalakshmi in Chapter Two of Govardhanram Tripathi's *Sarasvatichandra*. The picture does not suggest any deficiency or lack of felicity in the relationship between the couple: the man is absorbed in his work, the woman engrossed in raising her children. So there aren't very many occasions for them to meet; the chances therefore of the shine

---

[71] Translated in accordance with the author's Gujarati rendering.

fading from their marriage are slight. A faithful wife might say of her husband, 'He is what he is, but may he always be safe!' Or, 'Be he handsome or be he loathsome, I honour him as my beloved husband, and so my mind is not agitated'. Such feelings played in women's minds. Just as Shakuntala, finding herself removed to an alien land, does not fault Dushyant for forgetting her, so also women, even those rejected by their husbands, did not allow the men's faults to enter their minds. However, should a husband interfere with the complex web of household management, verbal darts would keep him at bay: 'You really have no understanding of women's work!' With these words the harridan would shut him up; and, having swallowed the wife's taunts, the husband too would fall silent. In this way, a couple established the boundaries for each other and avoided conflict. Only if there are great expectations between husband and wife does the possibility of disappointment arise; no such expectations existed in those days.

Recalling Navalram's portrait of an ill-matched pair, my father commented that though husband and wife were often incompatible, there were fewer quarrels in earlier times. But was there an opportunity for transcendent joy in such couplings? Perhaps husband or wife experienced the pleasure of which only each was capable.

Men no longer incurred large debts. Frivolous spending had ceased, so had ostentatious displays for the sake of family pride. Because individualism was gaining ground, religion mattered less.

Father held that *Pustimarg* was most suited to the prosperous members of the merchant castes. 'Young mothers brought up in this tradition play with their children and sing lullabies that Jasoda once sang to Krishna. They create an image of Krishna in their imagination; joy enters their shrivelled lives when they watch the *gopi*s dance the *ras* with Him; charity enfolds them as they deck the god in jewels in the hope that prosperity would grace everyone's lot. The *Pustimarg* is a form of worship that places value on individual happiness and reveres enlightened men; it is an emotional religion appropriate for the common classes.

However, in order to reach out to the more cultured classes, the householder should banish the *goswamis* or insist that they stick to the renunciant's life!'[72]

'Vaishnavism itself does not advocate any wrongdoing; its core teaching is simple: your devotion to the gods and to the ceremonies dedicated to them will either bring you close to the deity, or if you so prefer, unite you with Him.[73] Their priests have ruined these precepts. They ought to be banished,' such was Father's opinion of Vaishnavism. There were many Vaishnava temples in his neighbourhood, so his views on the subject were based on extensive experience. 'Shaivism is on the decline', he maintained, and 'If people in the future remain theists, they will most certainly turn to the Vaishnava faith; otherwise they will largely become atheists.' Father was to change his views on religious matters in his later years.

This was the state of society when reports of the 1857 insurrection in north India and the defeat of the English forces reached the people in Surat. Tumultuous scenes at Andrew's Library followed. As soon as schools closed, students would head for the library to read the latest news bulletins. Both Muslim and Maratha rule had brought ruin to Gujarat; as mentioned in the previous chapter, Father had a low opinion of their methods of governance. He held that Rajput kings by and large made the best rulers. In the belief that the rebels were no more than empty bellies calling out to be filled, the Rajputs had kept the rebels at arm's length; holding fast to their clan's more elevated principles, they did not participate in the uprising. 'Even though it has been broken several times, it remains Bharuch!' the saying recalls the permanent achievements of the Rajput kings of Bharuch, he believed.

On the advice of Saint Ramdas, Shivaji fought in the hope of extending his own faith. And Guru Govind, having established a

---

[72] On the *goswamis*, see p. 82, note 57.

[73] In Vaishnava philosophy, *sarupya* is a stage along the path of liberation or *mukti* (see https://www.wisdomlib.org/definition/sarupya [accessed 5 May 2021]); *samipya* brings you close to the deity (see https://shodhganga.inflibnet.ac.in/bitstream/10603/159349/9/09_chapter%207.pdf [accessed 5 May 2021].)

kshatriya order capable of standing up against Muslim oppression, created the Sikh sect. The former dedicated his own country to a religious man, accepting it back as mere custodian. The other dedicated his kingdom to the Khalsa order. The result was that Shivaji harassed the mighty warrior Aurangzeb and brought about a hopeless end. The Sikh Sardar Harisingh Navla spread such terror that to this day, mothers from the frontier regions of the north-west shush their little children with the words: 'Quiet child, the Navla has come.'

The 1857 insurgency contained neither Shivaji's nor Guru Govind's high ideals. Speaking on behalf of his own community, Father said, 'If truth be told, we were enamoured of English rule even though the rulers were foreign. There was a thousand times more happiness among people under English rule than under the corrupt Mughals or the plundering Marathas. Almost ninety-five per cent of those who received modern education were against the rebels. However, there were indeed some stormy sorts who relish upheavals, and take pleasure in turning things upside-down; they were delighted, sensing in the events an opportunity for the plunder that lay ahead. Several ignorant people ordered books in Marathi, learnt to say "*Kasā kāy?* How do you do?" and to write in the Modi script.[74]

'It is not surprising that we regarded the Maratha general Tatya Tope (1814–1859)[75] as a valiant man; for Nana Saheb (1824–1859), however, we had contempt.[76] First, because Baji Rao II, who destroyed a Hindu nation, was Nana's adoptive father. Nana Saheb had one lazy eye, a fat body, and a cruel temperament; he did not even count as a distinguished warrior. So how could we take pride in him?

---

[74] Marathi was traditionally written in both the Devanagari and Modi scripts. There are various theories as to the origins of the Modi script, and why it was eventually replaced by Devanagari. See https://www. omniglot.com/writing/modi.htm (accessed 5 May 2021).

[75] Tatya Tope was one of the ablest Maratha generals of the 1857 Uprising. For an eyewitness account of the Uprising, and Tatya Tope's role in it, see Godse 2014.

[76] Nana Saheb was the adopted son of Peshwa Baji Rao II, and one of the leaders of the 1857 Uprising.

'There was a buzz in the Muslim community that the Islamic faith will awaken once more. Drums began to beat at Saiyyad Adrus'. Mianbhais gathered in groups: "What else to do, Saheb? We'll carry a gun on one shoulder, and a second gun on the other. Thus armed, we will march to Delhi and fight the white man." We expected riots to follow.

'Bankers grew frightened that the Government's promissory notes would become worthless. People bought bars of gold and silver and buried them underground. Shrewd investors made rich gains.

'The well-heeled were on the side of the English. They were convinced that India would remain united, and that her future prosperity rested under the umbrella of the English Empire. At that very moment, news of the rebels' defeat arrived.'

'Three months later,' Father reports, 'white men belonging to a regiment caught hold of a brahmin advocate and accused him of being Nana Saheb. The same lazy eye, the same twisted turban atop his head, the same height, and the same skin colour! Right away they produced him before their colonel, saying, "Here is Nana Saheb". One of them shouted, "Kill him, lest the rebels come to his rescue!" Another added, "Let's take him to the government officers". The poor brahmin advocate trembled and pleaded his innocence, fearing that he would be strung up a tree. He begged the soldiers to summon a judge and learn the truth from the judge's own mouth. In the end, a judge was called; he vouched for the innocent solicitor, and had him freed. White regiments moving through Surat looted its bazaars. We suffered their misdeeds in silence.

'We were extraordinarily happy when the Company Bahadur's rule ended, and India came under the sway of Queen Victoria. The human "cattle farm"[77] that was India would shut down, we felt, and we would enjoy a new kind of governance that recognised the rights of the people. The initial triumph of the rebels followed by their ultimate defeat left a deep impression on our minds; we realised that India was not one united entity. The large skeleton of her body lacked a heart through which blood could flow and

---

[77] The phrase 'cattle farm' is in English in the original text.

vitalise all the organs of her body. The ideal of nationhood will not be nourished so long as we are a country with multiple ideologies, without a common language, one in which there are continuing clashes between religious groups. A saviour able to spread his vast wings and fly across the whole territory will not emerge so long as there is general ignorance, and the strong feelings associated with caste remain. "A man in sorrow looks ahead to greater sorrows," and so the misdeeds of the Marathas and the Muslims returned to memory, and the current situation of Gujarat, by contrast, seemed to us marvellous like Vishnu's heaven.'

♊

Father talked about his travels outside Gujarat following the 1857 Uprising: 'In 1862, I was sent to study the system of schooling in Bombay. At that time Madhav Govind Ranade (1842–1901), Sir Pherozeshah Mehta (1845–1915), Vikaji, Bal Mangesh Wagle (1839–1888), men who were to become outstanding lawyers in the future, were students at Elphinstone College'. Many years later, when I myself happened to meet Mr Unwala in Benaras, he remembered my father's visit. 'One day we saw a stranger seated near our mathematics teacher. At the end of the lesson, he mingled with us, chatting. When we asked who the man was, we were told that he was the visiting headmaster of the Surat High School, who was here to see the educational methods practised in Bombay.' Father met people like Sir Alexander Grant and Mr Harkness before proceeding to Poona. After examining the teaching methods practised in these parts, he travelled all the way to Pandharpur.

Mr Erskine (1821–1893)[78] and Sir Theodore Hope (1831–1915),[79] both members of the Indian Civil Services, took leading

---

[78] Claudius James Erskine was Director of Public Instruction, Western India from 1855–1859. See: https://tinyurl.com/29rjk3nm (accessed 5 May 2021).

[79] Theodore Hope was a civil servant of the Bombay Presidency, and served as inspector in Surat's Department of Education and in later years as Collector of Surat. With the help of local writers he created

roles in reforming Gujarat's educational system. Mr Erskine, who was extremely fond of my father, created opportunities for him to meet new people, and to observe different types of educational practices in different parts of the country—all at Government expense. In the course of these visits, Father noticed that prose writing in Maharashtra was far more developed than in Gujarat; he believed that the easy-going people of Gujarat could not even imagine the diligence that the Maharashtrian brought to both learning and teaching.

Around this time, Erskine Saheb urged Father to visit England, suggesting that an acquaintance with the educational practices in England would benefit Gujarat. Father reports what ensued: 'My old father wept, saying, "I will not allow you to be removed so far from me". My in-laws were equally old-fashioned and said, "There isn't much money in the house". And I myself thought, suppose that something untoward were to happen, how could I afford to have strained relations with them? So even though I was keen to go to England, I declined the offer. Had my father not been alive, I would certainly have gone. Many years later, Mahipatram went to England.'

Father said, 'I had little direct acquaintance with civil servants trained at Haileybury College. From friends who were in the revenue (*Diwani*) and administrative (*Mulki*) departments, I had heard about both their strengths and weaknesses. Motiram Mehta, my great-grandfather on my mother's side, his son Vidyaram Mehta, Aditram Mehta, Manekram, and Dolatrai had served as head clerks in court. They were given to repeating Herbert Saheb's words in my presence: "I have been young and now I am old, yet never saw I the righteous man deserted, nor his seed beg for bread".'[80]

---

textbooks and readers (Gujarati *Vachanamala*) for schools in Gujarat. See https://en.wikisource.org/wiki/The_Times/1915/Obituary/Theodore_Cracraft_Hope (accessed 5 May 2021).

[80] Psalm 37:25, King James' version of the Bible. See https://www.biblegateway.com/passage/?search=Psalm+37%3A25&version=KJV (accessed 5 May 2021).

Father considered Kinloch Forbes (1821–1865)[81] a sort of *laird* (landlord) of Gujarat, both courageous and accomplished in his dual role as collector and magistrate. Forbes was a first-class historian. Of sympathetic heart, he wrote a history of Gujarat's Medieval Age, having researched the songs accompanying the *ras* dances. Forbes Saheb invited the poet Dalpatram to live in his house and had him collect folklore, which he later published in two volumes under the title *Rās Mālā* (A Garland of *Rās*). Father had seen the illustrations in this collection, drawn in Forbes Saheb's own hand, and he said that the style of writing adopted by Forbes Saheb reflected the style of the chroniclers of the time. So how could my father, the author of *Karan Ghelo*, not remember the debt he owed the man whom he considered his guru?

To elevate the standards of education in Gujarat, Forbes Saheb set up various societies across the state. Towards the end of his life, he established the influential Vernacular Society in Ahmedabad. 'Inhabitants of Gujarat, if you want to write with distinction, use your own native tongue,' he advocated. Narmadashankar writes that his first poem was in English. Romesh Dutt (1848–1909)[82] initially wrote in English, and Behramji Malabari (1853–1912)[83] also, in the beginning, danced with the beauteous English muse.

---

[81] Alexander Kinloch Forbes was a civil servant in the Bombay Presidency, a significant part of whose tenure was spent in Gujarat. His interest in literature led to a friendship with the poet Dalpatram, with whose help he collected the bardic lore of the local *charan*s and *bhat*s, that eventually resulted in his *Rās Mālā* (see Forbes 1924[1856]). He established the Andrews Library in Surat (see Yagnik and Sheth 2005: 82–84).

[82] Romesh Chunder Dutt was a member of the Indian Civil Service who, after retirement, served as Diwan of Baroda. *The Peasantry of Bengal* (1874) is his earliest work in English. He translated the *Mahabharat*, the *Ramayan*, and *Lays of Ancient India: Selections from Indian Poetry Rendered into English Verse*. His best-known work is the *Economic History of India Under Early British Rule* (1892). See *Life and Work of Romesh Chunder Dutt* (Gupta 1911).

[83] The language echoes Behramji Malabari's, who published a slim volume of poetry in English titled *The Indian Muse in English Garb* in 1886 (see Karkaria 1896).

In order to reverse this unnatural trend, Forbes Saheb encouraged collections of Gujarati language resources. 'In our unsettled times', Father concluded, 'some of us were not always conscious whether we walked on our head or on our feet. He woke us up from our nightmares.' Father believed that this advice was Forbes' greatest contribution to Gujarati literature. 'When he died, it felt as though a temple dedicated to the goddess of learning had suddenly collapsed—so great was our grief.'

Erskine Saheb, who headed the Department of Education, was extremely fond of historical chronicles. Packed on the back of a camel, his collection of books accompanied him wherever he went on camp in the districts. He, too, was responsible for encouraging the writing of prose in vernacular languages. The literati of the time actually looked down on prose written in the vernacular. Their view was that good writing had necessarily to have a metrical form, composed in either Sanskrit or the Vraj languages. Later, the poets Premanand and Samalbhatt encroached on the traditional bard's livelihood and placed before the literate classes a large collection of poetry composed in the vernacular. Thereafter, poetry began to be written in Gujarati; but of good prose there was still no sign.

The situation was not very different in the Marathi or Hindi languages. To provide easy readers for Englishmen learning Indian languages, pandits were commissioned to write the first prose works in Hindi. According to Erskine Saheb, *Premsagar* was meant to serve this purpose, as were *Tota Kahani* and *Bagh-o-Bahar*[84] in Urdu. Sir Saiyyid Ahmed's revival of Mirza Ghalib's works firmly established prose writing in Urdu. In

---

[84] W. Hollings, who translated *Premsagar* from the original Hindi, writes the following in his 'Preface to the Translation of the *Prem Sagur*': 'The object of this translation is to render the work easily intelligible to the young Student:…The Hindee language is well worth the careful study of every public Officer in India, as being the one which is most commonly spoken by inhabitants of almost every part of the country. To the Military man this language is of special use, as it not only enables him thoroughly to understand his men on points of common occurrence and of duty, but by being able to converse freely with them, to study their habits, manners, customs, their general turn of thought and opinions.

fact, Ghalib's letters were in the vernacular, and so found wide currency among the people. Although books commissioned by foreigners did meet with momentary popularity among native speakers, the acclaim, however, was not to last long.

Father's novel was an inspired work of a very different sort. Even as the poetic imagination stirred with the bards' songs continuing to play within him, a magician pronouncing spells appeared and with his wand struck the stony surface of Father's mind. The stone split and out flowed streams of prose. These inspired streams took shape as *Karan Ghelo*. In other words, he brought a poetic quality to his prose.[85]

Narmadashankar and Navalram wrote the first prose compositions and critical commentaries in Gujarati. But Father was the first to experiment with the narrative form of the novel in Gujarati. Thereafter, because of connections in the Department of Education, he became friends with Sir Theodore Hope. This extraordinarily gifted civil servant worked strenuously for both uplifting and promoting Gujarati literature. Even today, the first readers in Gujarati bear his name.

When Sir Hope returned to Surat as Collector, he appointed Father, his friend of former days, to the Department of Education. My Father served him wholeheartedly. His concern for the common man's welfare, his outspoken ways and sharp intelligence

---

The Hindee of the PREM SAGUR is remarkably pure, and the book is, I believe, an Examination Book at all the Presidencies.' See https://www.sacred-texts.com/hin/psa/psa01.htm (accessed 5 May 2021). *Tota Kahani* by Haidar Baksh Haidari (1801) and *Bagh-o-Bahar* by Mir Amman (1748–1806) were taught at the College of Fort William. A copy of the original illustrated version in Urdu is available at: https://archive.org/details/totakahani00haiduoft/page/n10 (accessed 5 May 2021).

[85] Anticipating later nationalist critics of Nandshankar, Vinayak is at pains to distance *Karan Ghelo* from the primers meant for English officers. He traces the source of the author's inspiration to bardic traditions and to genius in the form of the magician figure. Romantic poet Samuel Taylor Coleridge (1772–1834) distinguished talent from genius and believed poetic genius to be a force beyond human control; see Coleridge's 'The Privilege of Genius', https://www.bartleby.com/209/967.html (accessed 5 May 2021).

convinced Sir Theodore that Father was not meant to be a mere school master. 'Come,' he said, 'I will appoint you to the administrative services of Government. Given your competence and integrity, you will soon rise to very high positions.' In the third chapter of this book, you will see how prescient this praise of Father turned out to be.

Sir Theodore Hope believed that administrative policies have to be thoroughly worked out: 'All your work, from the very lowest foundations up to the very top, ought to be clear, meticulous and solid'. He alone could have mapped the main road from Delhi Gate. Like a general in the army with a map of the ruins of Surat before him, he drew several routes through the city. Thereafter he faced many obstacles, despite which, like a good general, Sir Hope stood his ground. The union of Surat with the village of Randir, across the river Tapi, like the marriage of the Sun God and his bride the goddess Rannade[86]—so beneficial to thousands of people—was actually consummated by his bridge, the Hope Bridge.[87]

Father worked on numerous fronts to improve the city, but because he considered self-praise a vice, he did not particularly mention his work in this area. Given the significant lapse of time and the absence of diaries, how can one recover his involvement with municipal affairs, or unearth the articles that he then wrote for newspapers?

My maternal grandfather told us about a collector by the name of Bellasis (1822–1872) who was posted in Surat.[88] This poor gentleman was completely ignorant of Indian ways. He was a man of noble character, but his gait was that of Kumbhakaran's and his display of affection like Bhimsen's. Riding his horse at daybreak once, he came upon several men who, *lota* in hand,

---

[86] A temple to the goddess, sacred to a particular sub-caste of Nagar brahmins, still stands.

[87] The Hope Bridge has since been torn down and replaced.

[88] Augustus Fortunatus Bellasis was Collector of Surat. He wrote the Report on the Southern District of the Surat Collectorate. See https:// whowaswho-indology.info/636/bellasis-augustus-fortunatus/ (accessed 5 May 2021).

were on their way to emptying their bowels. They did not salaam the Collector Saheb. Further on, he saw several people seated on the threshold of their homes brushing their teeth in the usual, preferred way—spitting and puking. Irked by such behaviour and thinking such disregard an insult, he linked their conduct to the *lota,* and so ordered his police inspector to confiscate all *lota*s and deposit them at headquarters. The order was carried out; several petitions against it were received, which were summarily rejected. When Father heard of the event, he addressed a strongly-worded personal letter to the Collector, stating that the order was based on a misunderstanding and warning him that his action would be construed by the people as tyrannical. The Collector, used to the flattering ways of his subordinates, was astonished to encounter this directness; he sent back an immediate reply, inviting my father to meet him. Father armed himself with sound arguments before presenting himself.

On entering the Collector's office, his eyes met the terrifying figure of Bellasis. He was relieved when a smiling Collector moved towards him, and in a manner both serious and straightforward extended a friendly hand: 'How do you do?' he said. In the course of the conversation when the moment seemed right, Father explained the reason for his visit: 'From the very moment the need arises, an Indian feels himself polluted and impure. And so he will not greet his elders until he has bathed and cleansed himself'. A word to the wise is sufficient; the Saheb ordered the *lota*s to be returned. What a scramble followed! After this incident, before undertaking any 'welfare' measures Bellasis Saheb regularly consulted the Head of the English School.

Gujarat's revered religious reformer Bholanath Sarabhai (1822–1886) was appointed to Surat as district judge at around this time. Bholanathbhai was a pure-hearted, learned man, with a passion for classical music. Dedicated to reforming society and the current state of religious practices, he immersed himself in translating the works of the renowned Bengali writer Debendranath Tagore (1817–1905) and his reform movement, Brahmo Samaj. He was keen to establish a similar society of like-minded men in Gujarat. It is not surprising then that when

Father met this saintly man, mutual feelings of friendship and deep affection spontaneously sprang up between them.

Bholanathbhai was straightforward and uncomplicated. Indeed, he was a sage, with affection for all. My father and my dear mother would visit him often. He was older than my father; and even Bholanathbhai's elder son was older than my mother. She tells me that, being older than she was, he would address her in the familiar '*tu*'. He used to sing songs invoking The One Spirit without a Second, set in a classical *raga*. Even non-believers were naturally stirred by his singing.

Father read aloud his novel *Karan Ghelo*, as it progressed, to Bholanathbhai, Vidyarambhai and Dolatrai, who would assemble in our house to listen to him read. My mother recalls these occasions: 'I was shy and would not come into the room, but sat in the outer room, listening. The tragic scenes made me weep; hearing my sobs Bholanathbhai would invite me to the inner room. Had we not belonged to the same lineage, our large families would certainly have become entwined through bonds of marriage.'

In 1898, my father was in Ahmedabad to celebrate his grandson Dr Sumant's marriage to Bholanathbhai's granddaughter Sharada. During my father's absence from Surat, Bholanathbhai met his end. The songs our kinswomen sang on the occasion of the wedding included one with the words: 'Sharada, the merit your vast erudition has earned will accrue to Elder Brother', in a gesture invoking Motabhai. When I asked my father who they were referring to (since my brother-in-law Batukbhai was also known as 'Elder Brother'), I was told that the words referred to Bholanathbhai. The relationship now established between our families must indeed delight the eternal soul of the saintly man, for he was exceedingly fond of my sister Harsiddhagauri, Sumant's mother.

My parents went to Bharuch in 1869, where an exhibition was being held. They stayed in the house of the distinguished Desai family of Kalyanraiji. Caste rules concerning inter-dining were complicated, so uncooked rations were sent and brahmin servants hired to help in the preparation of the meal, which my dear mother then cooked. But with what welcoming hospitality the landlord's elder wife received us! Since she was barren, fearing that so distinguished a Desai lineage would end, Kalyanraiji became bridegroom for a second time. The first wife—it makes no difference whether you refer to her as mother or as mother-in-law—treated the other woman with an elder's care; the younger wife's children were in fact her own. Father maintained that hers was the deep truth earned by a true wife's utter devotion to her husband; indeed, if there was a woman who day and night sacrificed herself, verily a second Sita of the age, it was the elder wife of the Desai household, and Dahigauri, in the poet Narmad's.

Kalyanraiji's heart overflowed with generosity. Unfortunately, men of that age were shaped by adventurous ideas, and so instability often marked their conduct and decadence cast a shadow on their many virtues, overwhelming their noble character. Since there was no one able to control Kalyanraiji's self-indulgent spirit, the evil habit of alcohol took hold of the good man. Like a large fruit-bearing tree whose shade had sheltered thousands, he eventually succumbed to this addiction; like termites the addiction ate away at his substance. The tree fell, and people everywhere grieved.

We shall now examine the subject of caste. Authorities on traditional law declared that persons returning from foreign lands could not be received back into their caste fold, even if they were to perform purifying rituals. The ruling coincided with Rao Saheb Mahipatram's return from Europe. Even countries lying just beyond India's borders, that is, Sri Lanka and Afghanistan, were regarded as 'foreign'; so England was certainly a foreign land. Some 'experts' claimed that the returning person might be declared pure if he drank as atonement a measure of broken glass pieces passed through a sieve! There were several who, without a close scrutiny of scriptural injunctions, pronounced views for and against a variety of atonements; in fact, they twisted traditional authority to suit their own belief.

Father believed that scriptural texts should conform to the temper of the age. If the interpretation of the text, having benefited from a survey of the entire past, is extremely sharp, it will facilitate understanding in future. Indeed, such broad understanding alone enables one to plan for the future. 'I do not believe that the injunctions of the *shastras* are fixed or "eternal", in the sense of being "applicable for all time"', he said. A new age requires its own ethical regulations. That is why he maintained that if the purpose of expiation is to prevent ostracism from one's caste, then one ought to think of the expiation merely as a kind of fine; it is absurd to think that a person's character is in any way purified through such atonements.

The moment Mahipatram returned from England, Father invited him to a meal at Occhavrai's compound. He himself sat in the same row of diners, next to Mahipatram. Dolatram, Keshavrayji, and Jayashankar Rawal were helpmates in this enterprise. Since my maternal grandfather's own daughter, my dear mother's aunt, happened to be married to Rawalji, my grandfather did not show any hostility to my father's gesture, even though, being orthodox in his convictions, he had earlier taken a stand against my father's going abroad. Opinion in the caste was divided, so a rift within it appeared inevitable. Fierce battles ensued. After paying a fine of approximately Rs 2,700, Mahipatram was allowed to return to the fold. If a hero from Surat is to be identified in this battle, it would not be an exaggeration to say that it was Father. He mollified people, united a divided opposition, and drew everyone round to his own more moderate point of view.

It is appropriate at this point to discuss the issues leading to the ruin of trade during this period.

In his biography of Premchand Roychand (1831–1906), Mr Wacha has provided a good exposition of how speculation in the commodity markets between 1853 and 1854 ruined people.[89]

---

[89] See *Premchund Roychund* (Wacha 1913). See also *The Indian Biographical Dictionary* (1915), https://en.wikisource.org/wiki/The_Indian_Biographical_Dictionary_(1915)/Wacha,_Dinshaw_Edulji (accessed 5 May 2021).

Father maintained that Premchand was the Napoleon of this speculative enterprise. The outbreak of the Civil War in America had obliged textile factories in Manchester to buy Indian cotton at higher rates. Prices kept rising; as a result, small traders in cotton as well as farmers who grew it acquired wealth beyond their wildest dreams. They ordered a great deal of jewellery; rumours had it that goldsmiths began indulging in dishonest practices and in turn became rich. A well-known goldsmith from Gopipura boasted that during this hysteria, he managed bit by bit to mix a large lump of copper with the gold ornaments he crafted, and got away with the deception. There was an excess of money in the land and no one knew where to invest it. Truly the newly created wealth remained undigested! Wave after wave of possible options were tossed around, and even experienced traders got caught in this whirlpool of speculation.

The war ended sooner than anticipated. Cotton prices sank. Speculators were laid low; simultaneously various banks and business offices declared bankruptcy. Precious capital of helpless widows was dragged away in the ensuing flood. One cannot possibly imagine their grief. Mistrust of business practices was rife. People spoke contemptuously of Government's weakness: 'A native government would have squeezed in an oil press those who declared bankruptcies; it would have forced them to return every last penny to their proper owners. After consuming banquets of milk and honey, they declare themselves insolvent! The widow's capital ought to be regarded as inalienable; it should be on par with the wealth settled on her when she marries. Bankruptcy is one more of the thousand tricks dreamed up by dishonest traders!'

In this affair, Father believed that had the English been more paternalistic and not privileged England's commercial laws, the unjust business practices of Europe would not have become established in Bombay, and thence made further inroads into the country. This business upheaval resulted in the closure of older business houses, and investment in new enterprises. Older business networks were torn down, newer ones built, and innocent flies invited into these magnificent houses. 'Won't you come into my parlour?' said the cunning spider to the fly. With these words the rogue spider, ready once again to suck the blood of innocent flies, stood outside inviting them into his web.

Premchand was a courageous man, the enterprising son of a poor helpless widow. In search of work, he left Surat and moved to Bombay. Once there, he showed great business acumen, lending and borrowing money, buying and selling goods while keeping a sharp eye out, as if through a telescope, on the affairs of the world. Like an astrologer of the marketplace, his brain accurately predicted the future of money markets. Like an ocean, Bombay will become agitated: when the full tide comes in, fresh streams will begin to flow—he forecast all this. And as he had predicted, wealth flooded into India; those owning hardly a thousand became proud possessors of seven–eight lakhs.

As the ocean waves rose to their zenith, this quiet, simple man with an acute mind danced on the crest of the rising wave—a second Krishna subduing the serpent Kaliya! The people of Mumbapuri, right from the Governor down to our oil-presser Ganga, were like the *gopis* of yore, dancing 'thai-thai' to the sound of his flute.

During those halcyon days, Premchand Sheth once arrived in Surat on a special train. The residents of Surat, the Collector, government officials, and other prominent citizens were gathered at the station to welcome this business warrior returning to his motherland. My maternal grandfather describes what ensued: 'When the train stopped, Premchand descended alone. What grand images people had built of this man! Wouldn't a man who counts governors as traveling companions arrive in full regalia? But it was not that way. He wore a plain tie-and-dyed turban and a white tunic across which, shaped like a crescent moon, hung a silver chain with a watch dangling at the end, and an ordinary *dhoti*; on his feet were varnished patent leather shoes. A short man, sharp-eyed, with a modest face stood in our midst. Upon alighting he moved forward, first bowed politely to the common people of the land, who stood behind the leading citizens of the town. Only then, after greeting all the assembled Indians, including the prominent residents of Surat, did he turn and acknowledge the government officials standing nearby'.

As Father recounts, 'Premchandbhai was accommodated in a three-storeyed house. From dawn to dusk, on each of its floors, he met people. One couldn't really say how many came to see him. He asked Dolatrambhai, Vidyarambhai and myself to place in his charge the small capital we owned. "I will give you ten percent interest," he promised.

'In this Kali Yuga if there be a generous donor like Bali, it was truly Premchand. And he was invariably open-handed with those who asked him to donate to a good cause. His munificence was not confined to any one particular caste or group; one could, in fact, call him a Creator of Wealth. People were willing to worship him, despite which he retained his simplicity. And so, ordinary men were awed. "He is indeed some sort of god come down to earth," they exclaimed.

'Two months before his downfall, Premchand returned the money to the three of us who had invested with him. Attached to the money was the following message: "The rising profits we observe today won't last much longer. My concern is not to put at risk capital earned by the hard work of poor brahmins." We ourselves did not believe that Premchand would fall. But a thunderbolt hit this vast many-branched tree, and felled it. With his fall, all those thousands of individuals who clung to its branches and who stood under its shade were crushed. Not that he had told anyone, "Come, I shall be your refuge". Just as the *gopis*, swept away in Krishna's dance, scattered in the absence of the lead dancer, so it was that with Premchand gone, people were scattered.

'I certainly did not run after quick money in the demented fashion of the time. And, had Dolatrai not persuaded me, I would certainly not have thought of sending my four thousand rupees through him to Bombay. You might call me superstitious or anything else you want, but from childhood I had contempt for high-return investments.' Indeed, all of Father's savings were in government promissory notes, as I found out after his death.

In 1861, my father saw the birth of his first child. He was twenty-six years old then, his salary was fairly good, so a mind freed from anxiety and blessed with domestic happiness were now his. The daughter was named Harsiddhagauri. The eldest child is always well-loved, and my father and mother remained greatly attached to her, right up to her death in 1901. Harsiddhagauri had a serene, serious and straightforward temperament; wisdom and a sense of detachment marked her character.

My eldest brother Markandrao was born in 1864. He was a delicate child from the beginning; only after he reached the age of two did his health begin to settle down.

My father was a naturally affectionate man, but the rules of propriety required that he guard the entrances to his heart. Nor was my dear mother particularly exuberant in her display of affection. She was always anxious, afraid that might offend fate if what she did was wrong! But my maternal grandfather's love for his eldest grandson knew no bounds, and my elder brother reciprocated his grandfather's feelings.

In 1865, another son was born. This robust baby was barely a year old when he developed whooping cough while teething. My tearful mother tells me: 'After an illness lasting just two days, Dinkar took offence and left'. My second brother was born in 1868. From the moment of his birth, he was my mother's favourite. His tender, attractive and radiant features were gifts from my mother. He inherited Father's eyes and his nose was shaped like Father's; from the very beginning he was indeed a fine blend of both his parents.

This was the size of our family when Father left Surat to become a revenue officer in Ankaleshwar.

I now end this chapter.

'Glory, glory be to proud Gujarat! But alas, night has fallen, and the light is fading'—from Father's mouth I often heard Narmadashankar's despairing cry. Father's ardour for this land of Gujarat remained constant nonetheless: 'This beauteous province, this garden of the gods, this dwelling place of Lakshmi will be home to all virtue. Amen'. That love of one's country and love of one's state both spring from a love of the city of one's birth is not surprising. Suratis are an entirely different breed—this thought remained deeply embedded in all three of Surat's great sons, Nand, Narmad and Naval. The moment their wings grew strong, all three flew, just as the song sung by the maidens of Gorav has it: 'We are nestlings, bound to fly our nests come tomorrow, and be snarled in our family's affairs'. In the same way, these three great citizens of Gujarat, too, became entangled in earning livelihoods for their own households.

A great vessel sets sail from the port of Surat. At the helm sits an intoxicated poet, singing songs of heroism and love. His heartrending music is irresistible and draws thousands of small crafts to the side of the vessel. Unable to face the tossing high waves, these smaller crafts begin to sink.

Seated beside the explorer, Navalram speaks in a gentle voice, 'Education is the death of superstition. Prepare yourself to serve the nation. Draw strength from the armour of intelligence. Listen to the poet's song and move forward'.

Mahipatram says, 'Be industrious! Persevere! Believe in the true God. Give up the worship of graven images! Listen, as I relate the tales of my travel'.

And Father with great passion advises, 'Be radiant. Cultivate joy and the love of wisdom. In the process, beware of becoming a loudmouth or a swollen head, lest you become a laughing stock. Listen, I will read you a novel. At the very least, it will teach you a love of your land. Come below deck into the ship's treasure hold—the waves strike less violently there'.

Parvatishankar advocates diligence and contentment, and Adelji gives vigorous speeches advocating hygiene, a sharp wit and improvement of the culture of caste. Several other individuals seated inside the vessel sing songs:

> Come together to forge new bonds,
> aboard a vessel of our own native land,
> flying the flag of reform.

To those on the shore who ask, 'Why are you being dragged away?' Narmad answers in Hafez's cautious but apt words:

> *śabetārīk bīme mauj, girdābe chunīt hāīl* |
> *kujādānand hālemā sabuksārān ne sāhil-hā* ||

The night is dark, the waves fearful, with currents swift.
What do you on shore who walk the narrow paths know of us?[90]

Others are ambivalent.

Darmīyāne kāre dariā takhtā bandam karda ī |
Bāz mī goyi ke dāman tar makun husīyār bārā ||

Wooden planks have been laid across the deepest parts of the river.
And they tell us to be alert lest our clothes get wet.[91]

To them Navalram says, 'It matters not that we get wet. It is far better to have seen the world than to have merely lived in it.'

Overcome with doubt, all of society asks: 'But where are you going? Why are you leaving?'

Father replies, 'One after the other, where the currents of culture mingle, dipping and churning to come together.'

'Live by the rules and with radiant mind, and make others do the same.'

'Come back! Come back, whilst there is yet time!' they all shout from the shore.

The three answer together: 'We have slid the boat into the waters. Whatever will happen is right.'

In an instant the vessel disappears from view. 'The worth of a pearl is revealed only after it is brought out of the sea.' The ocean that was Surat contained many precious gems whose worth was revealed only in distant markets.

[90 and 91] My translations are based on the author's Gujarati translations of the Farsi originals.

Chapter III

MIDDAY
The Administrator

The fortunes of the Gaekwad and the Peshwa swayed as they fought for supremacy in Gujarat, writes Kinloch Forbes in his *Rās Mālā*.[92] Each, in turn, sucked Gujarat dry. With two death-dealing oppressors feeding on one host, Gujarat lay in ruins. If the inhabitants of Gujarat did not even dare to wear fine clothes in public, you can imagine how agitated they inwardly were. The moment a person appeared in distinguished attire, tales would carry, and the ignorant generals of an ignorant raja would set upon him. Any object considered valuable was hidden out of sight, underground. Then, around 1800, when a host of misdeeds—intimidation, injustice, and outrage—flourished, light began to illumine the darkness.

It was the administrators of the Department of Home Affairs established by the English who tried to revive a Gujarat that, like a flattened fly, had been sucked dry by the Peshwa and the Gaekwad. To revitalise the institutions of a government in disarray, especially when the available administrators are honourable and keen to achieve results, is not really difficult. Indian administrators of the time were certainly honourable men; honour among them was perhaps greater then than obtains today. In addition, they were fascinated with the prospect of gathering new experience, for, with a new regime taking charge, a thousand new opportunities for gaining renown presented themselves. With such inducements in mind, Sir Theodore Hope appointed Father to the Department of Home Affairs. He conceded that initially Father would be

---

[92] See p. 107, note 81, and Forbes 1924[1856].

obliged to accept a loss of salary; however, in the long run, that too would be turned around. It is like mounting a horse: you get your foot in the stirrup; once the foot is securely placed, you swing yourself onto the animal, and then firmly seated on the saddle, you ride away!

Father's first appointment was outside Surat, in Ankleshwar. The district of Bharuch provided the chief impetus to trade in Gujarat; ginning presses, which are machines for tying cotton into bales, were to be seen everywhere, as were grinding mills. Although, prior to the 1857 Uprising, when Father arrived in Ankleshwar, it was paper-making that supported the largest number of livelihoods, cotton now was the bride people chased.

Bharuch was in the hands of the Scindhias, but the Peshwa cast covetous glances at it, and the Gaekwad was of similar mind. Since Bharuch lay in the Gaekwad's front yard, naturally both the desire to conquer it and the justification for such conquest remained possible threats. As a result, the people of Bharuch were agitated. Had there not been a splendid crop of cotton, and had the price it fetched in the market not exceeded the price of gold even, this district could not have been self-supporting. Farmers were equally well-placed—the land was fertile; they worked hard; the rains were timely, and the prices high. It is not surprising then that the profits were large. Trade with Nandod was uppermost in Father's mind at the time. He believed that even if Bharuch was in ruins, Ankleshwar would be the new hub for trade.

Father was preparing for his higher and lower civil service examinations. Lely Saheb,[93] Fulton Saheb[94] and Muir-Mackenzie

---

[93] Sir Frederick Lely served as assistant collector magistrate in Bombay and Surat, and as an administrator in the state of Porbandar. See *The India List and India Office List* (Great Britain India Office 1902), https://archive.org/details/indialistandind00offigoog/page/n552 (accessed 7 May 2021). He finds mention as an administrator in Porbandar in M. K. Gandhi's *Autobiography*. Anxious to earn a barrister's degree in England, the young Gandhi journeys to Rajkot to meet Sir Lely, hoping for financial aid, only to be brusquely turned down; see: https://www.mkgandhi.org/autobio/chap11.htm (accessed 7 May 2021); see also Yagnik and Sheth 2005: 97.

[94] Edmund McGildowny Hope Fulton was a member of the Indian

Saheb (1854–1916)[95] sat the examinations with him. When the results were announced, it turned out Father had stood first. Lely Saheb stood first among the candidates for the covenanted services.

Around this time, Father became acquainted with the Bohra community's wrangling ways. Whatever wealth the community earned in foreign parts was lost at home in internecine quarrels. For them, the option of marching to court was never as a last resort. Father was friends at the time with a Parsi gentleman belonging to the Ginwala family. The Parsis are an affectionate, enthusiastic and greatly helpful people. He used to talk about the tensions between the Parsi and Muslim communities of Bharuch at this time. As Father noted, 'The Parsi community had become prosperous. While the Muslims made money, they were also quick to squander it; the capability of generating wealth was theirs, but they lacked the talent for conserving it. The rule that says generation and preservation, like light and shadow, must be equally balanced is indeed correct. The Parsi community's increasing prosperity angered the Muslims.[96]

'Given this scenario, a certain athletic Parsi gentleman named Dhanjishah began an adulterous relationship with a wealthy Muslim woman. How could this be tolerated? A large and unruly crowd gathered around the house where the couple was making merry, both blinded by wealth and blind to the rules of their own faith. The crowd accused Dhanjishah of entering a mosque under false pretences and polluting it. Realising that the game was up, the Parsi swung athletically onto the rooftop and, leaping from

---

Civil Service; he served in several parts of the Bombay Presidency, was President of the Asiatic Society of Bombay; and in 1902 was a member of the Bombay Legislative Assembly; see https://www.wikiwand.com/en/Bombay_Legislative_Council (accessed 7 May 2021).

[95] J. W. P. Muir-Mackenzie was a member of the Indian Civil Service and held several posts in the Bombay Presidency. See Great Britain India Office 1902: 517, https://archive.org/details/indialistandind00offigoog/page/n552 (accessed 7 May 2021).

[96] I have changed the original order of sentences in this paragraph to highlight the contrast the author draws between the Bohra and the Parsi communities; the contrast serves as an introduction to the account of the riot.

one roof to the next, fled. Reaching the end of a row of houses, he jumped down from a two-storey bungalow, and then kept running despite a sprained foot. The crowd saw him run, and then pause in front of a wide trench that blocked his escape. If only he could cross it, his troubles would end! With cheetah-like agility he leapt. Unfortunately, because his wounded foot failed to provide sufficient bounce, Dhanjishah failed to clear the gap and fell into the trench.

'It is hard to describe the fury of the men who came after him. They fell on him, then proceeded to lynch him and drag his corpse onto the street. The bloodthirsty rioters then entered the Fire Temple and killed the white-skinned, white-robed priests tending the holy fire. Alexander Rogers Saheb, who had been deputed to Surat, hanged two culprits, and so ended the riot.'

In 1871, Father was transferred from Ankleshwar to Dhandhuka as the chief administrative officer. He decided against taking his family with him, for Dhandhuka was remote, and there were fears that its waters were unsafe. He travelled alone up to Ahmedabad by rail, stopping there at Bholanathbhai's.

My revered mother, along with my brothers and sisters, could visit him in Dhandhuka only occasionally. True, a brahmin servant prepared his meals for him, but not being used to the half-cooked food the man served him, Father was obliged to cook his own. 'I made thick *rotlis*, which I used to fry in plenty of ghee, and eat dipped in a soft *dahl*.' The waters of Dhandhuka contained salts that helped digestion. There wasn't much work and he got plenty of exercise walking. Very quickly his health improved and his body filled out. On a visit to Surat, those who were acquainted with Father's delicately built frame pointedly remarked that the waters of Dhandhuka did indeed suit him!

Dholaka was the stage setting for Gujarat's history. The Rajput princes had built tanks, wells, ponds and rest houses there; unfortunately, the wheel of fortune turned, and the region became the scene of many battles. Partly due to Muslim religious intolerance, but also due to the ignorant Marathas' greed, the few who survived continued to live broken lives, as you can still see. The time had now arrived for the author of the novel to directly experience in reality what he wrote about in *Karan Ghelo*.

Father arrived in Dholaka at a time when trade in cotton was flourishing. The only problem was an acute shortage of water, for well water had turned brackish, and people were forced to drink from ponds. In summer, the ponds went dry and what remained were mere puddles, to which sheep and goat found access. The water, mixed with their droppings, soon turned fetid. For the governing classes, guards protected the puddles; they slept there and kept out intruders. The water was then strained, boiled and purified before it was drunk. Father used to say, 'One could indeed say that for me the experience was a foretaste of the waters of Paliya, which destiny had written into my future'.

Father's chief duty as *mamlatdar* was to arrange provisions for troops passing through the region. The work was supposed to be difficult. As he described it, 'A job in the Home Department meant swallowing insults, merely in order to lord it over the few below you. I really did not appreciate this attitude. From the very beginning I decided that should the commander of the troops show disrespect, I would show him the door; as they say, *Chalte phirte najar āv*: Get a move on, be gone'. An occasion for testing this resolve arose when Father was the *mamlatdar* at Ankleshwar.

'Once the commanding officer of a troop with the rank of major arrived. I rode up on my horse to welcome him, greeted him politely, and immediately told him the following: "Salaam, Saheb. Everything is in order, please check for yourself. I will be away inspecting revenue lands." With equal politeness the major replied, "Rogers Saheb has commended you warmly, and advised me to get to know you better. I am aware of your interests in history, and am curious to learn more about the ancient ruins of the locality. Do please postpone your inspection tour of the revenue lands and join me at camp." Thereafter, we spent three or four days pleasurably discussing scholarly matters.

'After this incident, there was a rumour that the actual burden of imposing a license tax fixed by Government on businessmen would fall to the *mamlatdar*'s lot. Looking at the matter in general, as well as from the point of view of the joint family, I for one was entirely convinced that the tax on family income is in many ways unjustly computed. If we take as norm the principle that there ought to be "equality of sacrifice",[97] I just could not comprehend how a man who supports scores of children should pay as much tax as a man without progeny. Even if their incomes are equal, how can their sacrifice be equated? Even if a trifling sum were deducted from his income it would profit the former; while for the latter the deduction would make no discernible difference.

'Independently of these concerns, it was clear to me that under British rule the trading classes had not only benefitted monetarily, but also improved their standing in society. Consequently, the argument that businessmen ought to contribute to the imperial treasury held up; but, apart from a license tax, how else could Government secure additional funds from them? So, although I did not favour the idea of my having to impose it, one couldn't hold that the tax was entirely unjust. But consider the consequences: people might hide their property holdings from the government, might falsify their accounts and utter a hundred falsehoods—so, while truth tellers would earn less, liars would prosper. Viewing the matter differently through the maxim "a hundred are punished for the sins of one", let us suppose that a large number of account books were all to claim lower levels of tax, everyone's accounts would then appear as having been cooked up, and an innocent few would have to pay higher taxes.

'A law that metes out justice to thousands but harasses even one counts as distinctly unjust according to the principles laid down in our law books. Even the public, where the new rule is increasingly being discussed, consider the tax oppressive. From the moment I heard that the tax was going to be imposed through coercive means, and that its execution would fall to my lot as *mamlatdar*, I resolved to oppose the ruling. I prepared a letter of resignation and carried it in my pocket wherever I went. Not having inherited any money from my forefathers, and being middle-aged, how would I support my four children

---

[97] The expression 'equality of sacrifice' is in English in the original text, and is possibly a reference to John Stuart Mill (1806–1873), who wrote: 'Equality of taxation, therefore, as a maxim of politics, means equality of sacrifice' (see Mill 1848).

were I to lose the job? What could I do?—all these thoughts
did not enter my head. It is normal that waves of fantasy speed
through your mind in such situations: "The wheat is ripening in
the field, my sons need my support, my wedding is on the fifth
day of spring." But men with a naturally commanding character
do not act with an eye on the ultimate result; they focus on the
ideal that is immediately in front of them, and all their energy
drives forwards toward it. I have to concede that I held in high
esteem Englishmen's dedication to the law. So, deep down, I felt
that I was right, that the law was unjust, and that my resignation
would not be accepted.

'At this point, Rogers Saheb (1825–1911)[98] arrived in the
district. I was considered Hope Saheb's protégé; Rogers Saheb
was not on good terms with Hope Saheb. It could even be said
that Hope Saheb had little regard for Rogers Saheb, and he did
nothing to hide his low opinion. I was therefore quite decided that
Rogers Saheb would find fault with my work. How wrong I was!

'Rogers Saheb was fair-minded, learned, and an altogether
good man. One could truthfully say that he had extensive
knowledge of Farsi and his study of Indian religions was deep.
He was kind-hearted, mature in years, and mature in learning.
Unfortunately, he died only two years later. Rogers Saheb
appreciated my work and even recommended that I be employed
in areas that required pioneering effort.

'And so, we began working to repair the harm done by the
Marathas. Mr Baines writes that the Damaji Gaekwad died before
he was able to consolidate his domain.[99] Just as a rat sucks a

---

[98] Alexander Rogers was an officer of the Bombay Presidency. He wrote
a two-volume work titled, *The Land Revenue of Bombay* (Rogers 1892).

[99] 'The thin crust of Maratha dominion rapidly disappeared before
it was either assimilated into the system of the province or hardened
over it. A military occupation of a large and civilized district, at a
distance from the mother country, and prevented from the jealousy of
the central authority, and the shortsightedness of those in charge of
its exploitation, from either conforming itself to the elements it found
already established, or absorbing the vital forces of the government it
dispossessed—a System without the breath of life, without elasticity,
without the capacity of self-direction, imposed bodily upon a foreign

man's blood surreptitiously, so the Marathas had slowly sucked the lifeblood out of places like Bharuch, but Ahmedabad and Nadiad they ravaged openly. To get rid of a pillaging Kantaji on the one side was to invite a Pilaji to loot you on the other—you push out a goat, and a camel enters—the new arrival swallowed all that was fertile, leaving the land desolate and barren. Gujarat, this garden of Hindustan, had become a desert.'

When Father first visited Devgadh-Baria, not a single copper or brass utensil was to be seen; every metal object had been looted. The unprotected areas on the outskirts of Dhar and Devas, in particular, were ruined. Fearing pillage, even the small amount of cash people collected was hastily buried. Food was cooked in traditional earthenware pots; the floors in their houses were plastered with cow dung.

Sir John Malcolm's book *Central India* contains a realistic portrait of this mismanaged, leaderless place.[100] Mentioning the book, my father remarked that governance under the Muslims was a hundred times superior to what the Marathas offered. True, occasionally overcome by fervour, Muslims did slaughter the earth much as they might slaughter a cow, but usually they cared for her, washed her, adorned her and fed her properly. The Marathas on the other hand were like a host of locusts devouring every leaf in sight; so the cow became emaciated and stopped producing milk.

---

people, without even the care of preparing a foundation—such seems to have been the Maratha government containing within itself all that was necessary to ensure a precarious, but while it lasted, an oppressive existence' (Government [of India] 1877). Jervoise Athelstane Baines (1847–1925), a statistician and ethnographer, was a member of the Indian Civil Service in the Bombay Presidency. See 'Sir Athelstane Baines' (*Nature* 1925); and Baines 1912.

[100] Sir John Malcolm (1769–1833) served the East India Company Army initially as soldier, and later as administrator and diplomat. As administrator, he helped shape the Company's policy regarding its conquered territories. Malcolm was a historian of some note, and author of *A Memoir of Central India* (1828); see Harrington 2010. 'The people of India must, by a recurring sense of the benefits have amends made to them for the degradation of continuing subject to foreign masters' (Harrington 2010).

They brought no stability to the lands they conquered, made no effort to win the hearts of the people even for the sake of their empire. Perhaps they did accomplish something in the south of India, but in Gujarat it was all violence, pillage and disorder.

My maternal grandfather spoke of an incident to illustrate the arrogance of the Maratha governing classes of the time. 'A Major Walker once received orders that he should accompany the Gaekwad's Diwan when he was out collecting taxes in Kathiawad. "Help him", he was told. It so happened that a durbar over which the Peshwa's Diwan, the arrogant Vitthalrao, was presiding was in session when word arrived that Major Walker was to grace the occasion. An overeager peon rushed forward to fetch a chair for the visitor. Major Walker was hardly ten yards away when Vitthalrao noticed the peon carrying the chair, and turning purple with rage, shouted, "*Māzi chāti var thevā*:[101] Put it on my chest!" The peon promptly stopped. Without moving a muscle, the major proceeded to seat himself on the floor, chat for a while and then depart. Government servants watching the scene greatly admired the major saheb's forbearance; what they were witnessing, they thought, were the last gasps of a dying state, not an assertion of power, not Ravan's legitimate pride. There was otherwise no rationale for seating a commanding officer of the militia on the floor, and for so gratuitously insulting him.'

At this stage, Father rose to the status of Assistant Political Agent, and was transferred from Dhandhuka to Devgadh-Baria. It was now Father's turn to experience the inclement waters of Baria. Unlike his father, he had not fortified himself on free meals served at caste dinners in Surat. A feast in Surat would certainly have protected him from jungle fevers! In Devgadh-Baria, he came down with malaria and, towards the end, developed a bacterial foot disease usually associated with poverty. The parasite stings you from inside the foot and makes it swell so that you can barely get your shoes on. Until the very last days of his life, a tough layer of skin remained on the heel of his left foot. Glancing with good humour at his diseased foot, Father would wryly remark that

---

[101] The words are in Marathi in the original.

it was the 'corpse from Baria still clinging to me', a reference to the tale of the corpse that clung to King Vikram.[102]

Intense heat and intense cold were typical of the region. Father made plans to clear the thick forest. Land settlements were negotiated with all those who had legitimate rights, whether they be kings or commoners. Father's intentions were not to expel tenant farmers, nor did he want to fill the crown's coffers by harming the ruler's kinfolk; what he wanted was to bring larger areas of forestland under agriculture. The Kanbis and the Kachhyas were excellent farmers; forest dwellers counted as the worst. Father did not think it proper to fix separate revenue rates for each individual farmer; instead he settled rates according to the caste groups to which the farmer belonged. He would say, 'Experience taught me that to make life easy for the lower orders would only make them lazy. Should he be taxed less, the Koli will grow only enough food to fill his stomach; he will laze around the rest of the time. Only if charged higher rates will he exert himself, till his land and not abandon it time and again. In fact, when assessments are high, the yields double. As his primitive nature is subdued, as his needs increase, the creature improves. One should keep his real wellbeing in mind, including waiving taxes when times are bad.'

Baria's raja, the late Mansinghji, was a minor; so his mother the dowager queen acted as regent. The queen mother Majirajba was kind, unassuming and somewhat naïve, but she was under the influence of a Rajasthani woman named Motiba. Unfortunately, a Rajasthani woman of the royal stock values only one stage in life—the stage when she becomes regent. As a mere queen she is only one among many; she fears being dislodged by rivals; she fears old age; and when old age creeps up, she fears the pain of

---

[102] The reference is to the *Vetala Panchavimshati* or *Baital Pachisi,* a set of twenty-five nested stories about King Vikramaditya who is ordered by a wicked ascetic to fetch a corpse for a sacrifice. The corpse in question is inhabited by a *vetala,* a malignant spirit who entertains the king with stories, each of which ends in a riddle. Every time the king answers the riddle, the *vetala* flies back to its original location. See http://literature.syzygy.in/vikram-and-vampire (accessed 9 May 2021).

losing her good looks. On the other hand, as the royal queen mother she is in charge, she is the one who rules. The king's other wives fear their lord's death, they grieve his loss; but for the mother of the crown prince, widowhood counts as the crowning glory of life.

Motiba tried every trick she knew to bring Father under her control. In her brief experience of power, she hadn't come across anyone who did not succumb to the temptations of money, women or youth. In the end, however, she gave up trying to lure Father, and withdrew. Father personally arranged to have Mansinghji married to the daughter of Verisalji, the Maharaja of Rajpipla. At this time, Father raised the issue of gifts received by government servants and put his weight behind the decision requiring government servants to relinquish to the treasury gifts received from the bridal side. The ruling exempted the lowest grade employees from the order.

My revered mother related many stories of the forests surrounding Devgadh-Baria. Right in front of her house was a hillock where, like a policeman on his evening rounds, a tiger kept watch. The tiger was no man-eater, he did not attack human beings; even so, no one had the temerity to wander beyond the protected area of the fort. But what my mother found truly astonishing was not the tiger but the maize, for she had never seen anything like it before.

Mansinghji was a man of few words; by temperament he was placid, affectionate and a passionate adherent of the kshatriya code. Although not generally attracted to every frivolous revel, his love of hunting knew no bounds. The news of his untimely death grieved Father deeply.

In 1875, in the winter month of Magh, my elder sister Harsiddhagauri's marriage was fixed. At the age of thirteen and a half she was to marry Dr Batukram. The marriage turned out to be very fortunate, and my beloved father's love for his first-born soon embraced his son-in-law. Dr Batukram was the first doctor in the Nagar brahmin community. An upstart poetaster of the time sang, 'Dr Batukrambhai went all the way to England to pass the doctor's exam', because only a person who earns his degrees in England is entitled to the title of doctor. Dr Batukram joined the Diwan, Sir T. Madhavrao's services in Baroda and, until his untimely and grief-laden death, served the Gaekwad State with dedication. In turn, he received torchbearers and a regal umbrella as insignia of office.

The thread ceremonies of both my brothers took place in Bhavnagar at this time. The occasion might have been an empty ritual, had Father not been transferred at this stage to an area lacking educational facilities. So he sent both my brothers to Bhavnagar, where my maternal uncle was a judge, and where ceremonial rituals were observed. My brothers lived with their uncle until 1882, and respectfully fell in line with the strictest orthodoxies practised in a brahmin household.

In 1875, Father was transferred from Devgadh-Baria to Lunawada. He believed that unless the native princes changed their older way of life, their administration would remain partisan. Since he disapproved of the princes' manner of running their kingdoms, he vowed never to serve as principal administrator in states controlled by rajas. Nevertheless, he went on to hold several administrative positions on his own terms. Besides Lunawada, he was the chief administrator in Sunthrampur. While the Political Agent lived in Godhra, as the Assistant Political Agent Father was in complete charge of Lunawada and Sunth. A foot trail led from Lunawada to the pilgrim spot of Dakore, though the path was long and difficult. At the time he received a salary of four hundred and fifty rupees; prices were low, the land was thickly forested, nothing ostentatious was available and there were no inessential expenses.

Vakhtsinghji and Pratapsinghji, the rajas of Lunawada and Sunth, were minors. The young princes, affectionate, attractive and sharp young men, were students at Rajkumar College. Unfortunately, Pratapsinghji died in 1896 while Vakhtsinghji to this day rules Lunawada brilliantly.

Father spent five years in Lunawada; both my parents confessed that this period of middle age in their lives found them fulfilled and at peace. Lunawada enjoyed a pleasant climate, and my mother was able to move about freely without fear. Father was kept busy, the work was to his liking, nobody interfered with him, and he could work with concentration. 'My body filled out in Lunawada and my capacity for work grew. I read books on many different subjects, and even recovered older memories of books I had read as a youth,' he said.

On the 8th of January 1878, my second sister Sulochana was born. She was the image of my second brother Manubhai. No one I had met as a young man had a sharper intelligence, a more radiant and attractive countenance than my sister's. Later in life, while in Europe, when I beheld Raphael's painting of the Madonna in the Sistine Chapel, I was vividly reminded of my beloved sister Sulochana, whose name Father affectionately shortened to Susi.

My third sister Bahuvidya was born on the 12th of August 1879; it was the month of Shravan in the Indian calendar. She resembled my eldest sister; the same serene and serious appearance was hers. If there ever was a human being born to please our entire being, it was this third sister of mine. We affectionately called her 'Kiki', and, as she was a tiny little thing, her name suited her. If sister Sulochana spoke with sharp clarity, sister Bahuvidya's speech was all sweetness. Because I grew up in the company of these two sisters, there were strong bonds of affection between us.

In 1977, when Empress Victoria accepted the title of 'Kaiser-E-Hind', Barton Saheb attended the Delhi Durbar with a retinue of local rajas.[103] In his absence, Father temporarily held the position of Political Agent, and even lived for a period of two months in the Agent's mansion in Vadodara. In 1879, under similar circumstances, Father was nominated to the same position for another month. He divided the rest of his time between Lunawada and Sunth.

Officiating on state occasions as the queen mother, my mother presided over the thread ceremony of Raja Pratapsinghji. At the end of the ceremonials, soon after she left the palace to return home in a carriage, the bullocks stumbled and took flight; the cartwheel struck a boulder and the carriage fell into a ditch. My

---

[103] Lieutenant Colonel Barton, Acting Political Agent serving in Bhuj, Kutch, served at Rewakantha in 1876. See https://archive.org/stream/reportonadminis03statgoog/reportonadminis03statgoog_djvu. txt (accessed 9 May 2021).

mother's forehead and knees were badly injured. Superstitious folk murmured that the wandering ghost of the raja's stepmother caused the accident. We gave no credence to this superstition. My mother healed herself with massages, but the wound she received left a mark on her majestic forehead.

During the five years she spent at Lunawada and Sunth, my mother, whose beauty, vivacity and splendid bearing could grace any royal court, was instrumental in arranging the marriages of the two princes.

There were offerings made by the princes' kinsmen at the time of the *phuleka* ceremony. The very last offering was hers. Finally, after placing a *tilak* on the princes' foreheads, she bade them goodbye. My father with my brothers joined the bridegroom's party as it proceeded to the bride's house.

Vakhtsinghji married the daughter of a kinsman of Vanswada, the raja of Khandu. The road to Khandu was inaccessible, and it was a hot time of year. Adding to the difficulties along the way was the widespread fear of dacoits. Yet despite a large police escort, one cart which got separated from the procession was set upon by robbers, and a man was wounded by the brigand's arrows. As soon as the news reached them, the bridegroom's relatives and their horsemen armed with guns and spears rushed to the scene. But in vain; the dacoits had already fled the scene. So they had to return without arresting the brigands.

Besides this event, nothing worth noting occurred on the journey. On the return journey, however, after they crossed the river Anas, there was an outbreak of the dreaded cholera, and a great many of the poor cart drivers and musicians from Surat perished.

The very next year, in January of 1879, the Raja of Sunth, Pratapsinghji, married the Bhambhor chief's daughter. The chief belonged to the Salumbhara clan, of the main Udaypur branch. My brothers, joined by their fellow students (Shri Thakoreram and Shri Vasudharram), attended the wedding with Father. The road was equally difficult, but on this occasion, it also happened to be winter; so the party from Surat, used to a milder climate, suffered from the cold. Father describes what happened on the return journey from Bhambhora.

'Night had already set, and the cold held us in its grip. Accompanying us was the son of Mirza Yahya, a police officer. In weather such as this, Father usually wore an overcoat quilted with cotton padding and went about by *tonga*. For the occasion, the youth chose to wear an elegant *angarkha* made of the finest cotton *jamdani* weave. Anyhow, in the course of that journey the boy almost froze; he was barely conscious when we stopped by the edge of a lake. It was so cold that water left out in the open turned to ice. We lit a circle of small fires and placed him in the middle of the circle. Only after about an hour did he regain his senses.'

Father recounts his personal experiences at Pratapsinghji's nuptial ceremonies. 'During the *phuleka* ceremony, we almost met with a terrifying accident because of a conceited mahout. Fortunately, we were saved. This is what happened. To enter the bride's pavilion, we had to pass through a gateway made of clay bricks. Raja Pratapsingh and my two sons were seated on a tall elephant. The mahout said he had eaten his master's salt for a long time, during which he was able to train his elephants well; and so, as a token of gratitude to his master, and pride in his training, "I will drive the elephant on his bended knees through the gate. I will see to it that not for a moment will the bridegroom's feet touch the bare earth." Father argued with him, but to no avail. The mahout bowed and touched his feet. "Forgive me my lord," he begged, "I am willing to risk my neck should any harm befall."

'The elephant fell to his knees and, inch by inch, slid forward. It had just about reached the middle of the gateway when it decided to stand up. We don't really know the cause—whether the elephant's knees were injured or what, I can't say. Had the animal actually stood up, all three seated on the howdah would have been crushed. There were agitated shouts; spears were thrown from the back, goads hit the animal from the front, and the animal lurched forward. The rear end of the howdah, however, was completely demolished. Had the elephant not moved forward without standing up, the consequences cannot be imagined.'

The mahout did receive his wages, and even came forward to ask for a baksheesh. Father confessed that he had wanted to sentence him to a lifetime in jail, but this did not happen, for, in Nandshankar's words from *Karan Ghelo*: 'None dare strike a man who serves the mighty'. Just as Madhav, the saviour of Khizr Khan, could not be harmed, so also the elders thwarted Father's intentions.

At this juncture, it became necessary to assess the land revenues of Lunawada. Father had no experience in the survey and settlement of revenue lands, so Government appointed one Mr Hall to oversee the work. Hall Saheb was an exceedingly heavy-set man, and the heat in Gujarat was such that his brain got addled; so he was forced to return on furlough to his native lands. Since no one else was available to oversee the settlement, the responsibility was given to Father. Sir Theodore Hope, in a letter commending Father, writes:

> I had frequent occasions of meeting and conversing with him. He was a distinguished Mathematician, so I entrusted him with organising, translating or digesting for abridgment the *Manual of Surveying* based on the text-book of *Trigonometrical Survey of India*, which I published as a part of the Gujarati series. I believe it was used for a long time in the Department and in the Revenue Survey, by persons in training for employment.[104]

The opportunity to put his experience to the test now presented itself. Instead of awarding uniform rates across populations, Father assigned communal rates for different caste groups. In his official report to Government, he wrote: 'If a uniform system of rate is adopted for Kanbi and Koli villages, the pressure of the assessment may prove too heavy, except under the careful system of husbandry, in which the former castes are adept, and the latter deficient'. However, this suggestion was not accepted by Government, which decreased the taxes on Kanbis, increased rates for Kolis, and suggested that the rates be made uniform. Later on, Government must have realised its mistake. For now, in the United Provinces, the tax rates imposed on the lower orders is less than those on the Kurmi and Kachhiya castes. Nor

---

[104] The text of this letter, and other official government communications, reports and resolutions quoted hereafter in this chapter, are in English in the original, except where otherwise stated.

did Father honour the Government order and hurry to measure non-agricultural lands in the immediate vicinity of villages. In reviewing the report, Father eventually wrote that Government conceded all his points, and recorded its commendation in the following note:

> The commendation of Government should be conveyed to Mr Nandshankar for the careful and complete manner in which he has sent in his proposals.
>
> 24-7-1875   C. Gonne,
> Chief Secretary to Bombay Government

In a similar vein, in a letter dated 31 October 1876, the following resolution was passed: 'The careful way in which Mr Nandshankar has drawn up his report is creditable to him'.

Father, who did not skimp over his own household expenses, believed in stretching sixteen *annas* to twenty when it came to Government spending. 'I did not employ any middlemen as inspectors, because middlemen generally swallow revenue, harass the populace, create unnecessary work, and seldom admit to making mistakes. As a result, expenses were minimised. Trusting the man on the spot, establishing strict and appropriate controls, and providing adequate compensation were three principles in which I placed my faith. I had to work very hard, but the people were protected.' In all Father had spent Rupees 3809.4.9 on the survey of revenue lands at Lunawada, and Rupees 2935.8.2 on Sunth. With this, his surveys of the two principalities ended.

The following report of the Political Agent confirms Father's account of his work.

> The superintendence of these operations has been conducted by Nandshankar Tuljashankar, the assistant in charge of the two states, and his report will show how rapidly the work has progressed under his auspices. The entire cost of the survey and settlement operations during the year has been Rs 3809-4-9, and I trust the Government will consider that Mr Nandshankar is deserving of credit for the despatch and economy disclosed by his report.
>
> [Letter to C. Gonne, Esquire Chief Secretary,
> No. 1266/560, dated 26-12-1875]

In 1877, on the occasion of the Delhi Durbar, Father was honoured with the title of 'Rao Bahadur' and received a medal.

The time now arrived when the crown prince of Lunawada attained majority and his coronation drew near. So that young princes learn the art of governance, it was a practice in those days to give independent charge to princes only after a year's tutelage under an experienced government administrator. Father had stepped into the role of Joint Administrator in charge of Lunawada. The prince's education now complete, the Political Agent recommended that Father be sent to Sunth as Joint Administrator. Mr Woodward of the Political Department sent the following letter of recommendation on 28 January 1880:

> The assistant I ask for must be a thoroughly experienced and efficient officer, and such a man I should find in Mr Nandshankar Tuljashankar, now in charge of Lunawada and Sunth States, and nominally Assistant Political Agent. I have the highest opinion of this gentleman's qualification. As Government are aware, he has done excellent service in Rewakantha. He is a highly educated man, possesses a thorough knowledge of all branches of administrative and judicial work, has served in various capacities under British Government, has passed with credit the Higher Standard Examination—in short he is, in my opinion, capable of filling with credit any post that may be bestowed on a native gentleman.
>
> [Extract para 7 from letter No. 179 of 28-1-1880,
> from the Collector and Political Department,
> sent with Mr Woodward's compliments][105]

A few days later, a letter confirming the appointment arrived.

> Government have in their resolution, Confidential No. 956 of 18-2-1880, agreed to the Political Agent's proposals that Mr Nandshankar should jointly administer the state of Sunth with

---

[105] Hillersden Woodward served as assistant collector, magistrate and forest settlement officer in the Bombay Presidency, 1871–1898. See Great Britain India Office 1902: 589, https://archive.org/details/indialistandind00offigoog/page/n626 (accessed 10 May 2021).

the young Raja, from May next. Government have also, in the Resolution No. 910 of the 11th instant, on the revised establishment of the Panch Mahals and Rewakantha, recommended the appointment of a Political Assistant to the Collector and Agency. If the appointment is sanctioned, then I can only reiterate my hope that Mr Nandshankar may be gazetted to it. Government are fully aware of the very high opinion not only I, but all my predecessors in this Agency, have of Mr Nandshankar and I deem it therefore superfluous to recapitulate our esteem for him both as a gentleman and a public servant.

> [Extract para 7 of letter No. 250/20 of 18-3-1880,
> from Mr Woodward to the Secretary to Government,
> Political Department]

Astrologers declared the morning hour of the seventh day of the waning moon of the month of Shravan, in Samvat 1936, the auspicious moment for the coronation of Raja Vakhtsinghji. On that day, Father handed over charge to the reigning king. He would later say: '*Jāto mamāyam viśadah prakāmam pratyarpitanyās ivāntarātmā*: This great calm has entered my inner being now that my obligation to what I held in trust is fulfilled'.[106]

The people of Lunawada grieved to see Father leave. The Queen Mother of Lunawada earnestly and with great courtesy requested Father to let my mother remain in Lunawada, and proceed to Sunth without her. 'The waters and climate of Sunth were in no way more salubrious than Baria's', is how she pleaded her case; 'On the contrary, the heat there is more oppressive', she said. Father's affection for his family, however, made it impossible for him to leave wife and children behind, and so he did not accept the state's courteous invitation.

The same day Lord Shiva in his form as Lord Vikhteshwar was to be consecrated in Lunawada. My devout mother looked forward with delight to the pomp and ceremony attending the end of the celebrations. At that moment, Father received a private message from Khushalraibhai, saying that Reeves Saheb wanted Father's services for Kutch. He described the conditions

---

[106] From *The Abhjnāna Śākuntalam of Kālidāsa* 4.22 (see Kale 1969).

obtaining in Kutch, adding in a postscript, 'it seems that all of you will be settling down in Kutch'. The anxieties festering in my mother's heart, she admits, 'by God's grace, now disappeared. He left for Sunth, and I remained in Lunawada to organise the household. The merchants there, Sheth Moti Jani and Ranchhod Ludher, always remembered Father's friendship, and never failed to welcome him'.

In 1896, accompanied by his entire family, Father attended the nuptial ceremonies of the crown prince, Ranjeetsinhaji. Reflecting on the affectionate regard in which he was held by the Raja and Rani of Lunawada, I can well imagine the manner in which they would have honoured his return as an elder! Dolatram Kriparam Pandya was the Diwan of Lunawada, whose hospitality the family then enjoyed.

Dolatram records Father's achievements in Sunth in the following letter addressed to me:

> The administration of the state was handed over to the present Raja Saheb on the recommendation of your father. I did not succeed him, but it so happened that many important reforms which your father had initiated had to be completed by me. Besides, questions of great importance to the state on which he had prepared his minutes had also to be disposed of by me during my tenure of office. The work he had accomplished during his term of office, and which was accomplished on the lines laid down by him, when taken together forms a sum total of duties wisely and faithfully performed, of which all can be justly proud.
>
> I particularly remember a case relating to the state's jurisdiction over a village called Lambho; the line of argument which your father had chalked out, and which I had to adopt before the Border Court, alone saved the village for the State. Although I vividly remember that when I first represented it before the Court, I was ridiculed for adopting an untenable line of argument.
>
> Your father was trusted by Government, respected by the chief and his family and loved by the people. The impress of his work will long remain in the history of Lunawada, if it ever escapes the fleeting memories of frail men.[107]

---

[107] This letter is in English in the original.

Father's life was linked to the sea as if a debt between them had been incurred over several lifetimes. In accordance with this law, he received orders to proceed to Kutch as Diwan. A man who seldom spoke about his work nor knew how to boast of his achievements; indeed, self-praise in any form was alien to his very being. And though he often talked of his experiences as headmaster, I seldom heard him mention his work with Government. True, my mother, then totally absorbed in looking after her children, spoke about the time she spent at court, but without any real interest in its intrigues. So she wasn't of much help to me regarding the time they spent in Kutch.

When Father was still an administrator in Sunth, he received the following order:

No. 4547

Political Department
Bombay Castle, 22nd September 1880

Letter from the Political Agent Kutch, No. 96, dated the 11th September 1880, forwarding for information with reference to this Dept. No. 4295 of 8th instant, a copy of this letter to Rao Bahadur Nandshankar Tuljashankar in which he informed him of his appointment as Diwan of Kutch and requesting that Government will allow Mr Nandshankar to join the above appointment in Kutch with the least practicable delay.

Resolution copy should be forwarded to the Political Agent Rewakantha who should be requested to allow R. B. Nandshankar Tuljashankar to join his appointment at Kutch with the least practicable delay.

Chief Secretary to Government

No. 845 of 1880

Copy forwarded to Mr Nandshankar with a request that he may proceed to join his new appointment at Kutch, handing over charge of Sunth to the Deputy Assistant as a temporary measure.

Political Agent, Rewakantha

At the time of Father's posting in Kutch, the crown prince, Sawai Bahadur Khengarji, was a minor. A Council of Regents ran the government. The Political Agent sat as Head of the Council; the Diwan and the prince's maternal uncle Raosaheb Jalamsinh sat as members. The late Bahadur Manibhai Jasbhai was then Diwan; but since Manibhai did not get along with the Political Agent, Reeves Saheb, he was moved as Native Assistant to Vadodara. Reeves Saheb suspected that Manibhai belonged to the Dowager Queen Naniba's party, and further, that Manibhai wanted the young and impressionable prince to marry the princess of Jhala, and so remain trapped in the grip of his uncle, Jalamsinh.

Father was not particularly keen to go to Kutch as he had never visited the area. He believed that the approach to the state was difficult and that its inhabitants were reputed to be wily. But the position was prestigious and the salary good; it was a unique opportunity besides to be of service to the people. On the other hand, my revered mother, always keen to be admired at court, was enthusiastic about the new posting.

Father traveled to Kutch via Vadodara. Manibhai, the former Diwan of Kutch, met him at the station and gave him a detailed account of what had gone on in Kutch during his tenure. Father gave Manibhai his word that his intention in accepting the position was not to point fingers or to find fault with anyone's shortcomings. Indeed, he had not sought after the post; and therefore, there ought not to be any ground on either side for mistrust.[108]

Immediately upon arrival in Kutch, Father discovered that the atmosphere at the Kutch court was entirely different from what he had known in Rewakantha. He was a man who preferred a tough and direct way of dealing with issues, which was not the case at the court in Kutch. His deputy was Mr Bhagvat and the head of revenue was his old friend Khushalraibhai.

Major Reeves was an obstinate, zealous, competent, forceful and irascible man. Having worked in Kathiawad, he was well-acquainted with palace intrigues. A well-known rumour among

---

[108] Manibhai Jashbhai Desai (1844–1900) was Diwan of Kutch and later, Diwan of Baroda. See: http://www.theindianportrait.com/artwork/ diwan-manibhai-jashbhai-desai/ (accessed 10 May 2021).

the people had it that the late Prince Raosaheb Shri Pragmalji had left word on his deathbed that his heir should not marry the princess of Jhala. The Queen Mother Naniba, on the other hand, a clever woman of obdurate mind, belonged to the Jhala clan. She had vowed that if her son is to marry, he would wed none other than Jalamsinh's daughter. The result was a rift between Naniba and Major Reeves. And so, the impression grew that Manibhai was of the Queen Mother's party. Due to this supposed enmity, and for other reasons of state, Manibhai had had to move out as Diwan of Kutch.

From the very beginning, Father intended to serve at Kutch for only three years, that is, until the crown prince was installed as the ruling monarch. Further, he was determined not to serve as diwan under any prince. 'I always wanted to work for the people's welfare. This was my one opportunity to serve without being supervised from above,' he declared. However, Naniba mistrusted him, not that he paid her much heed. 'As time went by, she firmly believed that I was responsible for Manibhai's departure. Had I not helped him out, Major Reeves would have been forced to submit to Naniba's will. Intrigue—silent—abounded. To secure Manibhai's return, Naniba's brother Jalamsinh threw money around. I believed that for three years at least their plans would not succeed, after which the prince would come of age; and then, I thought, they would go their way and I mine.'

Nandshankar set about removing the practice of crony appointments soon after arriving in Kutch. He worked hard, remaining at his desk until almost six in the evening and sometimes even later. After the day's work he walked the short distance to his family and there, in a world unacquainted with either flattery or intrigue, he lost himself. Many tried their best to draw him out; those who came to the house to speak ill of the former diwan were rebuffed: 'I am not Manibhai's antagonist; I do not wish to hear ill of him'.

Father's experience in Kutch was novel, very different from his experience of the court at Rewakantha. If men would speak with such malice about an upright officer like Manibhai, whom would they not stoop to malign? The truth of the old Sanskrit adage, '*atyādarah śankanīyah*: exaggerated courtesy should be suspect', was brought home to him.

Echoing the words in *Mudrarakshasa*[109]—'*madhu tiṣṭhati jivhāgre hṛdaye tu halāhalam*: honey sits on the tip of the tongue, but there's poison in the heart'—he maintained that Kautilya's unethical policies had cast a shadow over the country's affairs, to the extent that trust between people was lost. If the habit of flattery takes hold, lies inevitably follow; there is a gap between your inner feelings and your outer expression. You feel one way and show something else.

At this time, Father would have recalled the words from *Karan Ghelo*, on Madhav's fall from power: 'His old friends, those who claimed kinship with him, those who acquired dignity through their friendship with him, those who took off their shoes everyday outside the door to his house, those who called out "Bapji, Bapji" whenever he passed by were nowhere to be seen'. Nor did Nandshankar realise when he wrote these words that he himself would come face to face with the very same reality one day.

His heart at this time was very full. Of measured wants and joyous heart, he put his trust in God, and led a frugal, pure and healthful life. Though he was forty-five years old, an extraordinary capacity for work still remained his. A report written by Major Reeves to Gonne Saheb, Chief Secretary to Government of Bombay, on 7 June 1881, reads:

> Rao Bahadur Nandshankar Tuljashankar, the new Diwan, is a protégé of Mr Hope's and his antecedents justify the expectation that his nomination will prove in the highest degree beneficial to the Province. [Para 73]
>
> In all these matters, the Regency has received very great assistance from the experience, tact and energy of R. B. Nandshankar, the present Diwan of Kutch, who by the laborious manner in which he works, the punctuality with which he hears appeals and petitions, the care he exhibits to do justice in every

---

[109] A well-known Sanskrit play by Vishakhadatta about realpolitik and diplomatic intrigue, dated variously between the fourth to sixth centuries CE, featuring the ruthless and shrewd minister Kautilya or Chanakya as kingmaker.

case brought to his notice, and the anxiety he displays to preserve all the ancient rights of the Durbar has given general satisfaction.

[Letter of H. N. Reeves, (Major) Political Agent
Kutch, to Mr C. Gonne dated 7-6-1881]

Proficiency born of experience, skill in acting appropriately according to what the moment requires, competence, well-regulated conduct, a determination not to delay justice, and concern for the welfare of the people were prominent virtues of his character. Father considered it disloyal to override the rights of the princely state in order to please someone in power; on occasion he even battled to secure the rights of the princely state. He could not care less if his actions displeased his English officers.

The Annual Report of the State of Kutch, Order No. 6145, of 16 December 1881 states:

> The Report of the new Diwan exhibits a well-ordered and satisfactory administration including many modern improvements on the model of the British Institutions, but preserving on the whole the characteristics of a Native State Government. The Diwan evidently bestows great attention on public instruction, as might be expected from his antecedents.

In *The Republic*, Plato wrote that if you succeed in turning a wise philosopher away from his role as teacher and prevail on him to take on the task of governance, it should be great good fortune for the kingdom. Just as elements are purified when passed through fire, passions touched by wisdom lose their coarser aspect and acquire grace. So also, Father, a teacher whose peaceable life was thrown into a whirl of activity by Hope Saheb, acquired the kind of grace that wisdom matures. If experienced men join government, what good would it not achieve for the people! This was the kind of thinking that had made Hope Saheb convince Father that it was his duty to turn away from a seventeen-year-old passion for teaching and enter into a new kind of life.

But can the residual traces of early experience ever be forgotten? Not only for the sake of show, but in order to really get every detail right, Father endeavoured to lift the standards of education wherever he was posted. The sentence from the Government Annual Report just mentioned—'as might be expected from his antecedents'—refers to Father's early life spent as teacher.

Father was convinced beyond doubt that the British system of governance was far too expensive, as salaries alone consumed a very large portion of revenues available to the state. He favoured employing a smaller number of well-paid administrators and clerks. With a smaller administrative structure there is a danger that those who hold the reins of governance might introduce extensive changes based solely on their own particular predilections; there is the additional possibility of one-man rule. Were this to happen, the administration would not run like a well-oiled machine, at uniform speed. Instead, at each step it would look for a clever decision-maker.

Despite these shortcomings, the administration is freed from the whirlpool of traditional bureaucracies. Indeed, if the yearning for liberation is fulfilled only at the end of eighty-four rounds of births and deaths, its value diminishes! Similarly, even if government's purpose is achieved after wandering through circle after circle of routines, it pleases none. Father avoided the faults of the British system of administration while simultaneously rejecting the unregulated freedom of working according to whim, which is a marked feature of administration in princely states. Moreover, he brought the top officials within control of the law.

He believed that the lower rungs of the administration should be bound by the strictest rules, and that department heads be given greater authority, lest their creative intelligence fall into disuse and they get used to spinning the time away. The chief duty of the diwan is to keep an eye on these low-level administrators by confining them within the circle of higher laws. In the annual 1881–1882 report on the administration of Kutch, the resolution of 9 October 1882 read as follows:

> The administration of Kutch in the year under report has been entirely satisfactory and reflects credit on the Political Agent, Col. Goodfellow and on the Diwan, R. B. Nandshankar, whose careful and elaborate statement is now before the Government.

Accordingly, in an annual report of the year 1882–1883, a Government resolution was adopted on 3 November 1882, which reads:

> In September 1882, the Council of Administration took the place of the Council of Regency in Kutch, H. H. the Rao being submitted to a share in the management of the state. The total income of the State was two lacs more than that of the year before, amounting to a gross aggregate of Rs 1,804,050. There was an increment in the Land Revenue by Rs 117,803 and this was due to careful management and good harvests of cotton and grain. The total expenditure was Rs 1,36,8386. Or Rs 1372 less than in the previous year. Mandavi Bunder has been improved, good roads have been constructed, and now remains the question of the establishment of good communication between Kutch and Kathiawad. A Modified Postal Code and Criminal Procedure Code were introduced.
>
> The abolition of certain import and export duties and revising others and the assimilation of weights and measures throughout the province are creditable to the administration. Education has made satisfactory progress. The attendance at the night school has improved and the Bhuj School of Art shows improvement both in efficiency and numbers. The Governor-in-Council is glad to bear testimony to the ability with which Mr Nandshankar conducted the administration of the province and to the benefit to Kutch, which has resulted from his careful and economic control over all the Departments of the State.
>
> C. Gonne
> Chief Secretary, Government of Bombay

Having once undertaken such Herculean schemes, Father implemented them successfully in a very short time. When Turgot (1727–1781)[110] was handed the responsibility for ordering men to

---

[110] Anne-Robert-Jacque Turgot was an administrator and economist of France. He was a Physiocrat, member of a group of French economists of the eighteenth century who held that agriculture was the main source of national wealth. In *Reflections on the Production and Distribution of Wealth*, Turgot argued against government intervention in regulating the economy. See: https://mises.org/library/brilliance-turgot (accessed 11 May 2021).

be hanged, he said that since the tenure of chief administrators is short, and there is much to do, he should do what is possible in God's name. Phillips Saheb was the Political Agent at this time. The Dowager Queen Naniba exerted pressure on him to bring back Manibhai as diwan. Not being a man of strong opinion, Phillips Saheb supported the queen and forwarded the request to Government. Government replied that Rao Bahadur Nandshankar was sent to Kutch on the understanding that he would hold the position for a period of three years. Should his time in Kutch be cut short, he would suffer monetary losses amounting to ten thousand rupees.

Sir James Ferguson, the Governor of Bombay, believed it would be improper to act against the inclinations of a native state. Not wanting to interfere in the state's affairs, he did not rule against it, although he did advise that Father be allowed to serve in Kutch so long as the crown prince remained a minor. The ruling infuriated Naniba, who would not be shaken from her original demand that Manibhai be immediately returned to Kutch as Diwan. So, on Colonel Phillip's recommendation, Government agreed to make up the monetary loss of ten thousand rupees that Father under the circumstances would suffer, and Father reverted to his earlier office as Assistant Political Agent of Rewakantha. The Queen Mother agreed, in turn, to make up the lost sum; she was convinced that until Manibhai was made diwan, her plans for her son's betrothal would not succeed. Mahipatrambhai, or 'Rao Saheb' as we called him, presided over the Council at this time; through him a message was sent which said that in appreciation of the excellent service rendered by him, Rao Bahadur Diwan Saheb Nandshankar was to be awarded a gift of rupees ten thousand in place of the losses he might have sustained. In accordance with the above settlement, the following notification was published in the *Kutch Durbar Gazette*.[111]

Kutch Durbar Gazette
The Principality of Kutch

On Sunday, the 2nd day of the waning moon of the month of Ashad, in the year 1940 of the Vikram Era.

---

[111] The notification is in English in the original.

Notification

Rao Bahadur Nandshankar Tuljashankar resigns his post of Diwan in favour of the former Diwan Rao Bahadur Manibhai Jasbhai who assumes charge from tomorrow. The President of the Council of Administration cannot allow Rao Bahadur Nandshankar to leave the province without bidding him farewell publicly and expressing the high sense of the obligation the State is under to him for the successful manner in which he has administered its affairs during his tenure of office. As a mark of their appreciation of the good work done by him the Council of Administration, including His Highness the Rao, unanimously voted that 10,000 Rs should be presented to Rao Bahadur Nandshankar on his leaving, and His Excellency the Governor has graciously recorded his approval of this gift. The name of Rao Bahadur Nandshankar will long be remembered by all classes in this province with respect and affection and in bidding him now farewell, the Council of Administration feel assured that he will again soon occupy a position commensurate with his merits.

Bhuj, 31-7-1883

A. M. Phillips (Lt. Col)

Below the official letter, Colonel Phillips added a personal note:[112]

President of the Council of Administration
   I have much pleasure in reporting that he has aided me loyally and energetically in all measures of reform that have been introduced and that it is mainly due to his exertion that the Revenues of the State have increased in all departments.

12-7-83

A. M. Phillips (Lt. Col.)
Ag. Pol. Agent

Phillips Saheb was aware that my revered mother was awaiting the birth of a child. So he wrote the following confidential letter[113] to my father regarding the official letter he had received from Government.

---

[112] This note is in English in the original.
[113] This letter is in English in the original.

Confidential

To Rao Bahadur Nandshankar Tuljashankar
Diwan of Kutch,

Camp Mandvi
10-4-1883

Dear Sir,

I have communicated to you personally the content of the Government Confidential Letter No. 1706 of the 6th instant, and request you will be so good as to let me know on what date it will be convenient for you to hand over charge of your office to Mr Manibhai Jasbhai.

You will bear in mind that I am instructed by Government to inform you of the necessity of terminating your tenure of office with all the consideration that is due to you. I am directed to make it clear to you and the Durbar that the concurrence of the Government to His Highness the Rao's wishes to see Mr Manibhai reappointed in no way implies the belief that you are less fitted for the Dewanship; also that to the best of H. E.'s knowledge you have discharged your duties in a most efficient and creditable manner.

I remain,
Yours faithfully,
A. M. Phillips
Ag. P. A.

Father wrote back to say that it would be convenient for him to hand over charge towards the end of July. Because of Reeves Saheb's obstinacy, Diwan Bahadur Manibhai was removed; due to Naniba's obstinacy, Father was removed, and Manibhai returned to become Diwan for a second time. Neither Father nor Manibhai on account of their personal virtues or faults was responsible for the conflict, nor were they antagonists. The conflict arose because Reeves Saheb and Naniba each wanted their personal opinion to prevail. In any case Father did not want to serve as Diwan beyond that year once the crown prince attained majority. He was recompensed for the monetary loss through a Government order. Reeves Saheb held that Government should forcefully intervene to reform administration in native states; Phillips Saheb followed a non-interventionist policy. Naniba died on the night of 28 May 1883, satisfied that the order to return Manibhai to Kutch had been executed.

When Father was offered the position of Diwan of Kutch, his friends and relatives had advised him to appoint trusted friends and close relatives to positions of power in the state, which they believed to be the chief instrument of effective governance in a native state. Father thought the advice improper. A partisan administration has its advantages, but also its drawbacks. Father told his friends that he wasn't going to Kutch to establish dynastic rule, nor had he been given a lifetime's appointment. 'When the crown prince attains majority, British control over the state administration ends; after that I do not wish to remain Diwan. "Once the prince attains majority, then what? Goodbye to me and goodbye to my government job; my friends out of Kutch, running hither and thither in search of new livelihoods." The thought does not please me. Nor is it correct that I, a foreigner, with neither a home in a village nor a farm within the state's boundaries, should position my own people in government while displacing local courtiers who since birth have stood to gain from the state's prosperity. I see no justice in this.'

'Kutch should be for the people of Kutch' was his principled stand. And so the people of the region remained satisfied, even enthusiastic, throughout his tenure. By conducting affairs strictly according to law he demonstrated that deceit has no role in a just administration.

That intrigue and deceit were high up on the scale in the administration of Kutch of that period was a widely held belief. It was a belief that Father was to prove false. The custom before he arrived was for Government officials to hover round the Diwan's residence twenty-four hours of the day, promoting secret schemes and spreading false rumours. Father put an end to these gatherings by establishing the practice of meeting only those who had genuine work to attend to, and that too at the Diwan's official quarters, not at his residence. As a result, along with the lower rungs of the administration, the power of those who carried tales and slander and spread rumours was broken.

Father did not take a single official with him to Kutch. When he met the previous Diwan's trusted officials he was warned to be wary, to keep them at arm's length. But he did no such thing. Insisting on getting the very same officials to work for him, he demonstrated through a straightforward and authoritative manner of administering the state that if the Diwan is honest in his dealings, there ought to be no grounds for suspicion, even if people around him spy on each other, intrigue and quietly sow seeds of discord. The generosity of his governance evoked the affection and gratitude of the administrators as well as the people of Kutch.

Father's elevation to the status of Diwan made him neither proud nor egotistical; his innate straightforward temperament remained with him throughout. If he happened to travel to Bombay on work, he stayed at the bungalow of his former pupil Bhimji, next to the Cawasji Patel Tank, and not in Walkeshwar, where wealthy merchants of Bombay lived. When visiting the Chief Secretary, he did not ride in a carriage drawn by two horses with a *jamadar*, whip in hand, seated by his side; instead he rode in a rented Victoria. And when Bhimji jokingly suggested that he ride with more ceremony, 'attended by a whip-carrying groom', his response was, 'To whom do these peons and police belong? They are mine only so long as I work for Kutch. Are they going to accompany me when I retire? There is value only in living according to what one can always afford'. He carried this simplicity with him to his house in Dumas when he retired.

I was born in 1883 on 3 June, in the port of Mandvi of the Kutch principality. My dear mother, desirous of fresh air, was visiting the port city, and so my pet name was Dariyalal.

In 1881, in the month of Mah, at seventeen years of age, my elder brother Markandrao was married. My maternal grandfather was enthusiastic about the marriage, as my brother would be marrying into his unfortunately widowed daughter's former husband's family. The marriage was celebrated with great fanfare; my dear mother enjoyed every pleasure that was her due. From Bhavnagar, Gagabhai and several others of my maternal grandfather's friends attended. Nandshankar's lack of ostentation, his astute judgement and dedication to duty impressed the elders of Kathiawad society. Nandshankar himself praised Gagabhai's extraordinary memory, his clear speech and his competence. 'Gagabhai was certainly a fair-minded Diwan', he used to say.[114]

In 1883, on 2 August, Father again took charge of the position he had previously held at Godhra.

> Political Department,
> Bombay Castle, 26-7-83

> Whether Rao Bahadur Nandshankar reverts to his position of Assistant Political Agent in Rewakantha on the 1st prox or whether some other suitable post has been found for him?

In response to this query raised by the Political Agent in Rewakantha, there was an official resolution which read as follows:

> Resolution: 'Rao Bahadur Nandshankar should for the present revert to his appointment of Assistant Political Agent in Rewakantha. It would however be very desirable to find some other suitable post for this officer. The Commissioners of Central and Northern Division should be reminded of the case.'

After handing over charge in Kutch, on their way to Godhra the family stopped in Gondal, where Nandshankar's childhood friend Jayashankar Lalshankar Rawal, who also happened to be my dear mother's uncle, served as chief administrator. Despite a somewhat ostentatious appearance, Jayashankar was an able and solid administrator, even though the responsibility for the prosperity of the population, together with the necessity of thrift, weighed heavily on him. Nandshankar's Bhavnagar friends believed Jayashankar to be a good prime minister, but that his administration lacked flair; it was dry, insipid, without colour. Father travelled to Bhavnagar next and enjoyed short visits with Gagabhai Samaldas and with my uncle Vitthalbhai. Governance in Kathiawad was a completely different matter. He would jokingly

---

[114] Gagabhai Samaldas was the dynamic Diwan of Bhavnagar State. In *Mari Hakikat*, Narmadashankar mentions a conversation in which Gagabhai lists his contributions to the state (see Joshi 2010).

say that the people of Kutch admire the Buddhidhans, while we on our part have respect for Vidyachatur's way.[115]

Father was next obliged to spend almost a year around Mevas in the Panchamahals. My mother spent most of her time in Surat while he travelled around the district, re-reading books on history, and writing extensive notes for the District Gazettes, which he then forwarded to its editors. Father also mentioned how much he enjoyed reading the novels of Meadows Taylor. It took him only a day each to finish reading *Sita* and *Tara*. He attended the nuptial ceremonies of Ramanbhai, the learned son of his good friend Rao Saheb Mahipatram. On returning to Surat, he unfortunately fell victim to the dreaded cholera, from which, through God's grace, he recovered. He took a month's leave and spent it in a house situated on the banks of a river belonging to his friend Dr Dolatram. The experience of living on the river bank convinced him that on retiring he would move to the countryside.

At this time the state of Rajpipla, ruled over by Gambhirsinghji, was in complete disarray. The treasury was empty, the people oppressed, and there was no concern for their welfare as the licentious Raja was completely absorbed in marrying one woman after another. The Government at this point stepped in to stop the mismanagement and ordered a joint administration between the Government and the principality of Rajpipla. In this new dispensation, Father was transferred to Nandod as Assistant Administrator and Chief Revenue Officer. He took charge of this position on 28 August 1884.

The Government of Bombay Presidency sent out dispatches in all directions of the Bombay Presidency, requesting that a position be found suited to Father's intellectual achievements and rich experience, where his work would prove most effective. Father thus became the pillar on which the joint administration of Raja Gambhirsinghji and Major Stace Saheb rested. A great deal of work

---

[115] Buddhidhan and Vidyachatur are characters in Govardhanram Tripathi's *Sarasvatichandra*. Both men occupy high positions in government, but their administrative styles are very different. While Buddhidhan uses flattery and pretense to manipulate his way to the top, Vidyachatur is wary of flattery and intrigue (see Tripathi 2015: 67–68; 255–256).

lay ahead. It was important to resolve the tangled dispute between Government and Sagbara with respect to the forest boundary. Nor was it easy to attract money to the state treasury, to define boundaries, and create faith in governance among the subjects. Several officials of Rajpipla were from Surat: Jahangirshah, who belonged to the well-known Modi family of Surat, was Chief Judge; the Police Superintendent was Jahangirshah Ardeshar Talyerkhan (Father's old friend Sheth Dinshawji's brother).

Mr Spence, the Collector of Godhra who was also the Political Agent for Rewakantha, wrote in his annual report:

> Mr Nandshankar has carried on the duties with marked ability and there can be no doubt he is drawn away in such an appointment.

The hard work now began to tell on Father's health, which had not completely recovered its earlier robustness after the dreaded attack of cholera. Now his eyesight became weak. At this stage he decided to draw on his pension and retire. He was fifty-five years old. He wrote officially asking to be relieved from government service. His superiors recommended an appointment as translator of oriental languages, but he rejected the offer.

In 1890, in the month of Vaishakh, we left Nandod for Surat. My thread ceremony was performed there, along with the marriages of both my sisters. My second sister Smt. Sulochana married Shri Veerprasad Taptiprasad's elder son; my third sister Smt. Bahuvidya wed Shri Harisukhram Manekram's elder son. The fathers of both grooms were former students of Father's.

Shri Veerprasad served in the municipal department of Home Affairs of the Bombay Presidency. His emoluments were more than a thousand rupees a month. He was considered clever, virtuous, and he revered Father. I remember well my father in his old age attending barefoot Veerprasadji's death ceremony; his eyesight was failing, he was weak and barely able to walk by himself.

Harisukhram, the only son of Father's old friend Makubhai, was a district judge. A person of few words and tranquil temper, he was a saintly man who met his end in 1902. God alone knows why the intellectual lustre that shone on the faces of both these men has disappeared entirely from the men of our caste.

The happy times that I spent in Nandod still echo in my memory. We frequently travelled with Father on camp duty. While he remained immersed in his work, we enjoyed ourselves. Both my brothers joined us in Shoolpan. Here, Father's earlier joy in swimming revived, and we had a great deal of fun at the waterfalls in Mokhdi.

Rumour abounded here of a brahmin who wanders about with wounded head, surrounded by buzzing bees. The Bheel people see him and say, 'He is Ashwathama!' Often on sighting a bee, a Bheel would say, 'There he goes'. But to our eyes brimming with civilisation, the image of Ashwathama with bees remains invisible.

The popular saying, 'The parrots of Shoolpan are beauteous' is not untrue, for parrots here are indeed enchanting. From bank to bank, we wandered along the Narmada. We visited all the pilgrim spots on the river bank—Shukdev, Vyas, Anasuya, Shuklatirth, Channod, Karnali and so on.

In order to convey the administration's view of Father's competence, I end this chapter with a reference to Mr Maconochie, who writes:

> In concluding my general survey of the revenue administration of the state, I must express my high sense of the valuable services of Rao Bahadur Nandshankar, Assistant to the Joint-Administration and Chief Revenue Officer. His ability, his power of work, his carefulness and accuracy, his long experience, his zeal, his absolute sincerity of mind and purpose render him a tower of strength to the administration. I feel that no words can add anything to the name and fame of a veteran officer who made long ago such a reputation for himself as Mr Nandshankar, but it is my duty to acknowledge with cordial thanks the admirable way in which he performs his duties, the constant support and assistance he has given me and the many occasions on which I have been indebted to him for his advice. His annual report is a model of excellence, distinguished ability, minute mastery of details, and broad grasp of general principles and forms a most interesting resume of the conditions and resources of the State.

31-7-1887

A. F. Maconochie (I.C.S.)
Joint Administrator Rajpipla State

After Mr Maconochie's departure came Mr Shewan Saheb (1887–1894).[116] A pious man, with an excellent knowledge of Greek literature, he held Father in high regard, and says the following about his work.

> The assistant administrator's tour was broken by leave rendered by the state of his eyes. The Rao Bahadur informs me that he intends to retire from Government Service in the course of a few months. He has been associated with the work of this administration since its establishment and successive officers have certified to the zeal and sincerity of purpose with which he has laboured for the good of the State. His experience, ability and capacity for work and his sound advice have always been of the greatest value to me. His kindly presence will long be remembered with affection by the people of Rajpipla.
>
> A. Shewan I.C.S.
> Administrator, Rajpipla State
> [Extract para 149 of the Rajpipla State
> Administration Report for the year ending
> 31-3-89]

When I decided to write this biography, I requested Mr Shewan to send me reminiscences of Father. He responded in the following letter.

> Dear Mr Mehta,
> It is indeed now nearly, when I think, twenty years since I parted from your father on his retirement from Rajpipla, and I fear my memory has become somewhat dim as to particulars of the excellent work which he did for that state. But I have never forgotten what a sense of security his great knowledge of Gujarat revenue practice gave to me who was a Deccani. The regeneration of the revenue system (so to call it) of Rajpipla was his work. A good deal of it was done before I joined. But I well remember his

---

[116] Alexander Shewan was a British administrator of the Rajpipla State from 1887–1894. See Great Britian India Office 1902: 554, https://archive.org/details/indialistandind00offigoog/page/n592 (accessed 11 May 2021).

report on the settlement of the alienations. It was a most valuable document and, if my memory serves me true, the proposals were adopted by Government *en bloc*. But it was not merely his great knowledge and experience that rendered him so valuable an assistant. Added to this were great soundness of judgement and an influence with the people which was remarkable and unfailing. His industry and uprightness and single eye to the welfare of the State had won their confidence from the first. To me, it was more than half the battle won to have such an authority to depend on. His retirement was a great loss to the State and to me personally but the work was done, one might say, before he left or at least he had laid the foundations on which others could build. I imagine the name of Nandshankar Tuljashankar has not been forgotten in Rajpipla by those who were cognisant of his worth and are still alive. I myself remember with gratitude the wise adviser and valued friend. I had the good fortune to be associated in India with many native officers, my connection with whom it is a pleasure to recall. None of them has retained a higher place in my regard than your father.

We, that is, Mrs Shewan and I, remember your mother well. I am glad to hear your father has a son in the Civil Service and we wish you all success in it.

Yours sincerely,
(sd.) A. Shewan

The above shows how Father won the complete trust, respect and affection from the people, and honours and high regard from the government. His capacity for work, his dedication to service of the people, his firm views, competence and conduct won everyone's heart. He demonstrated the truth of the belief that in the Nagar community, the gift for statesmanship is imbibed with mother's milk. If I were to name three individuals of the nineteenth century in whom this esteemed quality is supremely embodied, it would be no exaggeration to name Gagabhai, Manibhai and Father himself.

On 20 August 1880, Dadabhai Naoroji, India's elder statesman, wrote the following in a note to Gagabhai, Kathiawad's elder statesman: 'My view is and has been all along, as you are aware, that every Native State, if administered carefully and honestly, should share a far greater degree of prosperity than the British Provinces can ever attain. Everything is in favour of Native States'.[117]

Father shared Dadabhai's views. It is supremely important, he believed, to serve in the public administration of Princely States, lest our own administrative genius fall into disuse. Administering states according to native systems is far less expensive because the system does not require the long and hierarchical ladder of authority. Native governance is based on friendly understanding; for Indians realise where the shoe pinches, and provide easy remedies for the pain. However, our people undoubtedly must learn from the English that a sense of duty is all important, and must be venerated. Independent judgement must like a river's course be kept in check; if it is allowed to overflow, total destruction will result. Patronage must be rooted out, talent encouraged, flattery consigned to flames, and partisanship kept at arm's length. If we adhere to these principles, there will be no happier political body than the Princely State.

---

[117] Dadabhai Naoroji's letter is in English in the original.

MIDDAY
The Writer

In his preface to the first edition of *Karan Ghelo*, Father describes the impulse behind the book's writing quite simply:

> Most people of this province are fond of reading stories set in poetic form, but only a very few examples of these stories are readily available in prose; and those available are not well known. In order to fill this lacuna and to recreate versions of English stories and chronicles in Gujarati, the former Educational Inspector of this province, Mr Russell Saheb, urged me to write something along these lines. On that basis, I wrote the book, in approximately three years. (*KG* 0.10)

Once English rule was firmly established in northern India, the need for suitable material in Indian languages for the use of administrators of the East India Company arose, and so maulvis and pandits were commissioned to write books in both prose and poetry. In the wake of these directives from above, stories such as *Premsagar, Tota Kahani* and *Bagh-o-Bahar* were written.[118]

Father writes that his book is really the first of its kind in Gujarati. Readers can easily see the extent to which *Karan Ghelo* surpasses the Hindi and Urdu works listed above. Father's is a literary work, while the others are skits and tales in the style of the *Puranas*. His is a historical work infused with the power of a poetic imagination; it pleases the mind, and for that reason has earned a permanent place in literature. The others are pieces

---

[118] See p. 108, note 84.

written for specific occasions, which, having served their purpose, are no longer relevant. *Karan Ghelo* will be loved and remembered so long as the Gujarati language is spoken and read.

Intimations of the book first came to Father when he was headmaster of the Surat school. He was thirty years old at the time, his reading of English novels was extensive, and his love of history knew no bounds. In tune with the adage 'where the sun does not reach, there runs the poet's speech', he understood that the best historical novels use poetic imagination to present a true vision of the past to readers. So he steeped himself in the study of the poetic annals of Gujarat and her oral storytelling traditions.

Father believed that the sun of a new age floated on the horizon just as an older light was fading. 'Arrogance and corruption defeated; righteousness triumphant; evildoers destroyed—I wanted to select a suitable historical period to illustrate all these. In Lytton's novels *Last of the Barons, Last Days of Pompeii,* and *Last of the Tribunes,* the choice of just such dramatic moments in history is apparent.

He found three moments critical to Gujarat's history: the fall of Champaner, the destruction of Somnath, and Allauddin Khilji's conquest of Gujarat. A mother's wrath is the main theme in the fall of Champaner, but the woman's anger described there is disproportionate to what the occasion demands; in *Karan Ghelo* the wrath of a woman committing Sati fits the occasion, given the circumstances surrounding the event. In the case of the destruction of Somnath, the manner in which the cowardly king Bhimdev turned tail from the battleground would prevent a writer from drawing a true portrait of Rajput heroism. Arguing thus, he settled on the oral tales relating to Madhav and began his novel.

Father would say that ideas rushed past other ideas as he wrote, forcing him to slow down. 'Only occasionally did I have to score out what I had written. I wrote in the mornings and late into the evenings, my afternoons spent teaching at school.' My revered mother adds the following to Father's account: 'There was a room in the turret of the house where he sat, paper on knee, writing with abandon. The room contained neither chair nor table; alone, seated on a *chattai* spread across the mud-plastered floor, he wrote. So absorbed was he in the writing that the time to be at school would arrive, and I'd have to go upstairs and wake him from the trance into which he had fallen'.

Father read with flair and loved listening to others read. Though I myself had not heard him read, it must have been apparent to those who heard his spirited reading of *Karan Ghelo* that the author chose word-sounds with care. For sound and its meaning together are the true guides to a word's placement in specific parts of the text, for instance, where to place soft syllables and where the hard ones.

The first edition of *Karan Ghelo* was published at Government expense in 1868, the second edition in 1871. Father had handed over publishing rights to Government, and in 1882 even received a small royalty.

On 21 February 1881, he received the following from the Poona Educational Society.

Poona

To Nandshankar Tuljashankar esq.
Lunawada

Dear Sir,
I have the honour to draw to your attention this office No. 470 dated 27th April 1881 and to request that you will return the copy of your work called *Karan Ghelo* with the least possible delay as a new edition of it is required.

I have the honour to be,
Dear Sir
Your most obedient servant,
(sd.) K.M. Chatfield
Director, Public Administration

Father wrote back, 'I have forwarded by Book Post the Copy of my book called *Karan Ghelo,* sent to me by Rao Saheb Mahipatram Ruparam'.

Government next informed him that they would be willing to reprint the book for schools, provided all mention of spirits and ghosts is removed. Nandshankar turned down the offer indignantly: 'My book won't be repaired by censors,' he said. He then sent, by way of Major Giles Saheb and Major Chatfield

Saheb, the suggestion that the copyright revert back to the author. The suggestion was accepted; thereafter the book was printed at his own expense.

In the preface to the third edition of *Karan Ghelo*, my elder brother Shri Markandrao wrote: 'There are three goals that the novel writer should bear in mind: the emotional tone needs to be solemn, even majestic; the sense elevated and serious; and the subject matter or plot wide-ranging and of abiding interest to readers' (*KG* 0.10).

With an eye on all three factors, I will now give you a foretaste of *Karan Ghelo*.

As the plot begins to unfold, Vijayadatt's response to Madhav's question is the first sign of the mood of the moment. When Madhav asks the presiding priest: 'Reverend sir, was the sacrifice properly conducted? I trust confusion did not tumble into its performance', the old priest replies: 'I am astonished that these words should come from your lips. Your mind has changed its cast; and when that happens in men like you, I fear for the future' (*KG* 1.10–11).

Among us there is a belief that when family fortunes decline, the householder's psyche changes, his faith diminishes, trust fades, selfishness grows, and self-interest governs his actions. Following this very pattern, the attitude of the king and his minister changed, trust between them diminished, self-seeking grew and with it, the feeling that all others are drowned in selfishness. Given this state of affairs, when the loyalty of the king to his subjects and the subjects to their lord diminishes, decline and fall are inevitable. Corruption of the whole kingdom follows such sinful conduct; a kingdom's downfall is not an act of God.

On this note, sensing that 'the time is out of joint,'[119] the reader enters a scene of confusion. The conversation of the leaders of the farming and trading communities in *Karan Ghelo* suggests that despite Gujarat's prosperity and her overflowing wealth, selfishness has grown, the king and the people have forgotten their duty to each other; individuals talk only of

---

[119] This quote, from Shakespeare's *Hamlet*, Act 1, Scene 5, is in English in the original.

their own petty profits. Wherever the sense of individual rights grows, obligation to the common good declines and perilous times surely lie ahead. The state of affairs after the defeat at Qadisiyya when Iran surrendered to Caliph Umar (Al Faruk), the condition of Yazdgard (r. 439–57 CE) and his people was identical.[120] When Pompeii lay buried, and the Roman populace was caught in the tangles of Arbaces' intrigues, men became selfish and devoid of faith.[121]

At this point, Karan enters the scene. Following an impulse, he sets out incognito to observe his subjects. He encounters the witches and with courage subdues them, whereupon they favour him with advice: 'Be very careful about women, Oh King. Have as little to do with them as possible' (*KG* 2.43). With these words the witches, who can foresee what is to come, respond to the man searching for his own future.

Among us there is a belief that the goddess who presides over a man's fate clings to his back like his shadow. The family deity hovers over royalty; she rejoices in the king's joys, grieves in his sorrows; seeing King Siddharaj Jaisinh's hour of death draw close, the goddess wailed.[122] In parts of Scotland, I have myself witnessed complete faith in such beliefs even today; the clan's deity, known as a banshee, is ever anxious to foretell future events. Father believed that the witches were indeed family deities and were signalling what lay in Karan's future: 'We have examined your *nāḍi* (pulse); we sense the fault lines and realise that "the time is out of joint". Be alert' (*KG* 2.43). The great poet Shakespeare places in the witches' mouths just such warnings about the future. Banquo asks the three witches:

---

[120] Yazdgard, the last Sassanian ruler of Iran, was defeated by the Arabs at the battle of Qadisiyya (see Yarshater 1983: 72).

[121] Arbaces is an evil Egyptian priest in Bulwer-Lytton's *The Last Days of Pompeii*. 'Lytton paints a picture of Pompeii on the eve of its doom as a cesspool of vice, greed, gluttony, indolence…' (Stephan 2012).

[122] Siddharaj Jayasinh (1094–1143) belonged to the Solanki or Chalukya dynasty. He ruled over a large kingdom which extended over Gujarat, Rajasthan, including parts of the Konkan; Patan in Gujarat was his capital.

'If you can look into the seeds of time,
And say which grain will grow and which will not, then speak to
me.'
The witches answer
1st Witch: 'Lesser than Macbeth, and greater.'
2nd Witch: 'Not so happy, yet much happier.'
3rd Witch: 'Thou shalt get Kings, though thou be none.'[123]

No sooner do the words 'Thou shalt be king…' reach Macbeth's ears than he is driven to act—'an impatient temperament is truly impressionable', says the adage. 'Though king, you will not be happy; your descendants won't be kings'[124]—Macbeth hears these prophetic words but disregards them. From the beginning the reader is aware that Macbeth will kill Duncan and become king, that he will be unhappy, that he will be killed. Macbeth on the other hand remains convinced that by the power of his human will he can ward off what lies in store. He is aware that the end will be disastrous, but he is unable to turn away from disaster. In the same way, Raja Karan knows that his wives, the fair Kaularani, a figure carved in marble, and the nymph-like Fularani, each an embodiment of serene and mature beauty, await him in his palace. And yet, Roopasundari's tenderly blossoming beauty drives Karan to madness; he desperately wants to seize Madhav's wife. He knows that Nagar brahmins may lack an instinct for revenge, but are not wanting in the warrior's courage. Nonetheless, Karan seizes Roopasundari. It was like snatching the jewel from the hood of a king cobra (*nag*). The king cuts off the serpent's head and succeeds in seizing the jewel, but what will it avail him? The jewel dazzles only so long as it resides on the cobra's raised hood, otherwise it is ordinary snakeskin. Even so, with the passage of time, Karan's passion for Roopasundari cools. He cuts open the hood, but thereafter wherever he looks, he sees the serpent's spreading blood—a thousand *nag*s emerge from the one he has killed; the sight terrorises Karan. The goddess of vengeance meanwhile establishes herself at the entrance to his

---

[123] From Shakespeare's *Macbeth*, Part 1, Act 3, in English in the original.
[124] Ibid.

minister Madhav's heart. He is afire: on the one side there is the smothered smoke of regret, on the other the poisonous winds of revenge. Gradually, everything Madhav sees fans this revenge.

Madhav's brother Keshav is killed, and Keshav's wife Gunasundari commits Sati. As she is about to jump into the flames, a Rajput beggar comes before her and asks: 'Mother, from time immemorial there is the custom for the Sati to leave imprints of her hands upon the city gates, as though blessing the king and the people. Tradition therefore demands that you do the same'. It would not be out of place to recall here the full text of Gunasundari's response to the beggar's request:

> At that very moment the Sati rubbed her palms and, filling her hands with burning coals, flung them at the town. 'A king who desecrates an innocent woman, that too, the wife of his chief minister—not any brahmin woman but one belonging to the Nagar brahmin caste—*ekam apy anarthāya kimu yatra chatuṣṭayam*: even a single transgression leads to disaster, what about four together? A king who sends into permanent exile his loyal minister, one who had his king's wellbeing at heart, who worked for the welfare of the realm; a king who has a brahmin, holder of a high office, killed in order to abduct another's wife; a king guilty of having a *brahmin* killed—of having a *woman* killed! When a young woman for whom the wish to die does not come easily still chooses death, does the king comprehend the sorrow that her untimely end would cause her parents, her brothers, her sisters? A king who is the agent of such grave tragedy will soon become a wanderer in forest exile; his wife will be abducted by strangers; his daughters, after great suffering, will belong to alien men; the place of his death and the time will remain unknown; neither his name nor any other sign of him will survive; his enemies will inhabit his palace and, according to the law which says that a king's sins will be visited upon his subjects, the city of Anhilpur will be destroyed, her wealth looted, her traders totally uprooted, and in the course of time all signs, even the name of the once flourishing city will be lost. Oh, Mother of the World, may my curse bear fruit.' (*KG* 3.69)

Karan hears that death awaits him. He hears that his family along with his kingdom will be ruined. He finds himself drawn relentlessly into the jaws of Time. That even his ordinary virtues will propel him towards his downfall is all that remains for the reader to witness. In the same way that a lizard overcomes a parrot chick and makes a meal of the poor creature, Time and Fate gradually swallow Karan. Accumulated events wound around a reel gradually unspool. We, the readers, are aware of the results, but Karan remains unmoved. '*Yatne kṛte'pi na sidhyati ko'tra doṣah*: despite our best efforts if success eludes us, whose fault is it?'[125]—is a constant refrain that we hear from him. He wants to do good, but the results turn out otherwise.

Father believed that a novelist must work towards a sense of historical inevitability, which then takes on the appearance of fate. When the events described above occurred in Karan's life, it was still in Karan's hands to alter the course of his future. However, once they occur and become a part of the past, should the author want in some way to condemn the king's actions, he would have to attribute Karan's downfall to his past actions; in this case it is Karan's disregard of the witches' prophecy. Every man knows that he will die one day, and yet, through an effort of will, through vain endeavours, he thrashes about to remain alive. After he dies, his life appears as if it had been hostage to fate. The truth is however that in life, he was hostage to his own deeds.

Karan is not temperamentally a villain. He is a youthful, full-blooded Rajput. He is assertive, even tyrannically so; his courage exceeds a lion's, but his dependence on others exceeds even a woman's; his heart is more tender than a flower's; he is more impetuous than a child, always eager to act swiftly, impulsively and in complete disregard of others' feelings. Having acted, he does not fear the consequences of his actions; he is entirely satisfied by the immediate gain. And yet, he also wants to know the actual bearing of his actions on his subjects; that is why he sets out to walk incognito through the town; this is also why, dressed in rags, he addresses the woman who will be Sati. In short, Karan's is the portrait of thoughtless and reckless humanity.

> Regret follows the unreflecting man
> Joy ends when his adventure began.

---

[125] From the *Hitopadeśah, Kathā-mukham* 0.33.3 (see Pandita n.d.).

We see him live to regret his actions, and yet his humanity imprints itself upon our minds. He suffers, and we, the readers, in turn suffer with him. The human heart is indeed touched by Karan's humanity, and melts like the Chandrakanta gemstone when the sun's rays first strike it; this is a unique feature shared by the human heart and the Chandrakanta jewel. Karan is full of the 'milk of human kindness'.[126] But the milk curdles and spoils because of deep flaws in his character.

Karan is introduced to the reader in the first flush of youth.

> He was thirty years of age. His body, exercised from childhood, was, by God's grace, strong and slim. His skin was light brown, the colour of wheat. He was tall. He had an oval face and an aquiline nose. His lips were small and pressed together, lending him an earnest look suggesting firmness of purpose. His elongated eyes were usually tinted with red, which produced a fearsome effect and agitated evildoers. He had a noble forehead, and thick eyebrows that almost joined together; to all observers he had all the qualities of a resolute man. He had two major faults, however—he was of impatient temper and a slave to sensual passion (*KG* 2.26–27).

The royal priest, as was customary, counsels Karan on his duties. The king, who is reclining, responds with yawns: who listens to such sanctimonious advice? But that very night, like a flash of fire, he suddenly leaps up and decides he will go out and listen to what people are saying about his reign. Haroun al Rashid would similarly set out at night to hear for himself his subject's views of his rule. Devotion to his subjects had inspired Raja Vikram to do the same.[127]

Coming upon a group of aggressive spectres, Karan immediately discerns that they are witches and addresses them thus: 'I am a kshatriya Rajput, and because you dwell in my kingdom, you are

---

[126] The phrase, from Shakespeare's *Macbeth* (Act 1, Scene 5), is in English in the original text.

[127] Haroun al Rashid refers to the fifth Abbasid Caliph, a legendary figure also portrayed in the *One Thousand and One Nights*. Raja Vikram is a reference to King Vikramaditya of the *Vetala Panchavimshati* (see p. 130, note 102).

my subjects' (*KG* 2.42). Their hostility is subdued; thereafter the witches advise him to stay away from women. Hardly had their words ceased to sound in his ears when he catches sight of Roopasundari, and rushes forward as 'fresh fields and pastures new' open up before his eyes. Just as a child sees something new and howls to possess it, so Karan's innards cry out for her. 'She was created only to be mine' (*KG* 2.46) he says, echoing King Dushyanta's words upon first seeing Shakuntala in the forest hermitage—'*Asaṃśayam kṣatra-parigrakṣamā yad-āryam-asyām-abhilāṣi me manah*: Undoubtedly she belongs to a kshatriya, since my noble mind desires her'.[128]

Roopasundari's youthful beauty, like the tender petals of a still unfolding lotus bud, captures Karan as the allure of his chief queen's mature good looks has begun to fade. After that it is a case of, 'I came, I saw, I conquered'.[129] His desires swiftly push him forward. 'A woman is in reality a slave to jewels and clothes,' he thinks, and 'I shall have her with ease' (*KG* 2.46). Alas, unfortunate man, little do you realise that Roopasundari has no desire for wealth! It is your queen Kaularani (Kamlarani), who, enslaved by her love of clothes and jewels, will preside over Allauddin's palace. After your defeat, Kaularani will abandon you, but true to her name, she will remain chief queen. Garlanding with her own hands your sworn enemy, she will enjoy once again the pleasures of married life. Your daughter, forgetting your murderous love, will wed Khizr Khan and urge the poet laureate Amir Khushrau (1253–1325)—the parrot of Hindustan—to write a *masnavi* and call it *Ishqiya*.[130]

After what was to happen has happened, the demented Karan placates Roopasundari. 'It was fated,' he tells her. Filled with superstitious belief in good and evil omens, and keen to wash away his sins, Karan seeks the blessings of the woman who is to be Sati, only to receive a foretaste of his future! Remembering

---

[128] From *The Abhijnāna Śākuntalam of Kalidasa* 1.20 (see Kale 1969).

[129] The quotation, attributed to Julius Caesar, is in the original text.

[130] The *masnavi* is a poetic form used in Farsi courtly narratives. In 1315, Amir Khushrau wrote about the romantic story of Dewal Rani and Khizr Khan, also called the *Ishqiya* (see Losensky and Sharma 2013).

the Sati's dying screams, the miserable Karan sits on a rock and, filled with remorse, weeps like a child. Even when the moment of battle arrives, he does not wait to hear what his ambassador has to say. Nor does he heed the wise words of his battle-tested warriors. He antagonises the wealthy Jain community by lowering their flag. He plunges into battle and loses.

In sorrow, this very same Karan shines. His love for his daughter, for instance, redeems him in our eyes somewhat. 'The owl of Minerva issues from her nest when it is the dark of the night', says Hegel.[131] Amid the enveloping darkness of misfortune, the first rays of intelligence, a sense of what is right for the moment, begin to flicker in Karan's mind. Had he, in defending Anhilpur, adopted the earlier strategy of carrying on the battle from behind the Bagalan Fort, the outcome would have been quite different he now realises.

Around this time, Karan receives Shankaldev's proposal seeking his daughter Devaldevi's hand in marriage. His ancient Rajput blood boils, and in this frenzied state he rejects the suit. 'Don't kick a man fallen low!' he cries. Just then news arrives that his queen Kaularani is happy in Allauddin's palace. Is Allauddin summoning Devaldevi to his court to please Kaularani, to fill that single void that would complete her happiness? So thinking, Karan prepares to put Devaldevi to the sword.

King Karan, there is no end to your sorrows! Your eyes are robbed of their lustre, but what await you are further blunders, defeats, and the utter weariness which drive you to exile in Kathiawad. Even there you will learn from your own sworn enemy—unbeknownst to you and to him—that your queen Kauladevi is happy and that Devaldevi has given her hand to Khizr Khan. Oh Lord, put an end to this suffering!

In desperation, Karan throws himself into the water. But can he die? What kshatriya kills himself? And would one's bodily

---

[131] The quote from Hegel, which is in the original text, lends itself to several interpretations. Vinayak's reading, that wisdom dawns when the worst misfortune strikes, is not the standard one. See 'Owl of Minerva', in *The Oxford Dictionary of Philosophy,* https://www.oxfordreference.com/view/10.1093/oi/authority.20110803100258860 (accessed 15 May 2021).

instincts even permit it? A doped-up brahmin pulls him out of the water and a hermit reads Karan a Vedantic sermon on the illusory nature of creation.

Karan protests, saying, 'The Creator's word cannot be false' (*KG* 16.492).

'"I am the doer, I am the agent"—it is false pride that speaks thus. The supposition is as nonsensical as saying that a dog sleeping under the cart pulls it. False pride is at the root of the belief in human agency,' argues the hermit (*KG* 16.492). Karan debates the fatalistic philosophy, thinking it will help him bear the great misfortunes that have fallen his way. However, he disagrees with the sermonising and stands by human effort as a necessary condition for meaningful action.

Unlike Charles the Fifth, Gujarat's last king does not give up his throne to become an ascetic.[132] He does not renounce his wealth or punish his body. Instead, he is quickly misdirected to southern India, where once again the bugles of war are sounded, and within his wounded body Karan's kshatriya blood begins again to stir. But defeat and more defeat are written into his future. 'Time and again as each new misfortune strikes the body prepares to receive fresh blows,' so goes the saying. He bears the punishment but does not live to see happiness. Far from his own kingdom, deserted by his loved ones, unknown, he is killed on land belonging to his daughter's father-in-law. Dear Reader, do shed some tears over his dead body.

Father believed that in the past, abduction of another's woman had led to great upheavals. Even if we ignore the epic tales of the *Ramayan* and the *Iliad,* history's mirror reflects other examples. Bereft of his daughter Samyukta, Jaychandra of Kannauj sends fire and water, symbols of capitulation, inviting Mohemmed of Ghori to conquer his neighbour Prithviraj.[133] A year before Mohammed Qasim entered Sindh, a similar episode

---

[132] In 1556, at the age of fifty-five, Charles V, then the Holy Roman Emperor, abdicated his throne to join a monastery. See https://www/jansnirger/met/em/cja[ter/cjar;es-v-resignaton-and-abdication

[133] Prithviraj abducted Samyukta or Sanjogita, the daughter of Raja Jaychand, after a prolonged battle (see Talbot 2016).

took place in Spain. Roderick, king of the Goths, deflowered Julian's daughter Florinda, and so Julian invited the Muslim rulers of Algeria to conquer Spain. Tarik ibn Ziyad overran Spain, and so the crescent supplanted the cross.[134] When such causes for the uprooting of kingdoms is revealed, people are moved to pity; they do not look upon the ensuing events as implausible—this was Father's belief.

Madhav is an historical figure. The well he built still stands for all to see. The injustice meted out to him has worked its way into folklore. He was brought up, it is said, in poverty. A sharp intellect, a sense of what the occasion demands, the ability to scheme, and a certain tenacity allowed the once lowly clerk to rise to the position of prime minister. Indeed, this Nagar minister could make Raja Karan dance on the tip of his little finger. Of average height, white-skinned, with a body tending toward corpulence, Madhav had an oval face, with eyes lit by the brilliance of a quick and pliable wit. His was not an inherited position, despite which he had all the markings of a stern ruler: 'No one who set eyes on him walked away without due respect for the man—such was his stately bearing' (*KG* 1.8). Nor was there any lack in the king's regard for him. Nonetheless, Madhav feared losing his powerful position. He tried therefore in every way to win over his people's affection. He had no children, so accumulating wealth held no allure. Since it was impossible to be of one mind with his king, why not work for the people? Following this belief, he looked to his people's welfare.

This middle-aged minister had an eighteen-year-old wife, Roopasundari. Perhaps because he married late in life, or perhaps because Roopasundari was his second or third wife, Madhav was deeply attached to her. Among other caste groups disregard for women may have emerged at some time or other, but the Nagar community from ancient days has held its womenfolk in great respect. And the main reason is that Nagars have always been and still remain monogamous. The desire for progeny is not so great as to make them want to take on second wives: for them a wife is their children's mother.

---

[134] See *Roderick, the Last of the Goths* (Southey 1844).

When Karan orders Madhav into exile, his wife tries hard to dissuade him, saying, 'There are ill omens, beloved husband, don't leave town'. But 'it is the king's order, and Madhav was a Nagar, and Nagars are not superstitious men. So, ignoring his wife's appeal, he left home' (*KG* 3.52). He was neither weak nor superstitious, but a man who abided by his king's orders. Before he returns home, he hears from Jethashah's brother Motishah that his wife has been abducted, his brother Keshav killed trying to save her, and his brother's wife become a Sati.

Chapter Four of *Karan Ghelo* begins in a swirling poison of revenge.

> Karan! You destroyer of what we together built! You will not ever be happy. Like Death I will follow your wandering footsteps wherever you go! I won't let you rest. Revenge, thou son of rage, awake in my heart! And O' Keshav! Glory to you! You, a strong man met death defending a defenceless woman: the very thought shrinks my pain. Your wife, a Sati, has redeemed seven generations of our line. Now let revenge lead me on. Revenge at my own hands, but if not, only then at the hands of God. (*KG* 4.81)

When Madhav lies thus convulsed with anguish, dreaming perhaps or half asleep, a woman appears before him. Madhav addresses her, 'Goddess of Vengeance! Whoever you are, woman or demon, tell me how I am to avenge that deceitful king'.

The woman replies: 'I am Goddess Ambabhavani. You, a Nagar, have come to me for refuge. Come to Arasur, and I shall show you the way' (*KG* 4.81).

Madhav's mind grows still. He travels to see a vision of the mother goddess. She appears to him this time in the form of a *mleccha*. In one hand she is armed with a sword; in the other she holds a man by his braided hair. In that moment, the man uses his great strength to push away from the goddess' grasp, and she is left standing holding just a plait of his hair in her hand. Madhav grows alert to the meaning of this vision. Father said that the advent of the foreigner on the soil of Gujarat was occasioned by the goddess' anger, and therefore, our view of Madhav should not be entirely negative.

During this period in history, all roads led exclusively to Delhi. The hitherto dammed waters of Gujarat were to blend with the more powerful stream originating in Delhi. The glorious period of Jainism had ended, and the desolation in Ashapura thirsted for Islamic mosques crying, 'Delhi! Delhi!' In the course of a man's life, the future often beckons, even as an individual makes superhuman efforts to plunge towards it. Madhav is merely an instrument of historical forces, and these forces are not to his liking. On the way, he actually tries to drown himself in a well in order to deliver himself from the charge of theft. The Goddess of Vengeance restrains him. On reaching Delhi, he is mysteriously presented with the opportunity to save the crown prince Khizr Khan from a fire. Having saved the prince, Madhav is granted the boon. And Gujarat is overcome!

Shall we make Madhav responsible for Gujarat's fall? There is no causal connection between Allauddin's ascent to the throne and Madhav's humiliation; the two events merely occurred at the same time according to the same principle that if a crow were to alight on a palm tree and a coconut happen to fall, the connection between the two events is accidental. The invitation to invade Gujarat arrives when Allauddin is without cares. Having just murdered his uncle, he is nursing fantasies of imitating the heroics of Alexander the Great and thirsting after riches. So, he accepts the invitation.

Madhav's happiness does not last long. Alaf Khan's successor removes Madhav from his position of authority and dismisses him. Intent on spending his last days in some sacred place, Madhav and his wife seek the protection of Karan's cousin brother Harpal. Hundreds of insults are hurled at Madhav. He accepts them as warranted and silently bears them all. He admits his wrongdoing and says, 'I should have taken revenge on Karan, if it is revenge that I sought. As it is, I brought ruin to all my people' (*KG* 16.472–473). Husband and wife then see their old king. Though now emaciated and beggared by sorrow, they recognise Karan. Like the ripening fruit of an evil fate, unknowingly, they bring to the king news of his wife and daughter. How topsy-turvy is this world! The wheel turns, taking you up, then loops around, bringing you down. In the same way, Madhav's thoughts buzzed round and round like drones and then he sank into despair.[135]

Neither Karan nor Madhav lack the will to act. But it is as though some unseen force pushes them, as though a tidal wave from the past is sweeping them away in its wake. They imagine that they are swimming; but look—in fact they are being swept away by history. What Duryodhan says in the *Mahabharat* is true of both these men.[136]

> In the past you acted in certain ways, the fruit thereof now you taste,
> You cannot alter what you did, the Creator's words cannot be re-writ.

---

[135] *Rātrir gamiṣyati bhaviṣyati suprabhātam* |
Bhāsvānudeṣyati hasiṣyati paṅkajaśri ||
Ittham vicintayati kośagate dvirefe |
Hā hanta nalinim gaja ujjhāra ||

The night will vanish and a beautiful dawn arrive,
Lotuses will laugh following the rising sun.
With such fancies the drone clings to the bud.
Alas, alas! Just then an elephant uproots the flower.

From Sivasahaya's commentary on the *Bal Kand* of the *Ramayan*; my translation accords with the author's Gujarati rendition. See https:// tinyurl.com/4fu3zae8 (accessed 26 May 2021). This popular verse appears in several modern anthologies of didactic verse; see *Samskruta Mouktikaani*, https://sanskritpearls.blogspot.com/2011/07/july-22nd. html (accessed 26 May 2021).

[136] In Chapter V, Vinayak quotes the following verse, attributed to Duryodhan in the *Pandav Gita* 57 of the *Mahabharat*, along with his Gujarati translation, where he interprets '*devena*' to mean both 'by God' and 'by Fate' (*daivena*)—an ambiguity that allows him to interpret *karma* as historical necessity (see p. 210). For a discussion of its place in the *Mahabharat*, see https://hinduism.stackexchange.com/ questions/26141 (accessed 21 May 2021).

jānāmi dharmam na ca me pravṛttir |
jānāmyadharmam na ca me nivṛttih |
kenāpi devena hṛdisthitena |
yathā niyukto'smi tathā karomi ||

The Nagar is dependable; he is courageous and will not tolerate insults. He welcomes the chance for revenge; and being an able man, he succeeds in doing what he sets out to do. 'Hindsight is omniscient', and Madhav retains the backward look; he finds 'the immediate contemptible' and so he knocks it down with a blow. We should not judge Madhav too harshly. 'Karan broke the law, so his life was spent; because he crossed limits, Madhav had to repent'. Only reform banishes injustice, not revolution. One man's sins can sink the ship—this is the law.

Now we go on to study Roopasundari's portrait. To read the description of her delicate beauty is to behold moonlight frozen. She is a reflection in marble—a tiny oval-shaped face, deep and tranquil eyes, in whose oceanic depths how many ships wouldn't have capsized? Her beauty drew men unwittingly to her, spinning their already befuddled minds. So delicately built was she that an onlooker seeing her carry a silver pot would grow anxious lest it wrench her arms. Roopasundari was indeed like a lily created to give pleasure; you cannot blame her if she attracted men for she was not one to deliberately trail a seductive air. It could even be said that she was quite unconscious of her own beauty. When Karan abducts her, she is unable to take her own life. 'What fate decrees, can human ingenuity counter?' she thinks. The storyteller in his portrait makes it very clear that she was created for pleasure. So when Karan's obsession with her ends, she lies in a corner, robbed of lustre. A woman who is valued by her lord is valued by all, so she believes. 'When will my husband return? When will he put me through the atonement ritual and take me in his arms?' She might have burst with the intensity of her longing for Madhav, but she is not someone who, when pulled in one direction, pushes with equal force in the opposite. Her life with Karan is not happy; she yearns constantly for Madhav.

Bankimchandra Chattopadhyay's novel *Chandrakant's Will*, if read side by side with *Karan Ghelo*, evokes a comparison between the figure of his heroine Bhramar and that of Roopasundari. The one difference is that unlike the latter, Bhramar is not particularly good-looking. She lacks beauty, but possesses youth and dazzling virtue. To her, dying is easy, no more difficult than laughing.

Bhramar believes she was born to be faithful to one man, and so she dies by his side.

Quite different from these two women is Kaularani, who is based on an actual historical character. 'Kamal' becomes 'Kanval' in the vernacular; we often come across the name Kaunlin in north Indian languages. Kauladevi then is a vernacular version of Kamladevi. Muslim chroniclers claim that she had only one daughter, Devaldevi. We don't know why Father imagined a second one.

Kamla or Kauladevi is a Rajput. Nandshankar used to say that among Indians, one sees tall men and women among the Rajasthanis and Marathas. Every limb of their body is sinewy. Even though Rajput women remain locked up in palaces, their bodies are robust. Whether it is on account of caste or ancestry, we can't say. If one were to speak in metaphors, one might say Roopasundari was a delicate *champa* flower to Kauladevi's sturdy lotus—a tiny, fragile, girlish figure against a mature, strong and dazzling presence. Kauladevi's passions are equally strong. Unlike Roopasundari, Kaularani does not falter when calamity strikes; instead she fiercely declares that it did not matter to her if the palace burnt down or if she herself burnt to death. Saved from the fire, she flees disguised in male attire, only to fall into the hands of a Bheel. Destined to be a priceless treasure in the emperor's crown, she is captured and taken to Delhi. Here, Kaularani's true nature asserts itself: fickleness takes over and she forgets the past. In this way, rubbing salt into each fresh wound, a succession of misfortunes strikes Karan: 'Rips in the fabric of life multiply when misfortune strikes: *Duhkheṣu chidrāṇi bahulī bhavanti*'.

Devaldevi's beauty is of the rich 'oriental type'.[137] While Roopasundari is delicate and innocent, and Kauladevi has an elegance marked by boldness, Devaldevi is beauteous of limb and face, with a richness that grows and declares itself only to overcome the beholder. Unlike Ashrumati of Mewad, she is not created to renounce the world and practice asceticism. She pairs up with Khizr Khan and, in Gwalior the couple sleeps the

---

[137] The phrase 'oriental type' is in English in the original.

infinitely long sleep of the dead. No single human being has willed these events; they are the result of historical necessity—prophesied in Gunasundari's curse. Historical necessity is the god who drags events in its wake. The distinction between good and evil counts for nought.

The least of a poet's or novelist's responsibilities is to ensure that his characters retain their appeal until the very last. In keeping with that intention, both Devaldevi and Kaularani are depicted as holding on to their humanity. Kauladevi's lament at leaving Gujarat rends our hearts. The lyric: 'Karanraja where have you gone? Why have you abandoned the city? Where are you now?' played on musical instruments is so loved by the people that I have heard even a beginner sing the words in the Lalit Raga (*KG* 10.292). They say time heals sorrow. Kaularani forgets the past. Is a lotus able to stop blooming? What does it matter if the lotus blooms in a beautiful garden or in mud?

Virtue and vice, like shadow and light, are drawn into Allauddin's portrait. His character in *Karan Ghelo* emerges with far more immediacy than is reflected in the annals of history. A heroic, wrathful, alert and murderous man filled with adventure, yearning to be a second Alexander, though licentious is just; his arms are like Lord Yama's staff, bent on punishing the guilty and keeping the innocent fearful. Such a man is Allauddin, who, dazzled by Kauladevi's beauty, falls into Kafur's trap.

Malik Kafur is portrayed with zest. His efforts to rise above his station, his drive to overcome the stigma of slavery, his zeal to prove his courage, and his intrigues! This corrupt officer, a man who murders his own uncle, who forces men to drink from his cup of cruelty, handsome, superstitious, afraid of dervishes, like a snake he slithers before your eyes. You have held him like a son close to your heart; beware lest he destroy your progeny.

Shankaldev is patterned after the hero who is an aesthete. However, when the surroundings are on fire, who lends ear to the sweet strains of love? That is why the passion between Devaldevi and Shankaldev is played out in a lower key. Harpal, Karan's cousin, is the truly brave and tested Rajput warrior, who is given the role of an advisor.

In the first edition of his novel, Father wrote the following:

> My intention in writing the book was to draw as accurately as possible a picture of how things were in history at the time of the story—the manners of the men and women of the time and their ways of thought; the principles of governance of the Rajput kings of Gujarat and the Muslim emperors of Delhi; the heroism and pride in caste of the men and women of Rajasthan, and the passion and religious fanaticism of the Muslims. To what extent this intention succeeds I leave to my readers to decide. (*KG*0.9–10)

In what follows we examine aspects of the novel in light of the above statement.

First, the writing style is straightforward and simple, yet expressive, passionate and effortlessly ornamented. In his choice of words nowhere do you see the author struggling to substitute a commonly-used Farsi expression with newly-minted Sanskrit ones. The result is a language that is both natural and universally understood. One sees the same straightforward approach in Govardhanbhai's *Sarasvatichandra*. In the context of weighty debates, at certain junctures, the language is difficult, but the fault lies in the reader's imperfect command of the vocabulary, not in the language used. When new ideas are presented in new apparel, the clothes may appear rough or awkward at first, but with the passage of time, people get used to the new usage. It is sufficient here to say that Father was contemptuous of attempts to banish Farsi and Arabic words, then current in everyday usage.

Language (*gira*) is no one's ancestral property; it belongs to the native speakers who inhabit a country or region (*mulak*); it must bear the stamp of their ways, their customs, their religious beliefs and so on. Should one pretend that Muslims never did enter Hindustan, and that their language, their ideas and their ways have in no way influenced Gujarati speech (*Gurjargira*)?[138]

---

[138] The word for 'language' here, *gira*, is from the Sanskrit, and almost never used in everyday Gujarati speech. As also mentioned in my Introduction, Vinayak's use of the word in this context is ironic.

This kind of talk is pure illusion, perhaps realised only in the imagination. In Hindustan, Hindus and Muslims will always live side by side and move together.

Here and there in *Karan Ghelo*, one comes across Farsi words then current in Gujarati. With reference to these, someone writes: 'It is like finding "iron filings served in a plate of gold"'. The use of Farsi words is not a fault in *Karan Ghelo* but a virtue—it is proof of the author's respect for people's everyday speech.

In discussing the chain of events that forms the novel's plot, we notice the great ingenuity with which the narrative is worked. We don't ever see any but the most necessary connections. Every scene naturally morphs into the next, as though following a law of necessity. When Vijayadatt speaks, he alludes to Moolraj's gift to brahmins, and the invitation from north India. Jethashah's vivid sketch of the trader's life and Bhano Patel's portrait of the farmer are both true to the times and to the occasion. The statement in the *Mahabharat* on the king's duties finds an appropriate place in the novel. The thrust and parry of debate between the Jains and the brahmins, which is drawn from a biography of Kumarpal,[139] signals the decline of Jainism, and so is not inappropriate here. There being numerous readers of *Karan Ghelo*, it is not necessary to further illustrate the felicity with which the author has constructed the plot.

The author's descriptive powers are displayed at many points in the narrative. In Chapter Nine, there is an account of the terrible consequences of war. The thirty lines beginning with, 'That year, neither man nor woman will celebrate the Spring Festival with joy' could well have emerged from the pen of a positivist. The words perfectly suit what is being described, and the meaning has a certain simplicity; and yet, as sentence piled on sentence rushes forward with urgency, the author's intention to turn the reader against war is also realised, and the reader becomes convinced that 'bravery hides a thousand faults' (*KG* 9.244–246). Bodily strength combined with courage usually fills men's minds

---

[139] Kumarpal, the king who ruled Gujarat from 1143 to 1172, was a disciple of the Jain *muni* Hemachandra, and converted to Jainism in the latter part of his reign (see Majumdar 1956).

with such wondrous joy that they see virtue in no other quality: 'In this world, names of those men whose courage brought only disaster have become immortal instead of being erased. Some of the world's great murderers are worshipped like gods; others have become the shining lights of history' (*KG* 9.253). The above passage shows that Father truly imbibed some of the beliefs of the positivist philosopher Comte.

There is a wonderful description in Chapter Eleven of the book where Kanakdevi and Devaldevi lovingly nurse back to health a wounded Karan racked with pain:

> Observing Karan's suffering, the ever-compassionate God was moved to pity. Like faint rain in the forest wilderness, like a ray of light in darkness, amid all his sorrow, joy and peace appear. Comfort, like drops of dew on parched earth, fills this doomed vessel as two ministering angels descend from the sky to replace the evil spirits who torment Karan. (*KG* 11.297–298)

Karan Ghelo the novel is a daughter of narrative poetry. The reader does not easily forget the succession of metaphors found here; this linguistic influence can be traced to our traditional ballads. But observe how simple, how apt and how natural these metaphors are! Of all the short paragraphs in *Karan Ghelo*, the passage above is the one I myself like best.

Moving forward, we are shown Devaldevi's feverish love, its fulfilment, her *gandharva* marriage, her vows and so on in language that is lyrical, restrained and elevated. Here, Father's efforts were directed at restoring people's aesthetic sensibilities, which were tainted by the vulgar ways in which erotic love was depicted in this period. And his efforts did succeed.

In Chapter Twelve, Biharilal enters the scene crying, 'Oh Lord! You are able to transform a tiny ant into an elephant, and a blade of grass into a mountain. No one fathoms the depths of your reach'. The rule of Hindus ended, Muslim rule began and the rise and fall of power within Muslim dominions was there for all to see. Instability and uncertainty now became part of lived experience. Reading Father's portrayal of the *jizya* tax imposed on Gujarat gives the reader an idea of the insult and dishonour felt by Hindus when Aurangzeb revived this evil tax.

Following Kaularani's desire to have her daughter Devaldevi brought to Delhi, the Muslim emperor sends an emissary to Karan. Should you, dear Reader, wish to become versed in speech that is effusive, in words that have the power to please and to flatter, besides being lyrical, then read the emissary's speech given below. Father maintained that the use of metaphor is basic to Muslim speech. Muslims are able to illustrate moralising statements with amazing skill. Their conduct, however, is quite another matter.

Referring to Devaldevi, the emissary begins:

> She is young, and very much in need of a mother's care. Even at this moment she must be mourning her mother's absence. Send her to Delhi, and her needs will be met. She now hides in the darkest corner of a room; bring her into the light so that the fame of her beauty spreads across the world. The priceless and brilliant jewel lies deep in the corner of the dark and boundless ocean; it needs most certainly to be acclaimed by an expert jeweller able to set it in a ring. How indeed can an old man like you be a suitable companion to her? As long as she remains with you, Devaldevi will be like a deer separated from its herd. Like a fish removed from water, she will surely die struggling unless you return her to water. You have distanced a moth from light; away from the light how will she regain her joyful calm? You have uprooted a flowering plant from the garden and planted it in the desert sands of Marwad. How do you expect it to grow there without water? You have dragged into your house a tiny parrot which once played in a garden full of flowers. Instead of flying in the open sunlight, she walks on the ground. How will she be happy? So do as I say. If you do as I ask, as vassal to the Emperor, you shall regain your kingdom. (*KG* 13.370)

Karan's response to the emissary is expressed in words appropriate in the mouth of a scion of the famed Sisodia clan. It would not be out of place to belabour the point here.

> Should the vaulted sky collapse, should the earth sink into the nether regions, should even the emperor or the great God above ask for my daughter, I would not willingly part with her. I have fallen so low that I do not fear any man. I have lost everything and have nothing more to lose. The only thing that awaits me now is

death. All kinds of misfortune have already fallen my way. There is nothing more left for me to suffer. That is why I neither fear your emperor, nor Malik Kafur with his unlimited army of soldiers.

The Rajputs have not yet sunk so low, their honour is not so completely destroyed, their pride in clan and caste so lost as to give away their daughter to a stranger in return for protection, for gain, or for their personal happiness. That day has not yet come; indeed, it will not come for a long time. No! No! Send my daughter to a foreign king, entrust her to a low wicked people, one who is her father's sworn enemy, who without reason snatched away her father's kingdom, who brought him down to this miserable state? That will not happen, ever. So long as my body has breath, so long as blood flows through my veins, so long as my hand is capable of wielding a sword, I will hold on to my daughter's hand. I am willing to sacrifice my life to protect her. After I die, what is to happen to her will happen. Will the world say that Karan lived to sell his daughter for profit? Never! I shall kill with my own hands whosoever says this. That this tender flower should fall into impure and wretched hands! I would rather break her and cut her up. That she, a priceless, flawless pearl should adorn a vile body! I would rather reduce her to ash. For us Rajputs there is no shame in that. I shall not lose face by such an act. From ancient times that is our tradition.

To preserve the pride of our clan, to prevent giving our daughters to men of lower castes, we smother them at birth. My mistake was to let her live, to allow her to grow. Even now, nothing is lost! One stroke of the sword and the deed is done. With one stroke I shall save the honour of my clan, my caste and my country. With one stroke your emperor's hope will come to nought. And that stroke of the sword will ensure that my daughter remains pure. (*KG* 13.371–372)

The words Karan hurls at Kaularani's hard-heartedness would melt a stone.

Kauladevi, you wretch, you vicious sinner! Why indeed should I address you as queen anymore? Did I not shower happiness on you? Did I not drown you in affection? Did I not gratify every word that fell from your lips? I made you my chief queen. And you repaid the debt in your own way: abandoning your husband, daughter, mother, father, relatives, caste, country—everything—

and defiling your religion. And now you revel in a barbarian king's harem! To wed another when your husband lives! In one lifetime to marry twice! Lust for wealth has wrapped you in an evil, irreligious man's embrace to rejoice in all manner of luxuries. Not that I am jealous of the man, but have you no pity for me? Do you not see the state to which I have been reduced? You don't even cast a glance at my limitless sorrow. Though steeped in pleasure, you seek yet more pleasure, and so wish to have your daughter too. I am utterly ruined. I have abandoned the world with all its joys. I sit in this *math* like a hermit, dependent on this daughter of mine for some small joy. But even that you snatch away from me! You sow! Having your daughter with you won't add in any significant measure to the sum of your joy. But without her I shall die an aimless wanderer pining for her. At present the sun of your fortune is at its height, but evening will eventually come, and soon thereafter your sun will set and the dread darkness descend. (*KG* 13.371–372)

Karan then takes up his sword and prepares to kill Devaldevi. But his sword falters against her innocence.

Further on in the book, there is a terrifying description of famine, which echoes the oral records of the Sudataḷa famine. The cavalry and the stampede following the destruction of Khizr Khan's birthday procession are all described and told to great effect.

How eerie and mysterious is the description of *kali chaudas*, the dark moonless night! When the corpse thrown in the water to be washed moves, the reader's heart is in his mouth! The awful suicide of the bard who prophesied the downfall of Hindu kings also presages the end of the whole bardic tradition.

Further on, there is much comedy hidden in Madhav's encounter with the thief. The French anarchist M. Proudhon (1809–1865)[140] writing on economics says that property is a form of theft: '*la propriété c'est le vol*'; in the same way, the thief announces the original Vedantic doctrine, which holds that the distinction between you and the other is an illusion.

---

[140] Pierre-Joseph Proudhon was a French anarchist. See http://anarchism.pageabode.com/anarcho/review-proudhon-what-is-property (accessed 16 May 2021).

Reading descriptions of the trader Jethashah's luxurious existence recalls stories of Akbar and his barber. The comic roguery of the brahmin couple, the association between the recluse and the opium-addicted brahmin come to us as gently rippling waves in the great ocean of sorrow that is the novel. Nothing in the novel is overstated. One notices Father's subtle use of the principle that declares: 'use only as many words as are appropriate to the situation—only as many as suffice—and no more'.

A straightforward answer to the simple question that Father raised in his Foreword is this: 'The poem is eternal'.

Chapter V

SUNSET

After twenty-two years of wandering, having fulfilled his obligations to the world, the seeker returned to the city of his birth. Father turned fifty-five (*panchāvan*) in the month of Chaitra, in 1890; it was the stage in life when men withdraw from worldly affairs to the forest wilderness. 'In my case, the world was the jungle from which I exited,' he joked with friends, 'it was a sign that I was saved'.[141]

As good fortune had it, old friends also retired the same year to return to Surat. Shri Vidyaram, his father-in-law, who had served as judge of the High Court of Bhavnagar, retired with a pension, and settled down in a mansion in Sanghadiavad. Shri B. Dolatram, retiring as *munsif,* flitted between Surat and Dumas, leaving Surat and returning to Dumas each year. Rai Bahadur Mukundrai gave up his position as chief judge to live contentedly alone on his private estate. Father had feared that a return to Surat in the absence of close friends would bring only desolation. That this did not come to pass, he believed, was due to Time's generosity.

It was usual for Suratis to take a turn in the fresh evening air. Accordingly, the four friends would stroll along the Civil Lines for about a mile and a half. I often accompanied them. Walking together they seemed to be two awkwardly joined ox carts. Mukundbhai, his gait so proper, with back so erect it would put any youth to shame, his steps slow and even, attire so distinguished, even if they might appear washed out sometimes;

---

[141] The word *van* meaning forest, affixed to *panchāvan,* the age of retirement, enables the play on the word *vānaprastha,* the stage in life when men leave the worldly life to retire into the silence of the forest.

his speech was sweet—in fact, he preferred to listen rather than to speak—and after the pithy words were spoken, any further exchange, as far as he was concerned, ended.

My maternal grandfather Vidyaram, though older than the rest of his friends who were more or less of the same age, had cultivated the habit of plunging headlong into conversation and declaiming his views with passion. At the mere hint of grandiosity, he would let loose a shaft of arrows. His angry eyes flashing greater fire than a penitent *brahmachari*'s, scorched whoever stepped out of line. On the other hand, Father, by habit a fast walker and not overly concerned about correctness, would occasionally step out of line, walk sideways, probably due to his defective eyesight, and so incur Vidyaram's ire. My grandfather was aloof, seldom spoke to the children, and that usually kept us at a fearful distance.

Uncle Dolat (that is how we youngsters referred to Dolatraiji) was the most athletic of the lot. He was of a muscular build, tall, broad-chested, he strode forward holding a bird-catcher's pole in hand, dressed very simply and often cultivated a deliberately rustic appearance. 'We are free folk, eh Master,' he would say, turning to face Father, 'Who cares about what people wear?' He stood completely outside worldly dealings. There is beauty in Creation and all is well with the world—such was his contented and optimistic outlook, reflected in his equally sanguine thoughts. He constantly alluded to his strength and said he was strong even as a child. Dolatbhai was a straightforward man; neither censure nor praise affected him. He was the last among his friends to die, perhaps because from childhood he had exercised regularly and led a simple life.

Mukundbhai was tough and sinewy, with an upright gait. He had an extraordinary memory and, on occasion when telling a story, his speech would effortlessly take on metaphorical turns, which were so precisely and so perfectly targeted that his audience could not help being amused. Pecking away continually at all perorations, he teased out comic details. Not that he'd written any books on humour, only that laughter dominated his being and appeared here and there in all his utterances. To respect rank in society, to maintain and display the dignity suited to his station in life—one could observe all these in Mukundbhai. He was in the habit of attending every social gathering; there wasn't a single wedding procession in Surat at which he was not present. Whenever I was with him, I observed the vigorous manner in which his gaze appraised all—his eyes took in everything and everyone, and savoured all that he saw.

The friends' circle usually met in the evening at one of the houses located on the Civil Lines, belonging to Ishwardas Store. Here Sheth Karsandas Purshottamdas Atmaram Bhukhanwala would also come to enjoy the pure air. Happy in the quiet of the countryside, he would busy himself welcoming visitors with zest and ordering the gardener to lay out chairs for guests. The friends probably hadn't developed the habit of chewing paan, and none apart from the Sheth smoked the hookah. Unlike other clubs where members eat and drink, here no refreshment of any kind was served. They conversed avidly, and my maternal grandfather blossomed in this company. His comments were always well-timed, and if he wanted to draw out a person, he would pointedly call upon him to speak.

The available water from the well was saline, so the surrounding vegetation was sparse, but an arrangement of large and small planters lent a decorative air to the garden. The place was perfect for those who enjoyed cool, fresh breezes. But Karsandasbhai himself did not find comfort in a life of retirement; so, like the Vardhamana of the *Panchatantra* story, 'one night anxiety arose as he lay abed. Even though my wealth is abundant, I should think of ways of growing it: *Tasya kadācit rātrau śaiyyārūḍhasya tasya cintā samutpannā /yat prabhūte'pi vitte arthopāyāś chintanīyāh kartavyāś ca iti*'.[142] Karsandasbhai decided that he must plan his investments, and so decamped to Bombay. Following his departure, the club closed down. Thereafter, the company of friends spent a large part of their time on the Muskati Estate.

After twenty years in the countryside, they found living in crowded urban neighbourhoods stressful. The difficulty of city life had struck Father even before he stopped working. Keen to

---

[142] From the *Panchatantra* 1.1 (see Mishra 1910).

live outside the urban life of Surat, he considered buying a house in the Civil Lines. But as the location bordered the river, the surrounding air was bound to be humid. If you want to be free of the entanglements of urban life, what is the point of living on the city outskirts where the air is damp? So he let the thought lapse. Someone suggested he live in the area called Hajira. But Hajira was too isolated, and not especially well-connected to Surat. So that too was ruled out.

Now Rao Bahadur Dolatrai pressed Father to follow his example and build a house in Dumas. Father's former student and friend Rao Bhimbhai, after retiring from his job as treasury officer, also encouraged Father to build a home and eat his daily *dahl* and rice in Dumas, where he too owned a house. To ensure that his advice was followed, Bhimbhai even accompanied Father to Dumas. My two elder brothers were drawn to the place, as they needed a quiet location to prepare for their law examinations. Under these circumstances, Father bought a vacant plot, belonging to Dr Dosabhai, across from Dolatram's house. Our bungalow was ready by the beginning of 1892. We spent a lot of time in the Dumas house—the entire three and a half months of summer, on and off during the winter months, and on Saturdays and Sundays during the monsoon season. Father referred to Dumas as his final resting place.

There were very few houses in Dumas at the time. Pure sea air, simple fresh food, waters promoting good digestion, walks in the open—in such pristine, unspoiled surroundings the mind remains alert, the heart overflows and the body is without disease.

In the year 1897, however, bubonic plague appeared in the cities, and the populations of Bombay and Surat spilled over into Dumas. Cottages and villas mushroomed everywhere. Dumas ceased to be a village, and acquired the appearance and allures of a city. The people of Surat are adept at turning wilderness into populous inhabited space. So, entertainment became a permanent feature of Dumas. A local poet had even immortalised Dumas as Suryapur in these words: 'With discerning judgement, Dumas was settled at Suryapur in the land of Gujarat.' At

Bhimbhai's urging, Harilal[143] identified the origins of Dumas with the Suryapur of the poem, which is set in the Harikatha metre.

When plague became endemic in Dumas, the people of Bombay ceased to visit. Even so, the place did not recover its earlier simplicity; prices remained high and with increased wealth came ostentation, horse and carriage gathered speed and pedestrian pathways were covered over in dust. Father, whose mind like Wordsworth's preferred a peaceful existence, was troubled by this ostentatious display of wealth. Bhimbhai, on the other hand, roared with anger: 'Whence have these upstarts come to ruin Dumas!' Dolatrai, like Diogenes, remained twisting and turning in his tub. And just as the Greek Cynic had cast a contemptuous glance at the great Plato's pride and thumped his foot ('I stamp on thy pride, Plato'),[144] so also Father and his friends retained their original rustic ways and regarded the wealthy tradesmen of Bombay and Surat with contemptuous eyes.

Twice a day, morning and evening, Father would set out for a stroll; he would walk two miles and then sit on the beach enjoying the sea breeze. Bhimbhai, on the other hand, would hold court at his bungalow, rarely stepping onto the beach. Fanned by the cool sea breeze, Shri Mansukhlal Solicitor would walk down to the seashore. An asthmatic condition made him weak, so he didn't much care for walks along the beach, preferring instead to play a game of chess. Soft-spoken and unpretentious, he was nonetheless gregarious; Father was very fond of him. So it was that the lives of the first and second headmasters of the Surat

---

[143] This possibly refers to Harilal Harshadrai Dhruv (1856–1896), a Gujarati poet and scholar of Sanskrit literature from Baroda State. See https://www.google.co.in/books/edition/Encyclopaedia_of_Indian_ Literature/zB4n3MVozbUC?hl=en&gbpv=1&pg=PA1005&printsec=fr ontcover (accessed 26 May 2021).

[144] Vinayak's English quotation: 'I stamp on thy pride, Plato' (usually rendered as 'I trample on the empty pride of Plato') is attributed to the Cynic Diogenes, who contemptuously rejected wealth and power in favour of an austere life, and is reputed to have lived in a tub. See https://sourcebooks.fordham.edu/ancient/diogeneslaertius-book6-cynics.asp#Diogenes (accessed 19 May 2021).

High School in many ways took a similar turn; perhaps because they shared a certain detached outlook towards life.

Rao Bahadur Jeevanrambhai retired to Dumas, giving up a prestigious position in the railways. Wearing the green turban of the merchant community, he was in the habit of holding forth in public, delighting his friends with old stories about his relatives' heroic foot journey to Shuklatirth. Father, Jeevanbhai and my maternal grandfather spent a great deal of time together.

Even after relinquishing his position as Diwan of Indore and retiring to Dumas, Khanderao Bedarkar retained his authoritarian ways to the very end. He lived in great style, was wont to tell elaborate stories about his past heroic deeds, while remaining an earnest scholar engrossed in his books; indeed, everything about him was superlative. Sheth Rajarama, a well-known merchant from Bombay now grown old, built a hospital in Dumas. He was a shrewd and happy man of the world.

Alas, they have all left the world and are gone! Dumas has lost some of its sparkle; the soil has become arid, the water saline; the garden where once bulbuls sang is silent.

Father's great anxiety on retiring was how he, who was used to spending all his time reading and writing, would occupy himself. His eyes no longer permitted him to read, and he found writing difficult. For one so attached to the pursuit of knowledge, so detached from the everyday business of life, such anxieties were indeed natural. He disliked gossip, whether about members of his own caste or those outside it. His savings were invested in promissory notes; so, unlike my maternal grandfather, he was not affected by the rise and fall of share prices. Nor was he interested in keeping household accounts. He did not in any way concern himself with financial matters. His way of life was typical of members of his class and caste.

I was seven years old at the time, and while I read books in Gujarati, my elder sister Sulochana read English primers. At first Father spent time tutoring us at home. But when I began school and she went to her married home, that period of our life ended. Then his attention turned to what had been an older area of interest. Some of his friends suggested that since Father, even prior to Sir Theodore Hope's time, had been drawn to the municipal affairs of Surat, he should once more work for the welfare of the people of that city. But Father entirely lacked a natural sense of entitlement, was completely disinterested in using his influential connections to further his prospects, and so thought it improper to be selected as a government nominee. Subsequently, the Government nominated Sardar Ishwardas Store and Doctor Dosabhai as representatives from the middle classes. Father had no inclination to elbow his way into the notice of Englishmen; he worked solely for the people's welfare, without seeking either government favour or public popularity. As a result, he was able to prevent tricky measures which were aimed at either immediate or short-term gain. Father was subsequently elected vice-president of the Municipal Council of Surat.

He once wrote the address for the ceremonies held to welcome His Excellency the Governor of Bombay to Surat; but even though the letters had been especially enlarged to render the reading easier, he insisted that Ishwardas present the welcome address.

At this time there was a discussion on the payment of property taxes. If facilities for water were widely accessible in Surat, there would be greater protection against fires, potable water would be available for those who did not enjoy the convenience of water tanks, and incidents of cholera would greatly reduce. On these grounds, Father advocated that water be piped into houses. He was entirely convinced that the burden of additional taxes that the measure might entail should fall on the public. He did not entertain the possibility that the public might turn against the project on these very grounds, for it was against his principles to use populist means to buy public approval. He referred to the ideals of Turgot, the Physiocrat from France who, for the sake of the general good, did not approve of government controlling the appointment of public servants.[145] Though Father held firmly to the view that the common man is ruled by self-interest rather than by the strength of intellect, he held that, 'for us, Vishnu is the lord of the people on earth'; in other words, he put his own welfare in God's hands.

---

[145] See p. 147, note 110 on Anne-Robert-Jacque Turgot (1727–1781).

Meanwhile, a member was to be nominated from the municipalities in northern parts of the Bombay Presidency to the Governor's Council. Bowing to the enthusiasm of both my elder brothers, and yielding to Shri Bhimbhai's pressure, Father submitted his name as a candidate for office. Shri Chimanlal Setalvad, too, was a contender for the position. Father had no comprehension of how caucuses work. The American method of selecting candidates based on a list put forward by contending factions, based on which the candidate who receives the most votes wins, was alien to the man who had spent his life in the mofussil areas of the province. Father received fewer votes than Chimanlal. Nonetheless, until the very end and despite his failing health, he thought it important to work for municipal affairs.

His principal advice was: 'Be sober. Be astute. Live purer lives. Cast your vote rationally. Work toward making your city sanitary and beautiful. Personal service is an imperative: service, rather than doling out of money, is a person's duty towards the city he lives in.'[146] When his eyesight grew weak, however, he began to withdraw from public life. Around this time he seemed to have suffered a mild stroke; his legs lurched, his hands shook, but the strict and salutary regime he imposed on himself kept disease at bay.

In response to some of my enquiries regarding this period in Father's life, Sir Frederick Lely wrote:

25, Hanover House
Regent's Park
London,
September 17, 1913

My dear Mehta,

I am glad to hear you are engaged in the filial duty of preparing a life of your father.

For a long time he was only known to me as the author of that charming book 'Karan Ghelo'. Later when he was living in retirement at Surat, I came into contact with him personally, and every year increased my respect and admiration for him. Reserved in manner and speech, he was keenly interested in popular progress. Wise in counsel, independent and steadfast in action,

---

[146] Nandshankar's entire advice is in English in the original.

catholic in sympathies, he was at that time an outstanding figure in the local world. With his shrewd and experienced eye, he saw that a certain policy was needed and he held to it with dignity and determination in the face of much odium, which I am glad to know was changed before his death into cordial appreciation.

It is a pleasure to know that you, the son of my old friend, have won your way into the Civil Service, and I wish you all success.

Yours sincerely,
(sd.) F. P. S. Lely.[147]

Having retired from public life, Father now revived his older interest in mathematics, and once again began solving problems from textbooks. He started with geometry, and there was not one problem in the book that he was unable to deduce.[148] My own knowledge of mathematics is limited; beyond algebra and trigonometry I had no knowledge of the subject, so I am unaware of further challenges he might have undertaken on completing his study of geometry. With slate and pencil he would begin work at seven in the morning, stopping only at ten or half past ten. Apart from an hour in the afternoon when he rested, he was always with pen and slate in hand. In Dumas, he spent less time on mathematics, as he went for walks in the morning.

When we were together, we read to him. He did not like stumbling readers. By God's grace my elder brother excelled in oratory and dramatic skills; I recall how much Father enjoyed Manubhai read Dickens' novels. When I gained sufficient fluency in the English language, I too read *Dombey and Sons* and *Bleak House* to him, and during my holidays, books on history, political economy and travel. We read T. H. Huxley and Herbert Spencer. In 1898, before I passed the matriculation examination, we read Milton's shorter works: *Il Penseroso, L'allegro, Comus, Samson Agonistes,* and all *The Task* poems of Cowper. When my brothers and I were otherwise engaged, Father invariably reverted to his slate and pencil. I am now convinced that the slate and pencil added years to his life.

------

[147] See p. 122, note 93, on Sir Frederick Lely. His letter to the author is in English in the original.

[148] The word 'deduction' is in English in the original.

'An idle brain grows feeble, and the brain's weakness significantly affects the body. One should dismiss the thought that old age is a time for reading,' he maintained. 'From early on in life one should cultivate a hobby; quite apart from working for one's bread and butter one should engage one's hands, learn carpentry, engrave printing blocks, design gardens, prune trees, cultivate beautiful, scented varieties of flowers and enter them in flower shows. As far as possible, foster interests that don't strain the eyesight. Should your eyes retain their strength in old age, then your time is well-spent reading; should they become weak then beware, for all creation will become dim.'

The drawing room in our home was furnished with sofas and chairs. And yet Father much preferred sitting on the floor, with mattress and cushions spread out. When I recall my childhood, that vast mattress with a bolster placed at the back, like those used by royals, appears before my eyes. He is seated exactly in the middle, while I either lounge or sit by his side. With one leg bent at the knee and the other folded, and the slate, rested against his bent knee, held close to his eyes, my father writes, and the sound of the pencil scratching the slate's surface reaches my ears. Writing in this manner, he sits motionless, except for his hand that moves on the slate. An hour or two pass; my childish mind tires; he remains absorbed in his work.

He was a man of disciplined habit. Despite the number of servants in our household, he did not allow anyone else to cater to his needs. He would wash the slate, sharpen the pencil himself, and if by chance we asked why he insisted on doing things on his own, his answer was: 'As long as I have the strength to do things for myself, I will not order servants around; only if I keep this resolve will I retain my strength.'

After drinking his morning tea, he would sit down alone to work in the drawing room, provided no visitor interrupted him. Writing and erasing what he wrote repeatedly, writing and erasing as if haunted by the mischievous ghoul Babrobhoot.[149]

----

[149] Babrobhoot, identified in *Karan Ghelo* (*KG* 7.190–191) as Madhav's murdered brother Keshav, who returned as a ghost to avenge Karan's misdeeds.

There was, I recall, a strong bond at the time between my elder brothers and my future father-in-law, Shri Thakoreram. Together they would frequent our home in the mornings bearing *The Bombay Gazette,* a daily recommended by Shri Jhaverilal that they would read to Father. Other visitors were few and far between.

Father was a life member of the Andrews Library, where illustrated papers arrived every fortnight. We would look through them first and then read them out to him. From childhood I worked as his amanuensis: my responsibility was to read his letters and write down his replies, even read books to him. However, until such time as I was able to read with some fluency and understand the meanings, he rarely called upon me to read. Father was a stickler for correct pronunciation. Reading in a monotonous voice, placing stress in inappropriate places or pausing at wrong junctures were unacceptable—in short, it pained him to listen when what he heard lacked that special tone which comes only with comprehension.

Come summertime both my brothers, Markandrao and Manubhai, would arrive from Bombay and Baroda. Then Father's joy knew no bounds. Time sped by in philosophical discourse, in discussing politics, in conversations about social reform in the country. There was never any kind of idle gossip or criticism, either about caste or concerning individuals.

After three in the afternoon, we would get together again. My mother would join in the conversation, and so would any visiting sister. Every evening we went out for walks. We would drive to the outskirts of the city in our carriage and then begin our walk. Returning home by eight, we would be together again until ten at night.

My mother was always present with some delicacy in hand, waiting to welcome us affectionately with a smiling face when we returned from school. Of frustration, if there was any, no one ever saw a trace on her radiant face. She rose in the wee hours of the morning, was the first to climb down to the ground floor to wake up the servants and begin establishing order in the household. She would then bathe and, dressed in fine clothes and jewellery, sit turning the beads of her rosary. Mother held the reins of the household firmly; not a thing escaped her keen eye. Every object in the house had to be clean and in its place; every child had to be taught cleanliness and to be treated with affection—it was her way of running her household. After lunch, she read the *Ramayan* or the *Bhagavat*. She slept little. Though generally thrifty, she was also keen on appearing gracious, so she spent freely when the occasion demanded. In the evenings in Surat, she would occasionally leave the house for an outing, but in Dumas she would be restless if she did not walk morning and evening. In Dumas she remained in the pink of health; in the absence of fresh air in Surat, she wilted.

In the year of 1899, in the month of Vaishakh, our entire family assembled in Dumas. Walking on the Dumas beach and watching his blossoming, smiling progeny spread about him like a lush garden, I distinctly remember Father saying, 'Not in my wildest dreams did I imagine that fortune would bless me so abundantly with the joys of a happy family'. Like a man who renounces the worldly life and sits meditating under the shade of an old banyan tree, gazing at the wonders of creation, detached from it all and yet in love with it, I saw him elated and gently smiling. My eldest brother had five children, my second brother four, my elder sister Harsiddhagauri six, and my second sister Sulochanagauri two—in this way from the solitary homes of Amritram and Tuljashankar had sprung an extended clan. There is a belief in the Shinto faith that our invisible ancestors help their descendants. May our ancestral hosts care for us!

Until 1901, the clouds of misfortune had cast few shadows on this happy family. It is true that in 1867, a nine-month-old son had died. But when one is young, the loss or gain of sons does not leave behind as much sorrow or joy as it does when one is past middle age. Father's fourth son died in Nanded; in an earlier chapter I have hinted at the boy's injuries. He was only sixteen years of age, but having suffered a wound to his brain as a child, his body did not mature. He suffered seizures, which, though few in the beginning, grew in intensity as he aged, and finally took his life. An innocent boy in the grips of disease had finally found release.

When Father was at Nanded, his nephew Vaikunthhram, a youth of only twenty-eight, died in Poona. Hearing that the bright young man, who had reached a distinguished position in government service, had died, leaving behind a child widow and four children, Father, who was very fond of his young nephew, was devastated.

My younger aunt's middle son died of tuberculosis. 'When it seemed that time was running out, I arrived from Godhra to see his life, a vessel tossed in a storm on the high seas about to capsize. By his bedside, holding two tiny girls in her lap, sat his young wife. She was Nandsukhlal Shirestadar's daughter, and a distant niece of mine. When my glance fell on her—a young tree with two tendrils hanging on the side felled by lightning—it broke my heart. The grief I felt for her, sinking unprotected in the sea of sorrow, was greater than what I felt even for the nephew whose life's potential had been cut short,' I recall Father saying. After the untimely death of these two nephews, I never again saw him don his red turban; thereafter, he only wore the Abbasi turban.

Then, in 1901, my own elder sister died of the dreaded pneumonia. Harsiddhagauri died in her prime, well before the full canopy of her life had unfolded. Not one given to displaying either sorrow or joy, Father showed few signs of outward grief, but the blow cut deep into his being. His eldest daughter, virtuous, calm, given over to piety, suddenly disappearing—it was like a limb had been cut off; the shock reverberated to the very end of his life. The wound inflicted by the loss of his first-born never healed.

My mother liked to go on pilgrimages while Father liked to travel in beautiful countrysides, so whenever possible we visited pilgrim sites. In the year 1899, we went on pilgrimage to Nasik, the source of three rivers. I was very young at the time, so I do not remember the visit well, but I vividly recall the tiny temples within the Godavari's profusely flowing waters. The area is historically associated with Panchavati where, according to the ancient epic *Ramayan*, Rama and Sita had lived in exile.

In Poona, we saw the hillock seated on which Bajirao Peshwa witnessed the battle of Khirkee. Across from that hill stands Shivaji's fortress Simhagadh (the lion's fort). 'The fort is won but the lion lost: *Gaḍh ālā simha gelā'*—Shivaji's words when Tanaji Malusare conquered the fort, dying a heroic death, are well-recorded in the chronicles of the time. While, 'Baji(rao) came, turned tail, and a kingdom was lost: *Baji ālā, pāji zālā, ne rāj gelā'*[150]—is unfortunately how the coward will always be remembered in history. Parashuram, although a brahmin, learned the use of weaponry, but proved unable to contain the burden of this knowledge within limits, and so he went on to eliminate the warrior race of kshatriyas from the earth. Assuredly, it is easy to acquire power, but to foster and hold on to it is difficult. Just as, 'To make love is easy but to nurture love is difficult: *Iśk āsān namud avval vale iftād muśkil hā.'*[151]

The following words—placed by Father in the mouth of brahmins advising a remorse-filled Karan Vaghela to journey as a pilgrim to Shristhal—reflect his settled views on the matter:

> Even if we set aside the idea that pilgrimages result in a vision of God, the effect of a pilgrimage on a person's mind is wondrous. Having read literature in praise of pilgrimages, the re-vitalised imagination stills the body; altered surroundings contribute their own share to this experience; new sites, and the stories attaching to them, add new impressions and become lodged in the memory, pushing aside earlier painful experience. When a change of environment offers relief to those who are physically diseased, why shouldn't it similarly alleviate the sorrow of those who suffer mental agonies?
>
> Moreover, our ancient sages chose beautiful and beguiling landscapes to locate our sacred sites; several are found on the banks of well-known rivers. At dawn and at dusk, alongside the different river *ghats*, one sees men bathing, women filling their pots, and brahmins reciting the Gayatri mantra. A soft breeze blows ripples across the glass-like surface of the clear waters even as, on the other shore, trees drift past; in between are boats large and small swaying with sailors. Observing these, the mind becomes still and joyous.
>
> Watching the flowing river, people are reminded of their life in this world. Just as a river is tiny when it emerges from mountainous terrains and then playfully rambles on for some distance through

---

[150] The chronicler's words are in Marathi.

[151] In Farsi; translated as per the author's Gujarati rendition.

a floral and pebbly course, so passes the childhood of man. As the river flows, it is joined by others, so also the grown man becomes related to others. And finally, at the end, the river merges with the vast unbounded waters of the ocean, so also man's life wanes and his finite lifespan merges with the infinite. In this way, standing on the river bank, a man's thoughts traverse his entire life, and in the face of God's wondrous creation, he feels himself reduced to a cipher.

Sacred sites are often located in great forests where, within a vast canopy of trees, men live in solitude. Several sacred sites are also situated near mountains. How can devotion not enter the minds of men surrounded by such beauty? Where God has so innocently and with such generosity given so much, where His great creation appears to mock man's petty works, where different forms of natural beauty are gathered together, where the earth is so sanctified by divinity that an ordinary man trembles to do evil, where so many forest-dwelling tribes imagine the earth to be a veritable heaven, imitating His example—it is in such places that man truly realises his own insignificance. Recognising that there is no power greater than his Creator's, he humbly bows down and submits body and soul to His keeping, praises Him with full heart and, with absolute devotion, gives depth to his own faith, convinced that whatever happens will accord with His wishes. It is, then, not surprising that the minds of men become tranquil and still when as pilgrims they visit sacred sites. (*KG* 206–210)[152]

My maternal grandmother, bathing at dawn in her old age, would recite:

Gangādvāre kuśāvarte Nīlake nīlaparvate / snātvā Kanakhale tirthe punarjanma na vidyate //

At the doorsteps of the Ganga, spread with kusha grass is Kanakhala, a sacred site surrounded by blue mountains. For those who bathe in the Blue River (Nilaka), there is no rebirth.[153]

---

[152] Vinayak embeds considerable textual material from *Karan Ghelo* while presenting a more concise form of Nandshankar's views on pilgrimages.

[153] According to Monier William's Dictionary, Nilaka is the name of a river.

My belief that beauty heals was confirmed when I first set eyes on Hardwar, and found myself murmuring, 'If there is to be rebirth for me, let it be here, let it be here!'

Walter Pater in *Marius the Epicurean* attributes similar beliefs to the Romans. When Marius falls ill, he is taken to the temple built atop a hill in honour of Aesculapius, the Physician. Here nature's beauty cures his disease: 'He was made perfect by love of visible beauty'.[154] In exactly the same way, many Indians seek relief from disease amidst the beauty of nature. Shakespeare, too, in *As You Like It*, has Jacques say: 'and man exempt from public haunt finds tongues in trees, books in running brooks, sermons in stone, and good in everything' (Act II, Scene 1).

In 1893, we went on pilgrimage to Girnar. My maternal grandfather and my mother were in Bhavnagar attending the marriage ceremonies of the Maharaja. We joined them in Junagadh. At the time, Haridasbhai, who belonged to the distinguished Desai clan of Nadiad, was Diwan. Accompanied by Purushottam Raiji, Nawabsaheb himself was present at the ceremony. We saw the sacred sites associated with Narasinh Mehta and, girdling the Girnar hillside, many monuments dedicated to Parshvanath. They seemed to proclaim the rising beauty of Jain art. On the top of the hill stands the temple dedicated to the goddess. Father climbed to the very top of the hill, accompanied by my elder sister Bahuvidyagauri and me. People say that the climb was easier before the path leading up to the monuments was paved with steps. But to my childish mind it was a feat as great as vanquishing a tiger.

On the way, we were shown the caves of the Aghori sect. Seeing these ascetic renunciants, with their single-minded doctrine, their elevated thought but base conduct, and their manner of punishing the flesh makes the very thought of renunciation abhorrent.

From Junagadh we travelled to Prabhaspatan. There, after visiting sites sacred to Krishna, we bathed in the Saraswati river. We saw the famous temple dedicated to Mahakali, All-conquering

---

[154] Aesculapius was the Roman god of healing. The quotation, 'He was made perfect by love of visible beauty' is from Walter Pater's *Marius the Epicurean* (see Pater 1910: Vol. 1, p. 106).

Time. We experienced the empty darkness that overcomes men who return after consigning a loved one to flames, the indifference and the world-weariness of cremation grounds. Oh Mahakali! You protected the moon from the grips of leprosy, and then allowed your own temple to be destroyed! You did not protect the brahmins' faith from the Turks—the truth is, however, that their faith was already enfeebled by the arrogance of wealth. Father addressed the goddess in the following words: 'Now you have just one message for us, "I am not stone. Worship me, not the stone. Elevate yourself. Abjure your petty lust for wealth. Do not falter from the path of righteousness."'

In *Karan Ghelo,* Father wrote that there is only one significant problem with idol worship, and that is: those who are devoted to images gradually begin to substitute the image of God for God. Not acknowledging their only true Master, men pay the obeisance properly due to Him to His underlings instead.

We spent a few days at Veraval and identified the source of Kathiawad's prosperity. The people there derive their adventurous spirit, their enthusiasm and their determination from their nearness to the sea!

I had heard about Haridasbhai several times from my maternal grandfather. At first, my grandfather had held a position above that of Haridasbhai, but that was before he left for Junagadh. Indeed, who didn't recognise the eminent Desai family of Nadiad? Father maintained that Viharidasji's family had a truly distinguished standing in the region; moreover, one hardly ever came across such a united family as his. Haridasbhai dressed very simply: a borderless pale pink *dhoti,* a tunic, a *paṭidar's* plain turban, and the simple shoes worn in the countryside. He was very fond of riding horses. We had occasion to meet him, and came away highly impressed by his hospitality, his simple straightforward ways and his intelligence.

In 1895, in the month of Chaitra, we set out on pilgrimage to Arasur, where Ambabhavani is worshipped. Father has provided a very realistic picture of the goddess in *Karan Ghelo.* The seed of the story is from Forbes Saheb's *Rās Mālā,* which Father embellished further with stories from the *Purana,* from oral traditions embedded in folk tales, and from several panegyrics in praise of the goddess.

The season we had chosen for the pilgrimage was quite inappropriate; it was summertime, so the journey by road was exceedingly hot, water was supposed to be scarce, and there was fear of being attacked by bears. The goddess keeps a kindly eye on us, so my mother believed. Courtesy of her protective presence, we reached our destination without any serious mishap. We were allowed to enter the innermost sanctum of the temple; my mother was able to offer her prayers to the goddess with her own hands, and we reverently lifted her *paduka* to our foreheads. The arrangements in the temple are courtesy Bholanathbhai's family, so *choghadiya* verses are sung every few intervals. During Navaratri the Nagars visit the shrine to sing *bhavai*s. My mother tells me that she experienced a vision of the goddess in the form of Ganesh for the first time here, at Arasur. A vision of Gauri's son, that remover of all obstacles, is considered a truly auspicious sign. We did not try to climb up to Gabbar, but we visited Koteshwar and, on the way, we saw the burned-out sites belonging to the Jains. We also saw an underground tunnel there, which, according to legend, leads all the way to the Dilwara temples. We were told how Ambabhavani had engineered a schism in the Jain order, but this is indeed false praise of the goddess; it is also a clear example of the growth of religious intolerance.

At the end of our devotions, we put twenty-five rupees in the hands of the head priest. The priest warned us that until he had received the full gift due to a priest, he would not certify the pilgrimage as being ritually accomplished. 'As you wish', responded my father, adding, 'not having your stamp of approval will not render our pilgrimage fruitless.' When we declined to plead with him, the priest was nonplussed. As we walked away, the *panda* called us back and gave ritual sanction to our pilgrimage. 'The public has only itself to blame for spoiling these *panda*s,' said Father. 'If you decide to go on a pilgrimage, then how can someone else certify whether your aim in undertaking it is fulfilled or not? So long as you believe that, failure to obtain the *panda*'s ritual assent will result in misfortune, and they will continue to extort pilgrims.' However, Father did not object to the priests receiving a fee in return for smoothing a pilgrim's passage through the scattered shrines, for assisting in the performance of religious rituals, and for being generally helpful.

Father maintained that the spread of artistic beauty in Gujarat was largely due to Jain influence. This leading merchant community accumulated wealth, fought battles, and built their magnificent shrines. In these shrines, the marble appears as though spun from silver thread; from every corner wafts the scent of saffron; the large domed interiors echo with the chants of monks and the hum of pilgrims; and tiny lamps emit the fragrance of camphor. In this suggestion of vastness, the self feels infinitesimal, is forgetful of its own separate existence and, following an impulse all its own, is naturally drawn to the infinite.

The best temples are those of the Jains at Dilwara; the best statues are of the Buddhists and the Jains. Their enlightened men, freed from the cycle of birth and death, are represented as absorbed in the deepest state of meditation, their hands held in gestures that say: 'There is naught to fear; there is forgiveness and redemption for the fallen'.[155]

Father himself was drawn to temples dedicated to Ram. As he would say, 'If there was a king who kept his vows to his people, it was that son of Janaki! If there was a king who renounced his own being to uphold his vows, it is Ramachandra! His worship is sacred, his praise is sacred, his temples are abodes of peace, and his images uplift the mind.'

Father recommended that temples be kept open all day, that stories from the *Puranas* evoking religious ardour and didactic tales of virtuous conduct be recited in temples; that times for viewing the main deity not be fixed as fixed timings see crowds collect and result in men and women being crammed together; that varieties of flowering plants like tulsi, jasmine and rose be planted all around the shrine; that a large tank with parapets where devotees can bathe be built across from the shrine, and wells providing drinking water be dug beside the tank; that large

---

[155] A translation of '*patita pāvana*', from the chant *Radhupati rāghava rājārām.*

trees with extended canopies be planted on all sides of the temple. In this way, a devotee entering the precincts at any time of day, in the morning, afternoon or evening, whether saying his or her prayers out loud or reciting them silently, may sit in a space filled with perfumed sanctity, to attain peace and salvation.

Returning from Abu, we dropped in at Vadnagar. This is the main seat of the Nagar community. The temple of Hatkeshwar, the deity we favour, is located here. There is no way of counting the sites sacred to Shiva in this region; shrines dedicated to each one of Shiva's names, from Bhensbadeshwar on, are to be found here, all arranged in hierarchical order.

I often discussed religion with Father, so I was acquainted with his views on the subject. For the common man, he believed, the inhibiting aspects of religious doctrine are more effective than the salvific. 'If you behave badly, Father Hanuman will devour you!'; 'If you anger Mother Goddess, the land will suffer!' Fears of this sort prevent men from swerving away from the righteous path, Father would say. He would add to the Socratic saying, 'Individual men should revere the gods of their own land and, if they have to worship images, they ought to keep their temples clean. The statues of the gods should be made of marble, without outer adornment; the chosen gods should convey a sense of purity and peace. Priests without learning, those of shallow intellect, should be kept far away; only good, noble men appointed to protect and beautify temples should serve temples. Priests should be stopped from charging fees.'

Then our talk would turn to the Prarthana Samaj. Father maintained that this order was most certainly not for the common man: 'It is suitable only for those who actually follow its tenets. Save for exceptional individuals, it has little impact on the general mass of people for it makes no difference in their lives. The general run of its members tends to be like any ordinary Christian who goes to church donning clothes specially set aside for the occasion, prays, takes part in the singing, returns home and hangs up his clothes on the same peg.' Father firmly believed that 'The devotional spirit is constant and requires no dwelling place, save for one's own home and a very few houses of worship'.

His view of the Brahmo Samaj was different. A religious doctrine that prepares to set aside bonds of caste and clan in order to unite all of mankind as the many children of one God is a formidable undertaking. Unfortunately, in the absence of a large following, the doctrine is not well-established in the general populace; it is like a tadpole's large head, supported by a small and shrivelled body.

Bholanathbhai was considered to be the moving spirit of the Prarthana Samaj. A river of faith flowed ceaselessly through his being, as though every act of his emerged from the depths of its sacred waters. Had he lived in the sixteenth century, he would most certainly have been considered a great saint today.

Mahipatram was by and large a tenacious man filled with the spirit of adventure, and keen to serve his people in religious matters. In the absence of the Brahmo Samaj in Gujarat, his need for a supporting and encouraging deity might have been met by the Unitarian faith.

Father had faith in the future of the Arya Samaj. However, its founder Dayanand Saraswati's conviction that demolishing his opponents' point of view should of necessity precede establishing his own did great harm. Moreover, though he revered the Vedas as primary texts, his views on cow slaughter clung calamitously to him. Due to this belief and despite great similarities between his new doctrines and those of monotheistic Islam, the division between the two religions widened. Dayanand's attempt to draw Hindustan back to its Aryan past is commendable, as were his efforts to uplift the lower orders through the devotional practices of Vaishnavism. His philosophy unified the common man's path of devotion with the path of knowledge meant for the high-minded. In the new temple, faith in our country will come alive, Dayanand believed.

Father accepted monotheism. He prayed with silent mind, taught men to grow in their own faith, and held that right conduct was the means to ultimate truth. Adhere with determination to the truth and be rational, he counselled.

In *Karan Ghelo*, he wrote: 'Men who in this world act righteously merely for gain stand on weak ground. That right action will bring beneficial returns and evil ones result in evil returns is a false carrot held out by moralists long ago; it is pure fiction. Those who desire to enjoy in heaven the fruits of their good deeds on earth and are convinced that virtuous acts produce virtuous results should not look for rewards on earth.' (*KG* 12.337–338)

Father's religious instincts were displayed not so much in his thought processes as in his conduct. He was an avid student of the life sciences, which is why he compared India to the hydra. The coral that we are familiar with is in fact hydra's armature. The hydra grows in one of two directions: it may grow in one direction; then meeting resistance it shrinks or, halting, moves the other way. Near the root of every division stands a transparent curtain showing a possible way forward; a small aperture in that transparent curtain ensures enduring continuity in the forward movement of the life force. So, even if each cell is unique and different, through the small hole in the curtain the organism still remains linked to the cells that lie before and after it. As a result, a vibrancy occurring at any one point spreads throughout.

In the vast ocean that is India's history, when the Dasyus, the native population, ruled over an ancient civilisation, the Aryan hydra appeared. The Aryans' ability to occupy space was so powerful that in whichever direction their two-headed hydra-like being spread, the native population was stamped out. Scientists have maintained that nature is cruel. But nature is neither cruel nor kind. The group comprising individuals in whom the life force is strong is bound to destroy those groups in which it is weak.

Father maintained that India would have been far better off if all its Dasyus had been entirely wiped out; a less satisfactory but acceptable outcome would have been if the two groups had merged completely. There ought to have been a complete confluence of the white waters of the Ganga and the dark waters of the Kalindi. If that did not happen, the Ganga should have abandoned the Jamuna at source. But at the time, men violated the laws of nature; and they suffer the consequences thereof to this day. There resulted an open order of Aryans, an order of pure Aryans, an open order of Dasyus, and an order of pure Dasyus, out of which four orders of the population emerged: a mixture of Aryan-Dasyus, with the Aryans predominating; a mixture of

Dasyu-Aryans, with the Dasyus predominant; pure Aryans; and pure Dasyus.

In Europe, three-quarters of the native population (Dasyu) was destroyed, and one quarter was completely absorbed, but the assimilation was reciprocal. By contrast, because in India populations were only partially assimilated, an inevitable tear in the social fabric remained. Slavery appeared as the lot of the lowest of the low castes. We see slavery emerge in some countries through the conquest of a people by another people, and in others as a result of commerce; but here, in India, it is as if a group of people was created just to be slaves. Something of the sort seems to be the case in the United States also.

This development resulted eventually in the Aryan way of life becoming weak. Brahmins, kshatriyas and vaishyas are considered to belong to the *dvija* or 'twice-born' order. The first presides over the brain; the second is considered dextrous in the use of arms; and the third, having eaten and digested the food, produces the precious substance in the form of blood and is associated with the belly. The legs attaching to the social body belongs to the shudras, who alone should, according to this design, engage in work that degrades!

Father did not believe that any kind of work is inherently degrading. Caste divisions began when society characterised certain kinds of work as demeaning, then allocated these tasks exclusively to certain castes, and finally decided that the castes engaging in degraded work are only worthy of low social ranks. Our first priority should be to rid ourselves of this infirmity, he advocated. Each individual must strive to become whole and to learn the skills best suited to him. Only when his hands become adept at manual skills will the digestive juices flow, and the brain bring forth a true conception of happiness. These thoughts ought to remain clearly stamped on everyone's mind, he said. All should honour the austerity of labour, and not consider some kinds of work as lowly or certain individuals as degraded by the circumstance of birth.

Further elucidating his thoughts on social structures, Father said: 'My intention in saying this is not to suggest that lions, lords of the forest, be made into beasts of burden or that donkeys rule in their stead. Men are not born alike nor are they meant by nature to be the same. Every individual inherits different ancestral characteristics. Additionally, through personal exertion men acquire their own capabilities. Society's only duty is to provide equal opportunity for all. Only individuals who fail to profit when opportunity presents itself are at fault. It is true that certain wombs are fertile with virtue, but to infer that only those who spring from these wombs are virtuous and that virtue cannot reside otherwise is a fallacy.

'When the Aryans first entered India, their social order lacked division of labour. It is when these nomadic herdsmen settled down and took to agriculture that division of labour arose. With the passage of time, the distance between the divided groups grew rigid and arrested the force that naturally and constantly moves in all directions. In the beginning, individual inclination was honoured. Eventually, however, the idea that only a particular occupation is appropriate for a particular group held fast; though uprooted, it never really lost its roots but returned like the corpse in Vikramaditya's story.[156] Where is the surprise then if the victors lost their valour?'

Father used to say, 'If an individual wants to be a brahmin, allow him to be a brahmin. If he wants to be a kshatriya, let him be one. If he wishes to be a vaishya or merchant, so be it. Do not label anyone a shudra. Instead, inculcate in each individual the habits of a shudra—of working for himself, for his society and for his country.' Father would draw upon historical examples to support his point. Amr (ibn al-As), the conqueror of *Misr* (Egypt), was lowborn; he belonged to the lowest of the low; but a touch of the precious jewel of Islam turned him into an intrepid soldier, a competent ruler, and an inspirer of civilisations. The same story is told about Nadir Shah. In our own Hindustan, such occurrences would be inconceivable.

Islam is a religion that uplifts the downtrodden; it is the only faith that raises the fallen and rescues the afflicted. A few drops of spirituality like dew fell in the desert; from their potency a majestic tree of faith grew in whose shade a more civilised social

---

[156] The reference is to the *Vetala Panchavimshati*; see p. 130, note 102.

order emerged, and a once conflicted people became peaceful. It was not the peace of the dead, but a peace that remained clothed in knowledge and art. Wherever the seed flew, it nourished a life-enhancing inner peace.

If someone asked him, are there no caste divisions within the Muslim order, Father's response was that caste was not an essential aspect of Islam, but was due to Muslim adoption of defective Hindu ways. Outside of India, caste distinctions do not exist in Muslim societies. Status based on wealth certainly exists within that society; there is, for instance, the division between landlord and farmer; but even within these ranks, persons are free to choose their own vocation. Function-based division of labour is not passed down the generations. In fact, poet after poet, from the very beginning to this day, writes homilies about the fickleness of fortune: nothing in creation is eternal; everything perishes. Their poets sing about the good and evil that kismet brings. In truth, one sees that real fervour in Islam is due to individual effort. Though, Islam also declares from on high what Duryodhan articulates in the *Mahabharat*:

> *jānāmi dharmam na ca me pravṛttir |*
> *jānāmyadharmam na ca me nivṛttih |*
> *kenāpi devena (daivena) hṛdisthitena |*
> *yathā niyukto'smi tathā karomi ||*[157]

I know righteousness, but my actions do not flow from that knowledge,
Nor do I desist from unrighteousness, though I know what it is;
I act following the command of whatever god (or fate) is stationed in my heart.

Which, in the context of Islam, may be rendered as: 'Should happiness come to me, it is Allah's will; if ruin comes, it is the hand of kismet'.[158]

Father believed that a person's temperament is properly adapted for one particular occupation. And even though

---

[157] See p. 175, note 136.

[158] Vinayak's gloss here is enabled with the aid of the two readings: '*devena*' and '*daivena*'—'by God' and 'by Fate'; '*devena*' is read as kismet in the context of Islam.

proficiency in varied subjects may enable one to prosper in several areas, sooner or later limitations generally show up. However, the belief that a brahmin should honour only knowledge led brahmins to neglect work of the hands. But, pray, why should a brahmin not be a sculptor or painter or an expert musician? Art is a daughter of the Vedas; in fact it is an essential part, and yet art is not respected in society today. After Ashvatthama and Parashuram, it was generally believed that a brahmin who is imbued with the warrior's spirit would only do grave harm. When the lustre of learning mixes with the warrior's brilliance, darkness will certainly prevail. Do particles of dust ever sparkle? The result will be total annihilation.[159]

The brahmin Peshwas established their power with the aid of their 'swords and curses: *śārpair api śarair api.*' In them the brahmanical spirit was eclipsed; but because the kshatriya temper had taken root in a few individual brahmins, the warrior spirit glittered. And because the glow appeared even after these individuals with the warrior spirit were gone, in due course it became established as a tradition within the group. But the power to bring down heaven's wrath dimmed; nor did the Peshwas truly master the art of war. Only if the well has water will it land up in the trough. And so the Peshwas' reign came to an end within a short period of a hundred years; Parashuram's avatar ended, and Ram the kshatriya prince returned.[160]

Since only the individual has the ability to judge his own limitations, it is important to provide a student with well-rounded education. Give him the gift of knowledge. Instruct him in the use of arms. Initiate him into business practices. In this way, the

---

[159] Ashvatthama was the son of Dronacharya. To avenge the death of his father, he slaughtered the sleeping Pandav kinsmen and let loose a world-destroying weapon. See https://sacred-texts.com/hin/m10/m10008.htm- and https://sacred-texts.com/hin/m10/m10016.htm (accessed 22 May 2021).

[160] Parashuram was a brahmin but took up arms against the kshatriyas, and so violated the brahmin's dharma. His conflict with the kshatriya prince Ram is from the *Bal Kand, sarge* 76, of the *Ramayan.* See https://www.indianculture.gov.in/srimad-valmiki-ramayana-critical-edition-commentary-sri-govindaraja (accessed 22 May 2021).

individual will discover the work he is naturally suited for, without having to squeeze him into some awkward pre-determined hole. When a square shape is forced into a round hole, unfortunate consequences are bound to follow.

Father was partial to Islamic history, and he was also exceedingly fond of the *Mahabharat*. Consequently, he maintained that our heroes should be scholars, even if the scholarship is in Islamic mould. They should be able, when the need arises, to build castles, but be equally ready to join working men, pick up the spade and dig the earth.

He maintained that caste solidarity no longer serves any purpose. Perhaps at one time there might have been a rationale for caste bonds, but times had changed, and they were no longer relevant. Within the modern social order, individuals run helter-skelter, each individual seeks ways to advance his particular goal, his character changes, but it is only his successive achievements that will spur him forward, and that too only if the chosen means are well-suited to the ends they are meant to serve. Since the native population, the Dasyus, needed to be subdued in the beginning, the kshatriya order was firmed up. And since knowledge at the time depended entirely on memory, it became the property of those with the capacity to learn by heart. The dark-skinned native inhabitants (indigenous populations) outnumbered the white-skinned ones; so effort went into preventing crossbreeding between castes (*varna-sankara*). To shun work that was considered demeaning became a way for the upper castes to establish their dominance. When the Aryan race first entered India, they spread out on the Doab, and the great sages of the time, with their sharp intellects, devised suitable means to further their own ends, and succeeded in achieving them. Those times have now vanished.

Just as the science of geology reveals a variety of raised layers emerging next to each other, so also caste divisions arose next to each other. Due to environmental pressures the layers continue to press together. A glance shows that the quality of the surface of each layer is very different from what one sees if we run our eyes down. Here each layer has a certain uniformity. As a result of the continuous pressure from the top and from the sides, the surface of each layer acquired different qualities.

The layers that are horizontally uniform were at one time made up of innumerable similar particles. As pressure on them grew, they bunched together and became disordered; laws governing union and partition came into effect, uniformity was replaced by multiplicity, and diversity spread. Each layer, no longer able to extend horizontally, acquired vertical depth.

In the same way, when the caste order was four-fold, each stratum would have contained numerous individuals of a similar type. When groups pressed together, the spread of each group diminished; some parts were pressed down and upper and lower classes emerged where once there had been no such division within the group. Clashes between classes resulted in the weathering process and the distance between the upper crust brahmin and kshatriya diminished.

To create homogeneity within each of the older caste orders is not the solution. Father's advice to those who wish to bring development for future generations is not to raise any single caste, but rather to altogether level out stratifications based on caste. Lower, middle and upper classes within each group are, however, bound to remain. He explicated his firmly-held opinions with the help of the above analogy drawn from geology.

'Don't allow brahmins to remain sheep-like reciters of the Vedas nor kshatriyas to become coarse, emotionally-barren fighters; don't teach members of the trading caste merely ways to multiply their capital. Strive to develop the whole person, one able to imbibe the nectar of life, rather than one who calls life a sorrow-filled burden. Strive to make individuals whole'—this was what Nandshankar essentially believed.

'Notions of untouchability should be rooted out,' advocated Father, 'But not at the expense of cleanliness, which should, in fact, be promoted. Keep the body clean so that the mind stays pure.' Indeed, in our family, we always changed our clothes after the evening walk, before sitting down to the evening meal. We bathed in the morning immediately before eating. Our conduct wasn't dictated by custom or religious sanction but governed by simple rules of hygiene.

'Competition between castes has wrought great damage. "Eat what I have touched…But what have you touched?—Ha! Ha!"

I don't approve of such ways,' he would say. 'Ostentatious caste attitudes of this kind cultivate narrowness of mind, caste and clan arrogance, and anti-social selfishness. The idea that there is nothing purer than those who cook their own food is quite false. When mushrooms were served as an offering to the Mahatma Gautama Buddha, how could the Buddha insult a devotee who held out the offering with love? This enlightened prince born in the Shakya clan accepted a sacred gift of mushrooms from a cobbler devotee without caring for the death of his body. He thereby stood by the principle that all human beings are equal.'

Father served as a teacher for almost fifteen years and then became headmaster. Throughout these years, he was keen to adopt educational practices current in England. He also strove to nourish the love of knowledge in a large number of people from Surat. Convinced that his views on education would prove valuable, I present them here to my readers.

'A child ought not to be educated in a haphazard manner. Do not send the child to school before he reaches the age of six. Don't allow him to remain in the first grade beyond four months, lest he grow bored', so he believed. Nandshankar held that the initial four grades should be so organised as to allow a child to finish each grade in four months. After the fifth grade, classes should be divided into two sections; English should be immediately introduced at this stage for those who wish to study in that language, since an additional two years is sufficient for improving the child's knowledge of Gujarati. 'One should keep alive the child's desire for knowledge. Never curb a child who asks questions', he would say. Not questioning is the disease; health wells up after generation upon generation of questioning.

Yah satatam pariprcchti śrunoti sandhārayaty aharniśam |
Tasya divākarakiranair nalinīv samvardhate buddhih || Panch. 5.93 ||[161]

Just as lotus buds open when touched by the sun's rays,
So also intelligence flowers in a person who constantly questions,
who ceaselessly listens and recollects.

---

[161] From the *Panchatantra* (see Mishra 1910).

'Do not adopt the English habit of praising children to their face. Do not encourage the habit of putting on good manners for the sake of appearance alone. Nor should you condemn a child in front of others. Nagging the child, constantly pointing out his shortcomings is wrong. Scold him by all means but, like gift-giving, this should not be done in public. It is not wrong to indulge a child, but the indulgence should be kept within bounds. Be openly affectionate but do not allow an unrestrained obstinacy to take hold. Control the shoots that awkwardly emerge from the root, otherwise at adolescence they go out of hand.

'We delight in calling children adventurous. The adventurous quality, useful when we were forest dwellers in need of protecting ourselves, is the inspirational spirit which now spurs us forward.' Father believed that the spirit of adventure should be cultivated in children because it is a means of uplifting them. Thoughts of greatness, he believed, are connected with a sense of honour; so if a child cries or does something that his own childish mind finds shameful, appeal to his sense of honour, and he will stop. If the child shows envy, becomes isolated, is greedy, untruthful, bullies those who are weaker, and seeks to get his way in crooked ways, invoke his honour, talk to him about the virtues of courage and so embarrass him. Above all, don't indulge him in inappropriate ways.

'I was brought up in my paternal home. My upbringing was quite unlike that of children brought up indulgently in a joint family in their paternal home, who are prone to uncivil conduct. Generally speaking, our child-rearing methods are quite strange. The mother is usually very young; the child she has borne is brought up and watched over by the grandfather, who in the presence of the child openly discusses his mother's character. If the fond mother becomes frustrated with her child and smacks him, the grandmother automatically comes down on the child's side. Sensing the grandmother's partiality, the child learns to be obstinate and disdains his own mother. So a well-behaved child in the maternal household becomes obstinate, demanding and given to tantrums in the paternal home.'

Father did not approve of the prevailing practice in Gujarat of children addressing their mothers in overly familiar terms, as sister, sister-in-law or aunt, rather than as mother. These are a throwback to the earlier days of joint families where the eldest male alone was addressed as 'Father', and the head of household affairs alone was called 'Mother', and the biological mother seldom allowed to display maternal feelings towards her children; she was just the unpaid wet nurse, not a mother but a foster mother.

The popular saying 'There is no love without fear' isn't entirely false. Even though it is wrong in general to thrash children, the fear of the rod has its advantages, but to allow occasions to arise when the rod becomes necessary is wrong. The adage '*panchavarṣāṇi lāḍayet, daśavarṣāṇi tāḍayet*': indulge your child for the first five years, discipline (literally, slap or thrash) him for the next ten/ in the sixteenth year, look upon him as a friend', like all old sayings, contains a germ of truth.[162] In the flow of a child's life, crosscurrents begin to emerge at the age of ten. It is wise to control these, but severe or frequent beatings will only serve to harden him. Fear, like a sword, should dangle from the sky; the sword does not descend, but the possibility that it might should always be there.

A child in its early years should be taught to learn good poetry by heart. Dalpatram is the greatest writer of nursery rhymes in Gujarat. 'A buffalo calf broke loose from the pen and scampered free to the village's end'; 'My babies, said the fly to her children, don't you try to fly or even lift your heads skywards until I return'; 'A naughty boy, Jeeva was his name'—all these rhymes are extremely well-suited for children. Their ingenious simplicity, penetrating message and their basis in the child's experience are rarely met with elsewhere. You can hardly find better ways to manage an obstinate and contrary child than by distracting him with these nursery rhymes. What child will not be sad when he hears the lines, 'Who heeds his parents' dying words finds his way; the heedless makes no headway'. Those who dismiss this great poet Dalpatram as a rhymester of dance music have no understanding of how difficult it is to write simple, unadorned lines that touch the heart. Dr Johnson once declared

---

[162] This is attributed to Chanakya's *Nīti Sāstra*. See https:// sanskritdocuments.org/ (accessed 22 May 2021).

that the poetic quality of Goldsmith's verse is of the common sort, whereupon Goldsmith in similar spirit countered, 'If you were to make little fishes talk, they would talk like whales.'[163]

Never make children learn the times tables beyond twenty, Father advised; encourage them to learn multiplication tables of halves and quarters, but don't press them any further in the direction of learning thirds and eights. From the beginning teach children to draw, encourage them to sketch in five or six pencil strokes the figure of some object placed before them. The teaching of arithmetic should begin at an early age, and should be taught alongside geometry.

Historical and geographical themes should be incorporated within prose readers, and just as we don't make students learn lessons by heart in a reader, the strategy of incorporating these subjects into the prose reader will ensure that history and geography lessons are not learnt mechanically. Do not impose any sort of homework on children. During the longer vacations, make them draw or trace pictures.

'To produce experiential learning in geography, demonstrate how water flows from higher ground to a lower level by actually creating a model. From the very beginning, develop skills of observation in young children; teach them to use their eyes, educate their hands, and encourage them to draw, carve or construct what they see.

'It is necessary to cultivate an interest in history. Indeed, starting with family history move on to the traditions of the village,

---

[163] Vinayak is alluding to an anecdote from James Boswell's *Life of Samuel Johnson L.L.D* in defence of Dalpatram's stories for children. The incident related by Boswell reads as follows. Oliver Goldsmith had told Johnson that he would write a fable in which animals talked in character. 'For instance, (said he,) the fable of the little fishes, who saw birds fly over their heads, and envying them, petitioned Jupiter to be changed into birds. The skill (continued he,) consists in making them talk like little fishes.' While he indulged himself in this fanciful reverie, he observed Johnson shaking his sides and laughing. Upon which he smartly proceeded, 'Why, Dr Johnson, this is not so easy as you seem to think; for if you were to make little fishes talk, they would talk like WHALES' (Boswell 2006).

the history of the province, and finally the history of the whole of creation; historical knowledge should be taught in ways such that the past appears vividly before the mind's eye. The teacher should never forget that history is not only about dates, or about a certain king ascending the throne and another king losing his kingdom; it is not the story of a succession of kings, but a vision of creation threaded together with truth. Stage settings change, newer characters play their part, but the plot remains the same—"humanity's eternal effort to reach its most desired goal."

'Pay attention to exercising the body. Not every man can be a scholar, but there is no reason why every man can't be strong. And after all, health is happiness (*nyamat*). If you want to digest instruction, strengthen the body, but don't carry bodybuilding to excess, beyond what the body can endure. Adopt those exercises that suit your body—walk, run, swim, jump, play Western games or Indian ones. Don't get old in childhood.' I myself loathed exercising, and so was subject to Father's sermonising.

Father claimed that the teacher should himself decide his instructional goals and abide by them in his teaching. How can you navigate the ocean of knowledge without the rudder? Despite the lack of direction, many a student is keen to be a sailor on the high seas, but however strenuously he rows, his rudderless boat tosses hither and thither on the open sea. Children are asked to write compositions on what they want to do in their future lives. There is nothing wrong with this practice. In fact, parents ought to ask their sons what they intend doing and what kind of work suits their temperament. What man, finding himself a square peg fitted into a round hole, does not find his life's endeavour to be in vain?

There is nothing wrong with rote learning; it brings a sharper edge to memory, Father said. Learn to memorise the sayings of great men; they make great companions and their sayings lend distinction to your speech. Of the supreme importance of good manners and right conduct in daily life, Father was emphatic. Learn to live by school rules, and if you happen to be in a position to give orders, be considerate to those under you. Those who have not learnt to follow the rules (*tabedari*) will remain incapable of governing.

Schools constitute a first step on the world stage; it is just a beginning, a first taste of the future. In school the person who is to serve his society learns to abandon self-interest for the good of the whole, to discover his authentic self without violating another's interests; it is here that he learns the non-violent laws that promote the welfare of his own caste; he learns that in respecting elders, one does not humble oneself but helps support a stable social order; he learns to observe from another's point of view.

Father's own temperament was such that he affectionately drew children to himself; children were not afraid to approach him. When I picture my own childhood, I am reminded of our drawing room in Nandod. Father is seated on a mattress on the floor, leaning his back against a bolster. My mother and one of my elder brothers are singing songs on one side while I and my two sisters loll on the same mattress, badgering him to tell us a story. 'Tell us the Alyababa tory'—even now when my mother reminds me of my childish words, childhood memories begin to stir. Tales of Alibaba, of the stupid crocodile and the quick-witted monkey, of the fox who fell into the indigo vat—we made him tell us all these. He had translated the *Panchatantra* into Gujarati, so his storehouse of tales was unlimited.

His welcoming manner did not intimidate visitors who called on him. Nor did his open friendliness diminish their respect for him in any way. I remember the time in Dumas when Father and I were alone, and my brothers' friend Shri Vijbhukandas Pakvasa came to call. Father spent a long time conversing with him sympathetically. Later, when I met Shri Pakvasa at the seashore, he wondered at my father's amazing capacity to look at others with kindly eyes as equals, and to focus on issues with which the other was familiar. He did not impose an air of superior wisdom—a consequence of either the maturity of experience or the prerogative of age. He did not allow the other to shrink or feel inhibited in any way. It was on such constant ground that Father's idea of friendship rested.

Some ships, heavy with the weight of experienced and wise men, ride out to sea on an even keel; in their wake several smaller vessels coast along at the same speed. It is however not unknown that much less heavily laden ships create enormous waves that sink tiny boats sailing close by.

Father's straightforward character sprang from his fine sense of what was appropriate to the occasion. You may call it what you like, a nuanced sensibility or some kind of inborn insight or intuition. In any given situation, he was always able to discern, naturally, how far to proceed and just when to stop. There was nothing pretentious about him, nor anything pedantic; his conversation was cultivated; falsehoods or pointless stories never fell from his lips. Those who came close to him did not leave without imbibing something of this refined sensibility.

As we grew older, he advised us to bring order, subtlety and kindliness to our manners, to our thoughts and to our conduct. In *Karan Ghelo*, after describing the fearsome asceticism exhibited in front of the Kali temple in Delhi, Father writes: 'The senses ought not to be destroyed; though controlled, they should be allowed to flower. The senses are like the river's flow: so long as the river flows steadily it brings benefits to all, but when it rages it destroys everything that comes in its way'. No sane person would conclude from the above that the river should be drained; but certainly there is wisdom in controlling the rising river, by raising its banks, deepening its course and constructing dams on it.

Father's views relating to women's issues were high-minded. 'Neither in terms of intellect nor in terms of age should there be a mismatch between the men and women who are contemplating matrimony. Thomas Carlyle's wife is reported to have written in great despair, "never marry a man of genius".[164] So long as the man does not respect the woman he marries, his household merely limps along. So long as he is unable to evoke love in the woman he marries, his own frustrated heart will remain parched, like desert sand. Our social order is not in total upheaval; when that happens, there will be greater division when men and women come together, since neither attraction grows nor mutual repulsion between the genders diminishes. In view of this, educate women as soon as possible so that they become equal partners in

---

[164] 'My dear, whatever you do never marry a man of genius' (see Nichol 1904).

marriage.' The traditional custom of marrying girls into families of a higher status had its beginnings in the conviction that the young wife will not look up to her husband and respect him unless she is convinced of the worth, the character and conduct of the family she enters.

Father invoked the image of a protective umbrella to describe the relationship between husband and wife—woman is the central post, man the overhanging cloth. Should the post break the household is lost; spread the cloth to cover as wide a space as you like, without the supporting post the household will not hold. On the other hand, even if the overhanging canvas is lost, the tonsured and widowed household will carry on, even if it is at the mercy of the elements. With great regret he would say that our ancient sages laid down rules forbidding widows to marry in order to limit female birth rates. By turning a whole section of the population into shudras, the sages broke the backs of the native population. By prohibiting widows to remarry, the women were sentenced to life imprisonment, with torture of the body as additional punishment. Each of these acts of injustice has ruined our society, Father rued.

From the moment of her birth, a daughter invites sorrow: '*Putrīriti jātā mahatīva cintā/kasmai pradeyeti mahān vitarkah/datvā prapasyati vā na na veti//*: A daughter is born—what a great worry that is! To whom should I give her? And having given her away, worry will she be happy or will she not? What a grave dilemma!'[165] Father would be displeased if he heard people saying it was a blessing not to have a daughter. 'What sins has the poor thing committed? If you are so anxious about finding a husband for her, leave her alone. Don't get her married. Why do you treat her like a child? Why are you afraid to let her venture beyond certain limits?' would be his typical retort. Some of his friends used to say, 'Better a daughter dead than widowed. A widowed daughter's difficult life will never torment us: you won't have to see her inauspicious face every morning; you are not always afraid, lest her shadow fall on you'. Father believed that such thoughts and numerous similar fears are at the root of our attitude to

---

[165] From the *Panchatantra* 1.222 (see Mishra 1910).

widows. He believed that widows should be allowed to remarry if they wish to do so. 'Don't prevent it. Don't say that women who prefer remarriage to widowhood have chosen an inferior way of life. Break the tradition that says asceticism is a necessary condition of widowhood. Once you annihilate this belief, only those who genuinely wish to lead ascetic lives will do so.'

In *Karan Ghelo*, Father ascribes to Gunasundari's mother the prevailing views of the time in Gujarat:

> It is far better for the daughter to die than to suffer widowhood. Widowed, she is a smouldering stove in your midst, her pain scorches her parents' heart; the very sight of her is ceaseless grief. On the other hand, were she to die, it is true that we would be overcome with sorrow, but sorrow has a short life. Since I will not see her face ever again, she will cease to rekindle my grief. But then, it is far far better that she, although widowed, live. To see her face is satisfaction enough, but when I am old and without strength, unable to get out of bed, my daughter will care for me; then her worth will rise to a lakh rupees. Time heals all wounds, so a widowed daughter who still lives brings deep satisfaction to her parents' heart. (*KG* 3.63–64)

Father said that committing sati was a far better option than living the ugly, dependent life filled with the humiliation and bodily torture that widows are subjected to at present. Here, the cruel people of Gujarat would do well to heed the words that he makes Gunasundari herself speak:

> To have to abandon my jewels and don the *rudraksha* beads of the mendicant, to bundle up my beloved saris and wander the earth wearing a widow's white weeds! And still to live on? And so living, to be banished from the world's affairs, which forbid even my inauspicious shadow to fall on ceremonial rituals? And so living, allow men to look at me as if I were available to them? To bear the sight of men, who on seeing my ill-boding face turn around to return home? And still to live on? To be a burden in the house and a source of your parents' sorrow? And still to live on? To bear the countless taunts of your brother and his wife, and become the lowest kind of dependent, only for the sake of your

bread and butter? And still to live on? What meaning, what joy is
there in such a life? (*KG* 3.65–66)

He might even have been justified in including the following
terrible passage, which he deleted from the manuscript for
fear of introducing a false note into the novel: 'To go on living
now? To sit next to an untouchable barber and have my head
shaved; to turn ugly; to suffer when men look at me as if I were
a pariah?' Father was completely opposed to the custom that
forced widows to shave their heads. The custom had travelled to
Gujarat from the south. You keep pouring water in a clay pot to
make it hard; similarly, a constantly humiliated widow becomes
hard-hearted and incapable of fellow feeling. She might even be
heard repeating the vulgar saying, 'a ha'penny (*nasari*) hag and
a penny for her tonsure'.

I once asked Father what sort of coin a nasari was. He told me
that a paisa would buy you a hundred almonds, while a nasari
would buy you twelve; so a nasari was one-eighth of a paisa. He
laughed and said, 'In those days life was cheap'.

Does a widow cease to be a mother, sister or sister-in-law?
In truth, she ceases even to be a person, a human being. If she
falls ill, people declare in her very presence that a hardened pot
seldom breaks, and that even if she does break, surely the widow
should be happy to be released from her wretchedness. Like
slaves attached to their fetters as if they were gold, grown pitiless,
widows are against liberating and uplifting their own kind. 'Allow
what has been there from times immemorial to continue,' they
say. Oh sister! Surely now is the time to abolish a custom that
began long ago.

On witnessing the death of his widowed mother in sheer
neglect and desolation, Pratap Chandra Mazumdar had uttered
the following heart-rending cry:

What need to bewail the world's hardheartedness? What need
to curse the selfish cruelty of men and women to the wretched
forsaken Hindu widow? To them she was a widow; only to me,
my dear mother, the sole guardian and friend I had in all the

world. I do feel that widows should be more loved, nursed and cared for more humanely. If men were more compassionate, and society recognised their right to the commonest necessaries of life, perhaps they would be less hard on themselves, and many a heart-stricken son would be spared the misery I felt when I found my mother's beloved life sink under the load of the world's neglect and indifference.[166]

A rumour is that early one morning a group of untonsured child widows crossed the path of Khandevrao, Maharaja of Baroda. He returned frustrated, without having accomplished what he had set out to do, and was wondering about this, when someone said, 'Maharaj! There were several child widows among the women who crossed your path this morning. This inauspicious sighting is the cause'. The thoughtless king thereupon promptly ordered that all widows should henceforth shave their heads. What callousness is this! What injustice!

Across from our house there stands a Vaishnav temple. The sight of women gathered here during festivals breaks one's heart—sixty per cent of the crowd consists of shaven-headed widows. Addressing them, Father said: 'Dried up, withered, pinched, you are unsexed of your womanhood. Your conduct has no tenderness; your speech is sour, not sweet; as you elbow your way forward in haste, your gait is gauche, not slow and sensuous. It is not as if you are shameless; rather you have forgotten what it is to have shame; you do not appear to be sorrowful; instead you make others suffer. If you are indeed devoted to religion, then rouse India's temples with your devotional songs. If you happen to be interested in an active social life, open schools and, with a mother's love, nurture children's minds. Or immerse yourself in women's education. Train to be midwives and doctors. Let wisdom flow through your hands. O terrible mother! Stop punishing your body and scorn as ridiculous the torture to which you subject yourself.

---

[166] Pratap Chandra Mazumdar's lament is in English in the original. A prominent member of the Brahmo Samaj, he was also close to Ramakrishna Paramhamsa. See https://www.ramakrishnavivekananda. info/gospel/introduction/other_brahmo.htm (accessed 22 May 2021).

Instead destroy your sorrowing self and surrender your whole being to the service of women and to society.

'Even today, women are educated as housekeepers merely with a view to making a man's life more complete. This is wrong. Don't treat a woman like a sacrificial beast. Don't feed her and adorn her with fine clothes and jewellery merely in order to sacrifice her at the altar of male wellbeing. Don't forget that she too is a person', Father would remind Gujarati society.

'In the beginning, my idea of social reform was outfitted in armour; compromise had no place in it. Of the four customary tactics of ensuring success, namely, persuasion (*sama*), bribery (*dama*), punishment (*danda*) and division (*bheda*), I believed only in using the rod. "Destroy" and "cut away" was the voice of public opinion in those days. Due to my reading of history, however, early on I swerved away from that path. At a time when, like an earthquake, revolutionary forces were rocking Hindustan, my vessel found safe ground. Throw away the rotted social layer by all means and rearrange the deeper layers, but do not destroy the root, which, like the *atman*, keeps the decrepit skeleton attached to life—this is what I believed.

'I believed myself to be someone who seeks to uproot as well as to uplift. Wherever the necessity arises, certainly do cut away at the rotting and the diseased, but I had no wish to destroy the social order in order to give it a newer, more civilised body, and drink the intoxicating nectar that emerges from such destruction. Since the beginning, Dalpatram had sung reform in verses set to the slow *mandākrāntā* tune.[167] "*Festina lente* or hasten slowly", as they say.[168] There is a marked difference between this gradualist's view of social change and change that is passive, dragged forward by time and circumstance. The difference is that the former moves toward an ideal that lies ahead, while the latter remains at the mercy of fate.

---

[167] *Mandākrāntā*, literally 'slow-moving', is a metre used in Sanskrit poetry (see Kale 1934: x).

[168] *Festina lente* from the Latin literally means 'hasten slowly'. The seeming paradox refers to progress that is measured and steady rather than radical or haphazard (see Pantazopoulos 2017).

'Society is made up of individuals. Only if individuals advance will society progress, but there is no independent force behind the individual which will force him forward. Reaction resulting from the mutual clash of two civilisations, however, is the singular factor which will result in a forward push. One could term this unplanned change, which is dragged forward by circumstance. Our countrymen of Hindustan prefer this kind of social change: to allow events to follow their own course and to face the consequences that come. "If we rise high, we rule; should we be oppressed, we are dragged forward; we honour deceit". In other words, individuals adapt to the times in which they live. "It will all happen in due course of time," they say.'

But Father clearly opposed this point of view, and said: 'You are endowed with the gift of intelligence—use it. Observe what is around you, act in accordance with the times in which you live, and then actively work to bring about changes in society. Time is not a substantial entity; other things move, time remains, and the change that things suffer is described as the Wheel of Time (*Kalchakra*). To accommodate yourself to this way of thinking is fruitless. However, the means you adopt to bring about change should be slow, open and targeted.'

> *Sāmnaiva yatra siddhir tatra daṇḍo budhena viniyojyah* |
> *Pittam yadi śarkarayā śāmyati ko'rthah paṭolena* ||[169]

The wise do not use the stick when the purpose is achieved by persuasion.
If sugar cures bile, what's the use of dosing yourself with bitter fruit?

If pleasant words accomplish one's purpose, nothing is served by bitter speech—this was Father's view. The Persian adage '*sakhun shīrīn mulakgīrī*: a sweet tongue conquers countries' is true as far as it goes, but he preferred to practice the injunction to be outspoken: '*spaṣṭa vaktā sukhī bhava*: may the candid speaker be happy'.[170]

---

[169] From the *Panchatantra* 1.409 (see Mishra 1910).

[170] My translation is based on the author's Gujarati translation of the Farsi maxim.

You should abandon the belief that life is divided into four stages in favour of only three stages, he advocated, which he believed was more appropriate to our times. This means not turning your face away from worldly affairs and giving up renunciation as the final goal of life. Correctness demands that you should remain celibate during the student stage in life when you are being educated, when the body is being strengthened, and the wayward mind being disciplined. The natural bent of body and mind should be properly channelled when one is a student. Since it is no longer possible to live in a guru's ashram, let us build dormitories close to schools or universities, so that student life fulfils its goal under the teacher's watchful eye.

Between the ages of twenty-two and twenty-four a young man should enter a householder's life. By this time a man ought to have gathered sufficient knowledge and skills, so that when the welcoming father-in-law is able to address him in the following words, 'ॐ *sādhu bhavān āstām archayiṣyāmo bhavantam*: Om, you are good, you are indeed worthy of being propitiated', the bridegroom should be able to confidently respond, '*Pūjaya*: Go ahead and honour me'. He should never forget the teachings his guru imparted when he was a student, '*Satyam vada, dharmam chara, svādhyāyān mā pramadah prajātantum mā vyavacchetsīh*: Speak truthfully, walk in righteousness, do not falter in your studies, do not cut the thread that binds you to community.'[171] When he sees a son born in his own son's home, he should detach himself from the protected shelter of home life to lose himself in the transcendental, and while still living at home work for the betterment of society; or, adopting the homelessness of the renouncer work to uplift ruined lives. Self-liberation depends on strenuous efforts to infuse others with the life force.

Father's friend Shri Navalram writes in his diary, 'After retirement I shall publish a newsletter and call it *Aryamitra*; I shall set up a drama company and call it Arya; I'll train a new group of bards who recite religious stories; I shall write ballads based on historic events—and in these various ways I shall strive to discover the sinews of this country. Finally, we will establish a society of

---

[171] From the *Taittirīya Upanishad* 1.11 (see Sastri 1903).

dedicated persons modeled after the Society of Freemasons. Father believed this was the true work of the *vanaprastha*, the third stage in life, when men prepare to proceed to the forest wilderness.

Subsequently, Shri Navalram designed a scheme to support the publication of his daily; his scheme assigned specific roles to Gujarat's literati. Father was given the role of writing about the 'History of Manners and Customs'.[172] His interest in history was universally acknowledged, so his friends had every expectation that Father would occupy himself with historical studies in his post-retirement years.

Men of letters who moved away from Surat to other places came under entirely different influences. Living amidst the poets and writers of Ahmedabad, Navalrambhai's speech acquired a cutting and jocular edge: he observed a 'cold formalism' in Dalpat's visage; he saw the 'dancing egotism of youth' in our Narmad.[173] Father declared that the Ahmedabadis, having been in close contact with the Turks, who even when fallen hold their heads high, had acquired some of their traits—or so it appeared to the Suratis. When the poet Mir departed from Delhi and went to a poet's assembly in Lucknow, the poets of Lucknow scoffed at his performance. On that occasion Mir declared:

> *Kyā budo bāsh pūchho ho Purab ke sākino |*
> *Humko garīb jānke hans hans pukārke |*
> *Dilli jo ek śahar thā ālam mein intikhāb, |*
> *Rahte the muntakhab, hī jahān rojagārke |*
> *Usko falak ne lūt ke virān kar diyā |*
> *Hum rahane vāle hain usi ujaḍe dayārke ||*

> O ye gentle denizens of the East!
> Knowing me a stranger, you mock me and raucously you laugh
> What savage place do I come from, you ask
> That great city of Delhi where once lived great men

---

[172] 'History of Manners and Customs' is in English in the original text.

[173] The phrases 'cold formalism' and 'dancing egotism of youth' are in English in the original text. See *Naval Granthavali* (Pandya 1891[1911]: 32).

> Was looted by Fate and into wilderness turned
> I am a citizen of that same great city, now ruined.[174]

If you substitute Surat, which once flew the flag of eighty-four counties, for Delhi, you will observe a similar instinctive pride in her citizens.

Father was good friends with Behramji Malabari, who had studied at the Mission High School in Surat. A poor widow's son, through hard work he rose to high positions in India. Holding aloft the flag of social reform, he has won acclaim from both the government and the people.

When Father was Diwan of Kutch, an Englishman accidentally shot a tribal man, mistaking him for an animal. Mr Malabari had the incident published in the daily newspaper. Father sent the newspaper report on to the Englishman, but failed to receive any response.

A month later, the same Englishman asked Father, 'What Nandshankar! Are there any more reports about that incident?'

'No,' Father replied.

'I have discovered an effective strategy to stop adverse comments in the press,' said the Englishman. 'I ordered twenty copies of the daily for Government use; the newspapers then stopped accepting any more attacks against Government.'

'Plunder, brothers, plunder!' Father murmured.

'I have lived in Kathiawad; I realise that it is fairly easy to receive good press in those parts. You simply order more copies of the newspaper, which wins over the newspaper editor, who automatically ensures that his paper sings your praises and, in future, only publishes articles in your support.' Readers of the novel *Sarasvatichandra* will here be reminded of the letter that Naveenchandra writes to the editor of the Bombay daily.

---

[174] My translation of Mir is based on the author's Gujarati rendition. Mir Muhammad Taqi Mir was an eighteenth-century poet from Delhi who moved to Lucknow. Another translation is available here: https://dsal.uchicago.edu/books/PK2155.H8413/194220d3.html (accessed 26 May 2021).

Mr Malabari published his book of poems on social themes by the name *Sansārikā* at this time, when the winds of insurrection, fraud, revolt and betrayal blew. The book was much debated in the pages of the Anglo-Indian press, which saw the seeds of sedition scattered across its pages. An angry Mr Malabari sent a copy of the book to Father, soliciting his views on the matter. I had previously read the book with Father, and so sent the response at his behest. I wrote: 'Mr Malabari's support for Government was indeed whole-hearted; there was nothing in the least mealy-mouthed about it. If action aimed at uplifting people is equated with rebellion, then who among us can be defended against such charges?' Acknowledging the letter, Mr Malabari sent us as a 'souvenir' an inkstand made in Austria, stamped on which was a facsimile of the front and back jackets of *Sansārikā*.[175]

On the occasion of my own marriage, in 1907, my elder brothers sent an invitation to the Malabari family. A note written in simple Gujarati accompanied Mr Malabari's wedding gift: 'Unless you write a biography of your great father, one that is within reach of the reading public of this land of Gujarat, you will not be absolved of the debt you owe your forefathers.'

Whether Father had met the late Govardhanbhai elsewhere I do not know, but to the best of my knowledge they first met in Nandod. Gokaldasbhai and Govardhanbhai were opposing counsels in a case relating to the forest of Sagbara in the tribal district of Bharuch; the litigation brought Govardhanbhai to Nandod. Occasion arising, Father had observed, 'Your philosophic vagabond is the true child of this generation, which thirsts after knowledge as such but is devoid of activity and still less capable of applying his knowledge to the rehabilitation of our social fabric.' And Govardhanbhai had said in response, 'Nandshankarbhai, you have truly hit the nail on the head—he is a child of his age, not above it.'[176]

---

[175] See p. 107, note 83. The word 'souvenir' is in English in the original.

[176] This exchange between Nandshankar and Govardhanram Tripathi, conducted in a mixture of Gujarati and English, has to be understood in context. The phrase 'philosophic vagabond' references Arthur Rickett's *The Vagabond in Literature*, wherein, according to Rickett, 'the term

Father held that among those who imitated Goethe, Bulwer Lytton was the most prominent. Both *Ernest Maltravers* and *Alice* contain the very same ideas which, going by Carlyle's judgement, Goethe's *Wilhelm Meister* expressed. Years later, after I myself had occasion to learn German, Father's firmly held belief, based entirely on Goethe's translated text, that Lytton owed a debt to Goethe, was confirmed.

In Goethe's numerous plays there is a foolish pedant named Wagner; instead of nourishment his learning produces indigestion. He pretentiously expresses the most clichéd views, boasts of his scholarship, all the while twirling his mustache. But when it comes to action, he loses motivation; weakness subdues his will. '*Die Kunst ist lang, das Leben kurz*: Art is long, life short', he mutters. This German aphorism has several implications, but essentially means that knowledge is at its most excellent not when it is stored but when it is assimilated; our understanding depends entirely upon the knowledge we absorb. Art that is daughter to true understanding is tardy. The German poet Ferdinand Freiligrath (1810–1876) wrote that Germany had become Hamlet-like ('*Deutschland ist Hamlet*'), in the sense that it was so caught up in logically weighing pros and cons in an abstract context that it was incapable of action, and so it failed to advance in the world.[177] Sympathetic critics are naturally able to accurately elicit the spirit of an era than those involved in the trifling business of governance. Not that Father ever abandoned his youthful dream of working for government, to fulfil which he accepted a leadership role in governance.

Vagabond is used in no derogatory sense. Etymologically it signifies a wanderer…[one] opposed to the routine and conventions of ordinary life' (Rickett 1906: 'Foreword'). Nandshankar's point here is that the hero of Govardhanbhai's celebrated novel *Sarasvatichandra* is a philosopher who is uninterested in social reform, and one in whom the 'wandering instinct is strong' (ibid.).

[177] 'In 1844 the writer Ferdinand Freiligrath declared in the famous first lines of a poem, '*Deutschland ist Hamlet!*'—like Shakespeare's dithering prince, Germany, still a loose confederation of princely states, simply couldn't make its mind up' (Dickson 2016).

Father liked the second part of *Sarasvatichandra* immensely—how different is *Sāsuvahu ni Ladāi* from *Guṇasundari ni Kutumbajālā!*[178] The difference between a chronicler who merely records events and one who writes history is that the former shows ordinary individuals whom we meet in everyday life through the eyes of the reformer; the other displays characters lit by the fire of imagination, clay figurines newly baked in the kiln. The sight of Dukhba will tear you apart. Who hasn't encountered the witch-like Chandika? At every step, you will be met by piteous child-widows like Sundar. The courage and wisdom of Manchatur is not unrealistic. It is seldom that one sees an entire household portrayed so well as in *Sarasvatichandra.*

The first part of *Sarasvatichandra* engages the reader's interest with descriptions of Shathrai raising his partisans to the status of ministers, and accounts of Buddhidhan's daily life.[179] However, Father could not comprehend Alak Kishori's delirious encounter with Naveenchandra. She is like fire; so how could she even be touched by the termites of base passion? Father thought this aspect of the novel unnatural. He held that the portrayal of Kusum was more natural than that of her sister Kumud, but Alak's was a different story altogether. Dharmalakshmi and Devi are depicted with veneration, which was quite proper.

In Father's opinion, the third and fourth parts of *Sarasvatichandra* hardly deserve to be part of a novel. Father maintained that a student is like a tiny insect that wanders through creation, searching for new experiences. Naveenchandra's wanderings are described in some detail in the novel; indeed, these two parts of *Sarasvatichandra* are entirely given over to the wanderer's experiences and his musings on them. Common rules of novel writing do not permit such lengthy and detailed rendering of this kind. *Wilhelm Meister* also suffers from similar defects, Father felt.

---

[178] Mahipatram Rupram's *Sāsuvahu ni Ladāi* (The Battles of Mother and Daughter-in-Law) is considered by some to be the first social novel in the Gujarati language; see Rawal 2002. *Guṇasundari nu Kutumbajālā* (Gunasundari's Household) is the second of Govardhanram Tripathi's four-part novel *Sarasvatichandra* (see Tripathi 2016[1892]).

[179] Part I of *Sarasvatichandra, Buddhidhān nu Kārbhār* (see Tripathi 2015[1887]).

Notwithstanding his opinion of the novel, Father was respectful of Govardhanbhai, and equally, Govardhanbhai held Father in high esteem—indeed, he revered him.

Having dealt with the main issues pertaining to social reform, namely, women's education, women's liberation, and widow remarriage, we will turn our attention to Father's view of brahmins who follow the ritualist part of the Vedas (*karmakāṇḍa*).

In *Karan Ghelo*, Father has modeled Vijayadatt Pandya[180] on a priest in the employ of a wealthy man. He is a heavyset man, in both body and mind. However, due to his contact with more serious-minded men belonging to a wealthier class, Vijayadatt has acquired a modicum of refinement. The man evokes laughter and also pity, but never contempt. 'His tummy was so large that you could fit a dozen *laddus* in it, and there would be space for more.' But when the householder, the one who presides over the ritual, begins to doubt the priest's loyalty, Vijayadatt flares up and says, 'Times have changed. Brahmins no longer count; their earnings have dried up. Both ruler and subjects are without faith. God forbid, but the decay of the kingdom is the result of the evil men do' (*KG* 1.12).

Unlike the lowly priest Murkhdatt portrayed in *Sarasvatichandra*, we observe here the image of a conservative priest of higher standing. Father paints an even more degraded priesthood, trapped in hopes of material gain, on the occasion of the festival of Dashera when the king's temple offerings are being distributed in front of the goddess Aparajita's temple. A melee breaks out among the assembled temple priests and the offerings are looted; it is a vivid picture of the brahmins of the time. Still lower down the scale is the village priest Joshi Maharaj, who accepts gold and silver coins to suppress Rahu's malignant influence on Roopasundari. Showering praise on the donor, he pronounces,

---

[180] The high priest who presides over the sacrifice to Mother Goddess Ambabhavani, and is introduced as prime minister Madhav's family priest (*KG* 1.9–10).

'The purpose of this bodily life is now fulfilled; he is saved from eighty-four-hundred-thousand rounds of rebirth; he will become a brilliant star in the sky' (*KG* 1.14–15).

Having looked at Father's description of different types of uneducated priests, the following question arises: did Father think that brahmins who conduct ritual ceremonies serve no social function in the present age? When I raised the question, he replied that ritual priests indeed have a continuing role. Every village needs at the very least a raised public platform or *chotro*, near which are located the village shrine, a tiny water tank, a sweet-water well, a man who recites stories from the *Puranas*, and a temple priest. From these material aspects of the village, a priest is able to draw out something larger and more meaningful. For this to happen, the brahmin has to be educated. If you need to broadcast any news in the village today, you ask the village headman for help; in Europe the padres perform a similar function. Why can't the village priest, adept at performing rituals, also take on the role of the schoolteacher? What is being written about currently in Bengal regarding the *guru-mahashaya*'s role as teacher proves that even today priests can perform a useful function in society.

Father related an anecdote that tells you what today's rustic priests are like.

Once visiting the holy Ashwinikumar Ghat for a bath, Father came upon a Rajput performing the rites for his departed ancestors. There was hardly much difference between the priest performing the rites and the Rajput: the poor Rajput was an ignorant man, and the brahmin was the lowest of the low, almost like an animal. Lighting the stub of his bidi in the sacrificial fire he shouted, 'Place five measures of sesame seed, five measures of *udad dāl* plus everything else before me'. With a piteous face, the poor man with the shorn head replied, 'How am I to obtain such large quantities?' The foolish brahmin's roar grew louder, 'Then get me three quarters of a measure of each!' Believing that the offerings would in fact reach his ancestors, the poor man met the brahmin's demand. 'Your forefathers like to suck on mangoes,' continued the priest, trying to diddle the poor man of mangoes.

He did not stop there. Father was disgusted with what he saw. 'I thought to myself, if this is a ladder to heaven, then beware of climbing it. It is rotten and might break.'

Another time Father recounted, once while he was travelling through the villages in north India, a blacksmith said to him, 'Your honour, the revenue to the zamindar is straightforward. I pay it twice a year; he even forgives me the rent if the crop happens to be bad that year. The debt to the priest, on the other hand, begins when one is in the womb and it continues till you die; his demands have no limit. Nor is he ever grateful; in fact, he is forever taking, because he considers it his birth right.'

Chandrashankar Dikshit was Father's original household priest; he was a godly man, totally unworldly. He worked exceedingly hard and passed his days without care, placing complete trust in his patrons. It is said of Leigh Hunt (1784–1859) that he considered himself free of worldly concerns; finding himself regularly caught in the moneylender's clutches, he would nonchalantly declare that he did not really understand what all the fuss was about. But when he gave King George IV the title 'Fat Adonis of Fifty', Hunt found himself jailed for libel.

Chandrashankar was a specimen of what could be thought of as a simple-minded family priest. He was poor, and of limited intelligence; he bears comparison with David Skimpole in Dickens' *Bleak House*. Father used to call every good man 'Chandrashankar'.

Father was passionately fond of Dickens' novels. 'Pickwickian humour' never failed to delight him. He was in the habit of picking out bits and pieces from the book, for example, the elder Weller's warning, 'Beware of widows'; Sam Weller's metaphors, 'Adding insult to injury—as the parrot said when he was not only encaged, but taught to learn English';[181] and when father

---

[181] Vinayak cites standard English versions from Dickens' novels rather than the dialect in which some of the original characters talk. *The Pickwick Papers*, Chapter XXXV, is the source of the quotation, which reads: 'addin' insult to injury, as the parrot said ven they not only took him from his native land, but made him talk the English langwidge arterwards' (Dickens 2009).

and son met in the bar, the father on seeing his son take a long swig from the bottle of liquor exclaims, 'Samuel my boy! You have an uncommon power of suction; you would have made an uncommon good oyster, had you been born into that station of life.'[182] Jingle's boasts, Windle's false pride, Snodgrass' poetic inspirations, Mrs Bordel's wicked ways and Pickwick's goodness; the foolish magistrate and the adroit advocate—Father loved the manner in which all these characters were drawn in the novel. If in the course of an ordinary conversation a person behaved like a character from the pages of *Pickwick Papers*, Father would give the person a Pickwickian name.

He greatly admired *Dombey and Sons*. He was particularly fond of the paragraph where Joseph Bagstock says, 'Cleopatra commands and Anthony Bagstock obeys'. At the drop of a hat he would recall the hook attached to Captain Cuttle's wrist and Bunsby's eye turned to the Greenland coast.[183] He believed that Betsy Trotwood, the character from *David Copperfield*, could well have been a familiar figure from Surat: 'the aging woman widowed in youth, the aunt scolding her nieces and nephews into submission'. He similarly loved the portrait of Peggotty, and shy Barkis, who as I recall was introduced as Adu Adgaro on the Bombay stage in a farce. He spotted the unctuously humble Uriah Heep whenever we came across him in real life. Finally, when I behold your face blossoming in laughter, Mecawber, I see the typical Nagar of the previous age, drowned in debt and yet contented, ever believing himself happy.

Mrs Jellyby in *Bleak House* sends woollen garments to black men in distress while neglecting her own progeny. The description reflects the situation in many parts of India today: 'Children of the household lick the grinding stone, and to the professor the flour goes'. So also, Chadband and Pecksniff's pompous lectures,

---

[182] *The Pickwick Papers*, Chapter XIII: 'Wery good power o' suction, Sammy,' said Mr. Weller the elder, looking into the pot, when his first-born had set it down half empty. 'You'd ha' made an uncommon fine oyster, Sammy, if you'd been born in that station o' life' (Dickens 2009).

[183] Bunsby and Captain Cuttle are characters from Charles Dickens' novel *Dombey and Son*.

their cupidity, cunning and pretense of piety are the way modern brahmins live today.[184]

In our family Dickens' novels were so well-loved that those who were acquainted with the English language read them over and over again. What is surprising is that though Father was passionate about Scott, we in the family really preferred Dickens. Father was equally passionate about Lytton. We read Thackeray to improve our language skills. In his novel *Esmund,* the incident of the hero marrying the heroine's mother seemed quite absurd to us. Father retorted that there was nothing absurd about the situation. If widows are allowed to remarry and if, as is the custom among Rajputs, the father is allowed to marry a girl chosen for his son, then why can't a widowed mother accept the man chosen for her daughter? Moreover, how could Thackeray conceive of Beatrice entering a prosperous home to meet a happy death? Nor could he possibly end the novel with 'and they lived happily ever after'. Thackeray keeps her forever an anchorless wanderer through the ocean of life. Is there any wonder then that Esmund, who initially chose an inconstant star by which to steer his ship, in due course steers it towards a steadfast and unmoving star and remains anchored to Rachel.

Father particularly admired *The Newcomes* by Thackeray. Should the reader wish to observe Anglo-Indian society of Warren Hastings' time, he would be well advised to enter this school of history. He pitied poor Becky Sharpe: when the roots are bad, the future is seldom good—in this worldly life, this is both a painful law and a pointer to the future.

We seldom read second-rate novelists. We did read Romesh Dutt's *Lake of Palms* to Father; he happened to be not overly fond of the portrayal of Sudha and Bindu in the novel. He preferred Dutt's *Madhavi-kankan,* only because of the way the author recreates the particular ambience of the age. 'The succession of events in the novel does not, however, communicate the sense of inevitability, which is an important feature of successful novels,' Father observed. He preferred *Jeevan-Sandhyā* and *Jeevan-Prabhat.*

---

[184] Chadband is a character from Dickens' *Bleak House,* and Pecksniff from *The Life and Adventures of Martin Chuzzlewit.*

He liked Meadows Taylor's novels. He read Bankim Chandra's novels, but only in Hemchandra's translation. He used to say that *Krishnakanter Uil* [Will], and to a lesser extent, *Kundanandi* and the *Poison Tree*, were his preferred choices.

Among Gujarati poets, Premanand and Dayaram were Father's favourites. Father had spent time in Nandod, where the air he breathed was infused with the lyricism Dayaram wafted across from Chanod; inevitably Dayaram's lyricism influenced Father. My dear mother recalled that in Chanod, a disciple of the Dayaram order, white-mustachioed old man though he was, covered his head with a sari like a woman, to sing Dayaram's songs: 'He is Krishna. He is the male and we female'. A Vaishnav devotee perceives all of creation through the eyes of a female *gopi*. Nowhere else has this sentiment been so truly embodied in lyrical words and reflected in meaning as in Dayaram's songs.

A reading of *Sarasvatichandra* tells us that Govardhandasbhai favoured Dayaram as well. That both these men of Gujarat, who had reached the highest level of intellectual and spiritual life, admired Dayaram in itself proves that his popularity was not merely due to his poetry's naked display of eroticism. The milkmaid comes face to face with Nand, Krishna's father, and addresses him thus: 'Your beloved son prattles, looks at me with dancing eyes, smiles his sweet incomplete laugh'. I myself vividly recall being in Nandod (I must have been five years old at the time) listening with great joy to two skilled brahmin women who would often sing his sweetly teasing song.

Father had great respect for Dalpatram. When we in our foolish childishness made fun of his verse, Father would ask, 'Do you notice anything either difficult or forced in his alliterative dazzle? If you are really interested in reading works of high style, then read his *Forbes-virah* or *Ven-charitra*. If there be a natural poet in the Gujarati language, it is Dalpatram. In the great storehouse of his work one discovers both diamonds and rubies.'

In an earlier chapter I have described Father's love of Narmad's writing. On occasion, it is true that Narmad breaks the unity of an aesthetic sentiment; nor is the poetic tone consistently sustained throughout his compositions. Since Father was not acquainted with modern poetry, I am unable to say what his views were with regard to either Govardhanram or Narasinhrao's poetry. He would say, 'Write if you must, but don't write about trivial matters. If you follow this precept, felicitous expression will naturally follow'.

In a previous chapter, I described Father's negative experience of Maratha and Muslim administrators. He was not attracted to the idea of self-rule that emerged after 1897.[185] It was Father's belief that, 'We have not yet learnt to control those under us, nor have we learnt to respect orders from above, that is, to execute their orders without grumbling. We will remain incapable of governance as long as we are either slavishly controlled by others, or continue to depend solely on our own authority. It is not that the English are endowed with higher intellectual powers, just that they have mastered the skills of administering society, which is the secret of a successful nation. So how is it possible to compare us with them?'

Father was similarly convinced that except at the very top, Indians ought to administer the lower rungs of the administrative bureaucracy. Not only would the expenses of administering the country shrink, but the fortunes of this new upper class would remain tied to English rule; so not even a shadow of sedition would appear.

He was an enemy of flattery, completely free of that worship of white men that afflicts so many Indians. He believed that all men are the same. After serving as deputy collector of a district, now, when I glance back at the past, I clearly see how much self-respect and seriousness marked his conduct; he was neither uncivil to white men nor was he obsequious.

He held that reform of government and social reform should move hand in hand. Being a government servant meant that he could not take an active role in the proceedings of the Congress until he retired. Meanwhile, he worked tirelessly for social reform. We should raise our people high so that the whole world respects us. Nor should we ever lose touch with our native genius; naught will survive if we allow ourselves to be dragged along the flood

---

[185] The date 1897 is obscure since it does not appear to be associated with any particular political event.

tide of the West. We ought indeed to grasp the fundamental features of their theories of social reconstruction, but ignore what is mere fluff.

Jeremy Bentham (1748–1747), in his *Theory of Legislation,* holds that individual self-interest and the aggregated interest of the community should be made to coincide. According to Father, this idea won Europe's lawmakers to Bentham's way of thinking. But Father was sceptical: who can really tell whether a particular measure actually serves the interests of the whole society? The gain or loss to particular communities can be directly seen, but the means of calculating what is good for society as a whole are always indirect. We should therefore be constantly mindful of our own tradition, which tells us that when you act rightly you are not doing so for the sake of the community but acting according to your dharma. In this way, you will uplift society and also secure your own welfare. It is not always easy to distinguish individual welfare from the welfare of society. It suffices therefore to act according to one's dharma and let others judge the results of your action.

One can neither say that laws governing society are transient, nor did Father maintain that they are fixed. It is absolutely necessary to modify them according to context, which means according to the direction in which the world is moving. Changing the basic structure of law falls within the domain of the law minister; ordinary men should act according to what their own dharma says.

Rule by the people is appropriate for village governance, so self-rule by village panchayats should be revived. Panchayats can easily settle frivolous lawsuits; moreover, the gain and loss to individuals as well as to the whole social group is directly seen. At the national level, his preference was for a liberal governance.

Later, as I read Nietzsche's poetic prose, I had the feeling that he was yet another philosopher who had dipped into ancient Indian philosophical systems. While Schopenhauer drank of the Buddhist stream in order to extinguish the great thirst for existence—the desire that spurs the ego—Nietzsche drank deeply of *soma,* the sparkling nectar of the Vedas, to take great delight in existence itself, and to lose himself in living a cultured life.

Affirm life and worship it—this tradition of thought prevails in
Europe today.

> *anyat śreyo anyat utaiva preyah |*
> *tayoh śreya ādadānasya sādhur bhavati |*
> *hīyate arthād ya u preyo vṛiṇīte ||*[186]

> Different is the good and different the pleasurable.
> The good and the pleasurable bind men to different ends.
> Of the two, one who accepts the good is ennobled
> One who turns to pleasure loses his purpose.

To frame rules and regulations keeping in mind what was
discussed is the exclusive task of elite liberal classes. From 1792
onwards, after an extensive study of mantras, European countries
conjured up a genie in the form of the Demos. Today the art of
subduing the hungry ghost which devours everything, both the
good and the bad, is forgotten. If a person is found who can put
this genie back into the bottle, a liberal government will emerge.
The new government will be superior to liberal governments of
the past, because reform does not happen in concentric circles;
rather it is an ascent in the form of an ascending spiral. The
coiled body of the Sheshnag symbolises this ideal.

When, occasion arising, we sought his opinion about the
present age, Father, who was not given to declaring his views
unasked, would respond in the following way: 'Self-interest has
grown and individualism has taken hold; in fact, one can even
say it has crossed all limits. In our time of spade and pick-axes,
individualism too was widespread. But in the past it represented
an adventurous spirit, for a transcendent spirit burnished self-
interest, which inspired men to turn to the spiritual life; today's
self-interest is an undisguised roar of the self. In the absence of
that turn toward the transcendent, individuals will not flourish
but remain forever discontented. A mind which is discontented
commits suicide.

'Faith too has diminished; there is a spillover into rank
individualism. And even though we ourselves had little faith in

---

[186] *Kaṭhopanishad* 1.2.1 (see Vasu 1905).

our ordinary religious practices, we believed that our lives were meant for a higher purpose. We were prompted to engage with the world, fight wickedness, and usher in the justice of Lord Ram's kingdom. The current lack of faith is like the pinnacle of a temple built on the shallow foundations of self-interest. Not only has faith in religion declined, but faith in caste, faith in the civilising aspects of life, faith in the very future of humanity has declined. As a result, wherever we look, we see lives smouldering in sorrow.

'There are, however, compensatory virtues to the present time. Persons are more independent; there is greater self-respect; and people are truer to themselves. Self-education has also made significant advances.

'Indeed, faith is the pole star of navigators. Never lose sight of it; let it be your guide whichever direction you may follow. Self-interest is evil; it turns sweet lives saline. Keep far away from it; do not allow it to dim your zest, which, like the rays of the sun, illumine your way. Only then will you fulfil your life's true purpose.'

Goethe's instruction at the time of Mignon's burial in *Wilhelm Meister* is eternal:

> Boys: Let us weep and remain here.
>
> The Chorus (invisible): Children, turn back into Life! Fly from night! Day and pleasure and continuance are the lot of life.
>
> Boys: Up! Turn back into life! Let the day give us labour and pleasure till the evening (vānaprastha) brings us rest and the nightly sleep refreshes us.
>
> Chorus: Children hasten into life! In the pure garments of beauty may love meet you with heavenly looks and with the wreaths of immortality. Travel, travel back into life! Take along with you the holy earnestness! For earnestness alone makes life immortal.[187]

Keep far away from the path which says, '*Babhūta lagāyo, alakh jagā yo, khalak kiyo sab khāro ve!* He smeared ash, evoked the nameless,

---

[187] Johann Wolfgang von Goethe, *Wilhelm Meister*, Book 8, Chapter 8. The quoted passage is in English in the original text.

and poisoned the whole world!' Instead, 'Evoke the nameless and fill the world with nectar.' If you are an able magician, show the world the wonders of heaven; never compare Creation to hell.

Julam mat karnā bacchā, |
Alakh kā khelan sab sacchā ||

Be not obstinate, child
The Creator's play is all real.

Explain to the people the wonders of the Creator. In France, despair shadowed the end of the century (around 1890). In Germany, during the time of Novalis, *Weltschmerz* and world-weariness became all-pervasive. A similar wind blows today in India. But Attention! Enterprise! Faith! Daring will be your 'lighthouse'.[188]

When I parted from him to travel to England on the first of October in 1903, a Thursday, in a tearful voice Father asked God to bless me. His blessings bore fruit, and I returned successful. I did not, however, have the good fortune to see his beloved and venerable face again. It was destined!

Fourteen days were left for my civil service examinations; Father's life ended before that. Three days before the end came, my elder brother requested Father to write words of blessing, so that I would have the strength and the forbearance to bear the loss. I am holding that letter. My hands tremble. To this day, the words draw me to his heart and allow me to plunge into the measureless waters of his love.

Goethe had the following verse inscribed on a wall of his small house:

Über allen Gipfeln
Ist Ruh,
In allen Wipfeln
Spürest du
Kaum einen Hauch;

---

[188] The word *kandaliya* is glossed in the body of the original text as 'lighthouse'. The words 'But Attention! Enterprise! Faith! Daring will be your lighthouse' vaguely echo Jules Vernes' tales of daring voyages.

Die Vögelein schweigen im Walde.
Warte nur, balde
Ruhest du auch.

Over all the hill-tops
Is rest.
In all the tree-tops
Ever less
Breeze leaves a sign.
The woods birds are no longer calling.
Quiet now—dusk's falling,
Rest will be thine.[189]

His name will not die, only the music animating it has ceased; the resonance of that music continues. To us—the people of Gujarat—he will forever continue to bring happiness. Amen.

---

[189] '*Über allen Gipfeln*', by Johann Wolfgang Goethe; the English translation is adopted from John Irons' text (see Irons 2010).

IN REMEMBRANCE

After Father's death we received numerous letters of condolence.[*] I quote from some of those that we received.

Dahyabhai Harjeevandas Nanavati writes to my brother Manubhai:

> I am extremely sorry to hear the sorrowful news of the death of your good and worthy father and my most respected Master Saheb.

Rameshchandra Dutt writes:

> Baroda, 18 July 1905
>
> My dear Manubhai,
> I am deeply grieved to hear of the death of your venerable father and I beg you will accept my sincere condolences and convey the same to the bereaved family. Gujarat has lost the most distinguished of its authors and also one of the ablest and best of its citizens.
>
> Yours sincerely,
> (sd.) R. C. Dutt

Vrajbhukandas Pakvasa Solicitor writes:

> By his simplicity of character and unobtrusive and retiring disposition and amiability, he commanded respect and reverence from anyone who came in the least contact with him.

---

[*] The text of all the letters of condolence quoted here are in English in the original, except for the last one, which is translated from the Gujarati.

R. Govindbhai Hathibhai Desai writes:

> In him Gujarat loses one of her brightest sons; and the good
> work he has done will ever remain a telling monument of it: For
> moral courage and probity, absolute integrity and devotion to
> the common weal as an administrator, he was unsurpassed in his
> generation and his loss to us all is absolutely irreparable.

Jamiyatram Shastri, Principal of the Training College, writes
from Ahmedabad:

> Gujarat must feel the loss of Master Saheb terribly as in him has
> been taken away the father of pure Gujarati prose.

Lallubhai Asharam Shah (presently known as O. M. Justice Shah)
writes:

> I need hardly add that I fully sympathise with you all in this hour
> of sorrow. We have to remember after all that it is our duty to
> accept without a murmur the dispensation of the Almighty. It is
> impossible, however, for any educated Gujarati to avoid the pangs
> of sorrow at the idea of the writer of 'Karan Ghelo' being no more.

Bhulabhai Jeevanji Desai writes:

> My dear Manubhai,
> The sad news has spread wide and has come to us that Master
> Saheb (true teacher of men he was) passed away peacefully the
> day before yesterday. But the loss, in this case, though it is bound
> to be particularly heavy to us as being above all a personal one,
> is on practically a universal character for Gujarat in general.
> His life has moulded the character and career of many a man
> that has lived and died to do service to this land. With him has
> passed away perhaps the last but the principal of the band that
> courageously shook off the yoke of the superstitions of ages and
> led a progressive school of independent thought and action. His
> powerful individuality and his deep-seated and earnest conviction
> are sure to leave for him a memory to be cherished with no
> ordinary regard or admiration.

In all this immense good that he lived to do, we have now to seek consolation and the sympathies of the whole of Gujarat and of the kindred thinkers of Master Saheb all over the country ought to count towards alleviating the immediate shock.

Yours sincerely,
Bhulabhai J.

Jamshedji Ardeshar Dalal, a former minister in the Baroda Department of Education, writes:

My acquaintance is wide and I have been agitating for some days if I could remember (bring to my mind rather) anyone whom I could put on a level with him of those now existing in this world. But I could think of no one. Highest wisdom and prudence, entire innocence of any deed or thought to harm, or even to offend the feelings of any human being, extreme contentment, dignity, justice, and repose in official life, these I do not find in anyone now, old or young; and in the past, I can think only of Mahadeo Govind Ranade, though I judge of Ranade only from report and not from long observation by myself. Since 1850 your father's character and career has been an example and a model of imitation for me; it would be absurd even to hint that I have approached the model in any way. We sailed in different seas and we weathered different storms. But whatever little of goodness I may have done or attempted was from ever looking up to him. I often wished to tell him of it; but I was deterred from the consideration that seeing me as I was, he would have shrunk from such a copyist.

I am,
Ever yours sincerely,
Jamshedjee A. Dalal

Gokaldas Karsandas Parekh writes to my elder brother:

To people like me who had the privilege of his friendship, his wide and varied culture, his sound common sense, his brilliant wit, the complete straightness of his life, and Spartan simplicity of his habits, always commended our highest reverence and in his death Gujarat lost one of its best sons.

R. B. Ramanbhai Mahipatram Neelakanth writes:

> In him Gujarat has lost one of her great and illustrious men whose place cannot be filled. A whole life of high ideals has closed its earthly career and we have to cherish its memory in sorrowing gratefulness.

Father's old friend R. B. Parvatishankar was indisposed at the time. His son R. Mohanlal writes on behalf of his father:

> My father wishes me to express his heartfelt sorrow at the sad death of your venerable father. As perhaps you know very well, my father was on very intimate terms with the deceased from his boyhood and it is but very natural that he should feel the loss of one who was endowed with high moral and intellectual capacities and was an ornament to our community.

The learned Narasinh Rao Bholanath, writing to both my elder brothers, expresses the following about our father:

> Master Saheb was one of my father's truest friends and I, who remember all the past days vividly, feel this as something like a personal grief.

D. B. Vasudev Mahadev Samarth, a former ambassador of Baroda State, wrote the following to my brother:

> I have not sent you a letter of condolence as is the way of the world. But I suppose you do not mind it, knowing how sincerely I deplore the loss of your good and eminent father; that 'secretly' I held him in high esteem and respect—secretly, that is to say, I was not effusive or demonstrative about my sentiments. Now I think you are quite fitted to do a duty to your late lamented father, and to the public. Can you not undertake to write a brief but instructive life of him, something on the model of Sashiya Shastri's life? I will send you the book if you have not come across it before. Such careers are bound to inspire some at least of 'the rising generation with a sense of value and urgency of unostentatious duty amidst circumstances not at all inspiring'.

Father's friend Zaverilal Umiyashankar Yagnik's son Madhavlalbhai writes to my eldest brother:

> The death of Nandshankarbhai must cause a void which it will be difficult to fill for years. A thoroughly self-made man, he made the best use of the powers that God had been pleased to bestow on him. His quiet persistent industry entitled him to claim a degree of scholar's life in his day, rarely to be met with in the best university now. His exemplary honesty, superior intellectuality and regular studious habits won him the regard and esteem of those who had to deal with him. To all this, it must be said to his eternal credit, he added an amiable nature, a quiet gentility, and a spirit of self-effacement which was as winning as it was able. It is but natural the whole of Gujarat shares your sorrow for the loss of one so gifted, so good and so learned.

A resolution sending condolences to the bereaved family was passed at a meeting of the Association of the Citizens of Surat, presided over by the Collector, Mr Westrop. In forwarding the letter of condolence, Mr Westrop added words of his own:

> I have the honour to forward in pursuance of the resolution passed at a public meeting of the citizens of Surat held in the municipal hall on 5th August 1905, over which I had the honour of presiding, the copy of the accompanying resolution.
>
> I trust it will be some consolation to you to find that the public of the city has shown its appreciation of the life-work of the deceased whom, I understand, it held in high esteem.

Reverend Shilidi, honorary secretary of the Andrew's Library in Surat, expressed his feelings in the following words:

> It is with much regret that the managing committee records here the death of Rao Bahadur Nandshankar Tuljashankar, who for the last ten years was the member of the managing committee of this institution. So long as the Gujarati language endures, his name will be known in connection with his famous historical novel *Karan Ghelo*, which is recognised by all as one of the few classical works our Gujarati language possesses. We need say nothing of Mr

Nandshankar's profound historical researches and his knowledge of the antiquities of Gujarat or of the grace of his literary style as all acquainted with his book are aware of these facts.

Krishnamukhram Atmaram Mehta, presiding over the Association of Surat Nagars, sent the following letter of condolence to my brother:

> With his great intelligence, his high moral principles and his calm yet decisive conduct, the late Raobahadur adorned the elevated offices he occupied in institutions run by British and Princely governments and, bringing satisfaction to both government and the people, served his country. All the people of Gujarat are grateful to him. The Nagar Community has always held in high regard such literary men of high intelligence and purity of life and leaders. And, today, on the occasion of his death, the whole Nagar caste shares in the grief of his departure.

In addition to the above, there were also resolutions of condolence forwarded from the Union of Nagar Brahmins, the Literary Society of Gujarat, the Founders of the Raychand Deepchand Girls' School, the Surat Mahajan Orphanage Committee, and the Rajputana Union Club.

BIBLIOGRAPHY

Aiyar, T. R. Ratnam and Kasinath Pandurang Parab, eds. 1903. *Mahākavisribhavabhūtipraṇītam Uttarramcaritam* (*The Uttara-Ramacharita of Bhavabhuti*. With the Commentary of Viraraghava). Bombay: Printed and Published by Tukaram Javaji. Available at: https://archive.org/details/UttaraRamaCharita/page/n37 (accessed 4 May 2021).

Baines, Sir Athelstane. 1912. *Ethnography (Castes and Tribes)*. Strassburg: Karl J. Trubner. Available at: https://archive.org/details/ethnographycaste00bainuoft/page/n7/mode/2up (accessed 7 May 2021).

Boswell, James. 2006. *Boswell's Life of Johnson*. EBook. Edited by Charles Grosvenor Osgood. Available at: https://www.gutenberg.org/files/1564/1564-h/1564-h.htm (accessed 22 May 2021).

Das, Paromita. 2008. 'Writing India, Writing Self: Beginnings of Indian Writing in English in Nineteenth Century Bengal'. PhD Dissertation, Department of English, University of Calcutta. Available at: http://shodhganga.inflibnet.ac.in:8080/jspui/handle/10603/156600 (accessed 4 May 2021).

Datta, Amaresh, ed. 1988. *Encyclopaedia of Indian Literature*, Volume II. Delhi: Sahitya Akademi.

Deshpande, Arvind M. 1987. *John Briggs in Maharashtra: A Study of District Administration Under Early British Rule*. Delhi: Mittal Publications.

Dickens, Charles. 2009. *The Pickwick Papers*. EBook. Available at: https://www.gutenberg.org/files/580/580-h/580-h.htm (accessed 24 May 2021).

Dickson, Andrew. 2016. '"Deutschland ist Hamlet": Shakespeare in Germany'. British Library. 15 March. Available at: https://www.bl.uk/shakespeare/articles/deutschland-ist-hamlet-shakespeare-in-germany (accessed 24 May 2021).

Dwyer, Rachel Madeline Jackson. 1995. *The Gujarati Lyrics of Kavi Dayarambhai*. School of Oriental and African Studies. PhD Thesis

presented to the University of London. Available at: https://www.
scribd.com/document/435174066/10673087-pdf (accessed 25
May 2021).

Forbes, Alexander Kinloch. 1924[1856]. *Rās Mālā: Hindoo Annals of
the Province of Goozerat in Western India*, Volume II. Edited by H. G.
Rawlinson. London: Oxford University Press. Available at: https://
archive.org/details/RasMala/page/n3/mode/2up (accessed 7
May 2021).

Godse, Vishnubhat. 2014. *Mazha Pravas*. Translated by Priya Adarkar
and Shanta Gokhale. New Delhi: Oxford University Press.

Government [of India]. 1877. *Gazetteer of the Bombay Presidency, Volume
II: The History of Gujarat, Surat and Broach*. Bombay: Government
Central Press. Available at: https://ia801604.us.archive.org/30/
items/in.ernet.dli.2015.106189/2015.106189.Gazetteer-Of-The-
Bombay-Presidency-Volii.pdf (accessed 9 May 2021).

Great Britain India Office. 1902. *The India List and the India Office List*.
London: Harrison & Sons. Available at: https://archive.org/details/
indialistandind00offigoog/page/n626 (accessed 10 May 2021).

Gupta, J. N. 1911. *Life and Work of Romesh Chunder Dutt*. With an
Introduction by His Highness the Maharaja of Baroda. London:
J. M. Dent & Sons, Ltd.; New York: E. P. Dutton & Co. Available
at: https://archive.org/stream/lifeworkofromesh00guptrich/
lifeworkofromesh00guptrich_djvu.txt (accessed 5 May 2021).

Hall, Manly P. n.d. 'The Four Idols of Francis Bacon and the New
Instrument of Knowledge'. From *Novum Organum*, Francis Bacon.
Available at: http://www.sirbacon.org/links/4idols.htm (accessed
4 May 2021).

Harrington, Jack. 2010. 'Sir John Malcolm and the Government of
India after 1818'. In *Sir John Malcolm and the Creation of British
India*, pp. 129–160. Palgrave Studies in Cultural and Intellectual
History. New York: Palgrave Macmillan. Available at: https://doi.
org/10.1057/9780230117501_6 (accessed 9 May 2021).

Heber, Amelia. 1830. *The Life of Reginald Heber D.D., Lord Bishop of Calcutta
by His Widow* (1830: 300), Volume II. London: John Murray. Available
at: https://tinyurl.com/3j56zpde (accessed 5 May 2021).

Henderson, Graham. 2016. 'Percy Bysshe Shelley: "Atheist. Lover of
Humanity. Democrat"'. 25 July. Available at: https://wordsworth.
org.uk/blog/2016/07/25/percy-bysshe-shelley-atheist-lover-of-
humanity-democrat/ (accessed 24 April 2021).

Hughes, James Edward. 2010. 'Catherine de Medici: Queen Mother of
France'. 15 April. Available at: https://www.jamesedwardhughes.
com/history-essays/april-15th-2010 (accessed 5 May 2021).

Irons, John. 2010. 'Collage of the English Translations of Goethe's poem "Über allen Gipfeln"'. 25 October. Available at: http://johnirons.blogspot.in/2010/10/collage-of-english-translations-of.html (accessed 20 December 2020).

Jacob, P. W. 1873. *Hindoo Tales, or The Adventures of Ten Princes*. Translated from the Sanscrit of the *Dasakumaracharitam*. London: Strahan & Co. Available at: https://www.gutenberg.org/files/11738/11738-h/11738-h.htm (accessed 4 May 2021).

Jayakar, Pupul. 1980. *The Earthen Drum*. New Delhi: National Museum.

Johnson, Paul. 2019. Review of *The Politics of Resentment: A Genealogy*, by Jeremy Engels. *Rhetoric & Public Affairs* 22, no. 2: 327–331. Available at: muse.jhu.edu/article/728925. (accessed 16 March 2021).

Joshi, Nileshkumar L. 2010. *Narmad's Mari Hakikat Part I and II: A Study Through Translation*. PhD thesis, Saurashtra University. Available at: http://etheses.saurashtrauniversity.edu/130/1/(7)%20JOSHI%20NILESHKUMAR%20L..pdf (accessed 20 March 2021).

Kale, M. R., ed. 1934. *The Meghaduta of Kālidāsa*. Third edition. Bombay: D. V. & B. D. Mulgaokar, Proprietors, Gopal Narayen & Co. Book-sellers. Available at: https://archive.org/details/in.ernet.dli.2015.367343/page/n9/mode/2up (accessed 24 May 2021).

———, ed. 1969. *The Abhjnānaśakuntalam of Kālidāsa*. Tenth edition. Delhi, Varanasi, Patna: Motilal Banarsidass. Available at: https://archive.org/details/AbhijnanaShakuntalamOfKalidasaMRKale (accessed 15 March 2021).

Karkaria, R. P. 1896. *India: Forty Years of Progress and Reform, Being a Sketch of the Life and Times of Behramji M. Malabari*. London: Henry Frowde. Available at https://archive.org/details/indiafortyyearso00karkiala/page/68 (accessed 5 May 2021).

Kiparsky, Paul. 2007. 'Panini's Razor'. 29 October, Paris. Available at: https://web.stanford.edu/~kiparsky/Papers/paris.pdf (accessed 24 March 2021).

Labhshankar, Narmadashankar. 1912[1933]. *Junu Narmgadhya* (Gujarati). Bombay: I. S. Desai, Gujarati Printing Press. Available at: https://archive.org/details/in.ernet.dli.2015.399481/page/n5/mode/1 (accessed 5 May 2021).

Losensky, Paul E. and Sunil Sharma, trans. 2013. 'Narratives'. In *In the Bazaar of Love: Selected Poems of Amir Khusrau* [E-Reader Version]. Penguin Global.

Macaulay, Thomas Babington. 1903. *Macaulay's Life of Samuel Johnson*. Edited by Charles Lane Hanson. Boston, New York, Chicago, London: Ginn and Company. Available at: http://www.gutenberg.org/files/42971/42971-h/42971-h.htm (accessed 5 May 2021).

Majumdar, A. K. 1956. *Chaulukyas of Gujarat: A Survey of the History and Culture of Gujarat from the Middle of the Tenth to the End of the Thirteenth Century*. Delhi: Bharatiya Vidya Bhavan.

Manusmṛti. n.d. *Manusmriti in Sanskrit with English Translation*. 3.56. Available at: https://archive.org/details/ManuSmriti_201601 (accessed 4 May 2021).

Mehta, Hansa. 1916[1979]. '*Sva. Shri Vinayakbhai Ne Anjali*'. In *Nandshankar Jeevan Chitra*, Vinayak Mehta, p. 9. Edited by Bhupendra Balakrishna Trivedi. Third edition. Bombay: Arvind S. Pandya, N. M. Tripathi Private Ltd.

Mehta, Nandshankar. 1866[1935]. *Karan Ghelo*. Ninth reprint. Privately published by Sir Manubhai Mehta.

———. 1866[2015]. *Karan Ghelo: Gujarat's Last Rajput King*. Translated by Tulsi Vatsal and Aban Mukherji. New Delhi: Viking/Penguin.

Mehta, Vinayak. 1916[1979]. *Nandshankar Jeevan Chitra*. Edited by Bhupendra Balakrishna Trivedi. Third edition. Bombay: Arvind S. Pandya, N. M. Tripathi Private Ltd.

Meredith, George. 1897. *An Essay on Comedy and the Uses of the Comic Spirit*. David Price, Archibald Constable and Company. Available at: https://www.gutenberg.org/files/1219/1219-h/1219-h.htm (accessed 4 May 2021).

Mill, John Stuart. 1848. 'On the General Principles of Taxation', Book V, Chapter II. In *Principles of Political Economy, with Some of their Applications to Social Philosophy*. London: John W. Parker, West Strand. Available at: https://www.econlib.org/library/Mill/mlP.html?chapter_num=67#book-reader (accessed 24 May 2021).

Mishra, Pandit Jwala Prasad. 1910. *Panchatantra by Vishnu Sarma*. With Commentary by Pandit J. P. Mishra. Bombay: Khemraj Shri Krishnadas, Shri Venkateshwar Steam Press. Available at: https://archive.org/details/PanchatantraSanskritHindi-JpMishra1910/mode/2up (accessed 4 May 2021).

Mookerji, Radhakumud. 1912. *Indian Shipping: A History of Indian Shipping and Maritime Activities from Earliest Times*. Bombay: Longman Green and Co. Available at: https://factmuseum.com/pdf/extra/A-history-of-India-shipping-and-maritme-activity-by-Radhakumud-Mukherjee.pdf (accessed 17 March 2021).

Moore, Thomas. 1839. *The Works of Lord Byron: With His Letters and Journals, and His Life. In Seventeen Volumes*, Volume III. London: John Murray. Available at: https://archive.org/details/workslordbyronw10moorgoog/page/n11 (accessed 5 May 2021).

Mukhopadhyay, Amiyo Kumar. 2018. 'A Brief Biographic Sketch of Dr. Bhau Daji Lad (1822–1874): A Forgotten Figure of Indian

Dermatology.' *Indian Journal of Dermatology, Venereology, and Leprology* (IJDVL). Available at: https://ijdvl.com/a-brief-biographic-sketch-of-dr-bhau-daji-lad-1822-1874-a-forgotten-figure-of-indian-dermatology/ (accessed 5 May 2021).

Narmadashankar. 1994. *Marī Hakīkat.* Critical Edition by Ramesh M. Shukla. Available at: https://archive.org/details/in.ernet.dli.2015.537875 (accessed 4 May 2021).

Nature. 1925. 'Sir Athelstane Baines'. *Nature* 116: 909. 19 December. Available at: https://www.nature.com/articles/116909a0 (accessed 9 May 2021).

Nichol, John. 1904. *Thomas Carlyle.* Available at: https://www.gutenberg. org/cache/epub/9784/pg9784.html (accessed 22 May 2021).

Pandit, Shankar P., ed. 1879. *Vikramorvasīyam: A Drama in Five Acts, by Kalidasa.* Bombay: Government Central Book-Depot. Available at: https://archive.org/details/VikramorvasiyamByKalidasa1879/page/n21/mode/2up (accessed 25 June 2021).

Pandita, Narayana. n.d. *Hitopadeśah, Kathā-mukham* 0.33.3. Available at: https://grantha.jiva.org/texts/hitopadesa_-_narayana_pandita.docx (accessed 14 May 2021).

Pandya, Navalram. 1891[1911]. *Naval Granthavali.* Compiled and edited by Govardhanram Madhavram Tripathi. Reprint. Ahmedabad: United Printing and General Agency.

Pantazopoulos, G. A. 2017. '*Festina Lente* and Failure Analysis'. *Journal of Failure Analysis and Prevention* 17: 167–168. Available at: https://doi.org/10.1007/s11668-017-0246-y (accessed 24 May 2021).

Pater, Walter H. 1910. *Marius the Epicurean,* Volume 1, Chapter 3, p. 106. London: The Library Edition. Available at: https://www.gutenberg.org/files/4057/4057-h/4057-h.htm (21 May 2021).

Ranganathan, Murali, ed. and trans. 2008. *Govind Narayan's Mumbai: An Urban Biography from 1863.* With a Foreword by Gyan Prakash. London, New York: Anthem Press. Available at: https://trove.nla.gov.au/work/8519290?q&versionId=9838906. (accessed 5 May 2021)

Rawal, R. L. 2002. *Mahipatram.* Makers of Indian Literature Series. Delhi: Sahitya Akademi.

Rickett, Arthur. 1906. 'Foreword'. In *The Vagabond in Literature.* London: J. M. Dent & Co. Available at: https://www.gutenberg.org/files/33356/33356-h/33356-h.htm (accessed 24 May 2021).

Rogers, Alexander. 1892. *The Land Revenue of Bombay: A History of Administration, Rise and Progress.* London: W. H. Allen & Co. Available at: https://archive.org/details/landrevenuebomb01rogegoog/page/n5 (accessed 9 May 2021).

Ryder, Arthur William. 1905. *The Little Clay Cart [Mṛcchakatika]: A Hindu Drama Attributed to King Shudraka.* Translated from the original Sanskrit and Prakrit. Harvard Oriental Series, Volume Nine. Cambridge, Massachusetts: Harvard University. Available at: https://archive.org/details/littleclaycartmr00sudruoft/page/n7/mode/2up (accessed 4 May 2021).

Sanyal, Sanjeev. 2017. *The Ocean of Churn: How the Indian Ocean Shaped Human History.* Gurugram: Penguin India.

Sastri, A. Mahadeva, trans. 1903. *The Taittirīya Upanishad.* With the commentaries of Sankaracharya, Suresvaracharya and Sayana (Vidyaranya). Mysore: G. T. A. Printing Works. Available at: https://archive.org/details/taittiriyaupanis00sankiala/page/n7/mode/2up? (accessed 24 May 2021).

Shelley, P. B. 1906. 'Essay on the Literature, the Arts, and the Manners of the Athenians. A Fragment'. In *Prose Works of Percy Bysshe Shelley,* Vol. 2. Edited, Prefaced and Annotated by Richard Herne Shepherd, in Two Volumes. London: Chatto & Windus. Available at: https://oll.libertyfund.org/title/shepherd-prose-works-of-percy-bysshe-shelley-vol-2-1906#lf1633-02_head_003 (accessed 4 May 2021).

Shelley, P. B. 1915. *Selected Prose Works of Shelley.* With Foreword by Henry S. Salt. London: Watts & Co. Available at: https://archive.org/details/selectedprosewor00shelrich/page/n6 (accessed 4 May 2021).

Siganporia, Harmony. 2018. *I am the Widow: An Intellectual Biography of Behramji Malabari.* Hyderabad: Orient BlackSwan.

Southey, Robert. 1844. *Roderick, the Last of the Goths: A Tragic Poem.* London: Longman, Brown, Green, and Longmans. Available at: https://archive.org/details/rodericklastofg00soutuoft/page/n11/mode/2up (accessed 14 May 2021).

Stephan, Annelisa. 2012. 'Apocalypse Then: Bulwer-Lytton's "The Last Days of Pompeii"'. *Getty,* 24 August. Available at: https://blogs.getty.edu/iris/apocalypse-then-bulwer-lyttons-the-last-days-of-pompeii/ (accessed 14 May 2021).

Stewart, Gordon. 1998. *The Marathas 1600–1818. The New Cambridge History of India II.4.* Cambridge: Cambridge University Press.

Tripathi, Govardhanram Madhavram. 1887. *Buddhidhān nu Kārbhār.* Bombay: N. M. Tripathi & Co.

———. 1892. *Gunasundari nu Kutumbajālā.* Bombay: N. M. Tripathi & Co.

———. 2013. *Sarasvatichandra* (Gujarati). Kindle edition. R. R. Sheth & Co. Pvt. Ltd.

———. 2015[1887]. *Sarasvatichandra Part I: Buddhidhan's Administration.* Translated by Tridip Suhrud. Hyderabad: Orient Blackswan Pvt. Ltd.

————. 2016[1892]. *Sarasvatichandra Part II: Gunasundari's Household.* Translated by Tridip Suhrud. Hyderabad: Orient Blackswan Pvt. Ltd.

Vasu, Sris Chandra. 1905. *Kathopanishad.* With the Sanskrit text, Anvaya, Vritti, Word Meaning, Translation, Notes and Index. Allahabad: Panini Office, Bhuvaneshvari Asram. Available at: https://archive.org/details/KathaUpanisad (accessed 25 May 2021).

Vatsal, Tulsi and Aban Mukherji, trans. 2015. Nandshankar Mehta, *Karan Ghelo: Gujarat's Last Rajput King.* New Delhi: Penguin/Viking.

Talbot, Cynthia. 2016. *The Last Hindu Emperor: Prithviraj Chauhan and the Indian Past 1200–2000.* Cambridge: Cambridge University Press.

Trelawny, E. J. 1858[2011]. *Recollections of the Last Days of Shelley and Byron.* Cambridge: Cambridge University Press. Available at: https://archive.org/details/recollectionsofl00trelrich/page/n20 (accessed 24 March 2021).

Wacha, Dinshaw Edulji. 1913. *Premchund Roychund: His Early Life and Career.* Bombay: Times Press.

Yagnik, Achyut and Suchitra Sheth. 2005. *The Shaping of Modern Gujarat: Plurality, Hindutva and Beyond.* New Delhi, New York: Penguin Books.

Yarshater, Ehsan, ed. 1983. *The Seleucid, Parthian and Sassanian Period. The Cambridge History of Iran,* Volume 3. Cambridge: Cambridge University Press. Available at: https://archive.org/stream/Frye1983SasaniansCHI03/Frye_1983_Sasanians_CHI03_djvu.txt (accessed 26 May 2021).